Praise for *At Her Majesty's Pleasure*

'A punchy account . . . such good humour and present-tense immediacy that you feel as if you are standing alongside him, scanning the prison wings for trouble . . . The effect is to humanise events that now live only in stark news headlines, and to make the reader want to know who Robert Douglas is going to meet next . . . characteristically frank'

Glasgow Herald

'A must-read . . . brutally honest'

Newcastle Evening Chronicle

'Robert's life behind bars at Winson Green in Birmingham, and then Durham Gaol, is described in stark detail . . . an eye-opener'

Hexham Courant

'As emotional, funny and evocative as its predecessors, this will make you laugh, cry – and buy copies for everyone you've ever known'

Daily Record

'Fascinating . . . lively . . . the final part of a well-received trilogy'

Bristol Evening Post

'This is my last autobiography but probably not my last book. I've got lots more to say'

Robert Douglas

Now retired, Robert Douglas worked as a prison officer and as an electricity chargehand. Although he has lived in Northumberland for many years, he says you can take the boy out of Glasgow, but you'll never take Glasgow out of the boy. His second volume of autobiography, *Somewhere to Lay My Head*, was a bestseller, and Robert has given many talks and readings both from that book and from his equally successful and much-loved first volume, *Night Song of the Last Tram*, since their first publication in 2005 and 2006.

Also by Robert Douglas

Night Song of the Last Tram
Somewhere to Lay My Head

Robert Douglas

At Her Majesty's Pleasure

HODDER

Some names have been changed in order to protect identities.

First published in Great Britain in 2007 by Hodder & Stoughton
An Hachette Livre UK company

First published in paperback in 2008

7

A CIP catalogue record for this title is available from the British Library

ISBN 978 0 340 93530 9

Typeset in Sabon by Hewer Text UK Ltd, Edinburgh
Printed and bound by CPI Mackays, Chatham ME5 8TD

Hodder & Stoughton policy is to use papers that are natural, renewable and recyclable products and made from wood grown in sustainable forests. The logging and manufacturing processes are expected to conform to the environmental regulations of the country of origin.

Hodder & Stoughton Ltd
338 Euston Road
London NW1 3BH

www.hodder.co.uk

Most of the photographs are from the author's collection.
Additional sources: Bristol Evening Post page 99,
Newcastle Chronicle and Journal Ltd pages 189 and 193.

To my wife Patricia, who's also my best pal

Acknowledgements

With gratitude to my gang at Hodder: Nick, Bob, Anne, Amber, Mark, Helen and Kerry.

A special thanks to all the authors, songwriters and movie makers who, since childhood, have kept me royally entertained – and often lifted my spirits.

Finally, there's my darling Ma, whom I never got the chance to treat. Only that last kiss. She's never far away.

Contents

Turning Myself In

Jeez, what a hot day! A day for sitting in the backyard, not for voluntarily walking into a prison. I put my heavy suitcase down and, somewhat apprehensively, reach for the iron knocker fixed to the wicket-gate of Birmingham Prison. Behind me, the driver of the blue and cream corporation bus snicks it into gear, revs the engine and slowly pulls away. I bang the knocker once – not too loudly. I glance up at the great wooden double doors. Flanked on either side by red brick, bow-fronted towers with small iron-framed windows, they look for all the world like the entrance to a medieval castle. The sun is warm on my back. It's 20 June 1962.

I hear the sound of a key being inserted into the other side of the small wicket-gate. It swings open. A plump, uniformed officer with a straggly brown moustache and a pipe clamped between his teeth looks at me. 'Yempth?'

'Eh, ah'm reporting for duty. Ah've been posted here from the training school.'

'Poor sod! Yumphyumphyumph!' He shakes with mirth at his own joke. The pipe never moves. I'll find out later he's called Arthur Mosely and is, by common consent, 'as daft as a brush!'

'S'pose you might as well come in.' He opens the small gate wider. 'Shame! Whatcha done to deserve to be sent to Birmingham? Yumphyumph!'

I can't help but smile. I take a last glance up the almost deserted Winson Green Road, its red brick terraces baking in the sun. I step over the high lip of the wicket-gate into the cool, dark area between the outer and inner gates. The solid door is shut behind me. 'A lad posted in from Wakefield, Mr Green,' he calls through the open window of the gate-lodge. He nods in its direction. 'Just give 'im your details, son.'

I step up onto a narrow pavement and look into the gatekeeper's fiefdom. The double doors of the large key safe lie open. The inside of the doors and interior of the safe are lined with 300 or more hooks. Keys hang from some, numbered brass tallies from others. A tally means an officer has his keys on him – therefore, he's on duty somewhere inside. Keys are NEVER taken outside the prison. If a set of keys (cell and pass) are lost, every lock in the prison has to be changed. I look at the gatekeeper. I immediately wonder how he got into the Prison Service. He's quite short; no more than 5 feet 5 inches. The minimum height for an officer is 5 feet 8. Eventually I'll find out why the height restriction was ignored in the case of Jimmy Green.

'What's your name, son?'

'Robert Douglas.'

'The bachelor quarters are full at the minute. Will you be needing digs?'

'Yes, please.'

'Uh huh.' He brings a well-thumbed notebook down from a shelf. 'I'll give old Gran Jackson down in Franklin Street a ring. I think she has vacancies. While you're up seeing the Chief I'll also ring the stores. Your uniform should have been delivered by now.'

'That's great. Thanks very much.'

'I'll tell you what set of keys you'll be allocated.'

I feel my face flush. After three months' training, the moment has arrived: I'm really getting to be a prison officer. I watch as he reaches for a ledger. It's leather bound; the edges of the pages are a swirl of red, blue and green. He runs a finger down a column. 'You'll have set 159.' He goes to the key safe. I can see both keys and tally hanging from the hook. He points to them. 'They're yours from now on.'

'Right, that's fine, sir. 159.'

'Okay. If you just stand away from the window, son, so's officers can get access with their keys, I'll get someone to come and take you up the Centre.'

'Right, thanks.' I move further along the narrow pavement. I can hear him on the phone. I look around me. The area between the inner and outer gates is cobbled. The inner gates are made from thick iron bars. It's dark and gloomy. The castle image is still in my mind. From my classes at the training school I know that both sets of gates are never opened at the same time – a passing con might be tempted to break away from his escort and make a dash for freedom.

As I stand thinking of such things there's a knock on the wicket-gate. Arthur opens it. A tall officer, handsome in spite of a pockmarked face, enters.

'Hello Art'ur.' Immediately I can hear the brogue.

'Dennis, my boy!' says Arthur. As the newcomer steps up to the window, tally in hand, Arthur draws his truncheon, tiptoes up behind him and 'gooses' him with it.

'JAYSUS!' Dennis obligingly leaps into the air, dropping his tally as he does so. 'Yah devil, Art'ur!'

'Yumphyumphyumph!'

In an almost reflex action Dennis bends down to pick up his tally. Arthur seizes the chance to goose him again. 'Yumphyum-phyumph!' He leans weakly against the gate. He waves his truncheon in the air. 'Beware all ye who pass through these portals!'

I'm dying to laugh out loud. Dennis looks at me and shakes his head. 'Have ye ever seen the loike?' Keeping a wary eye on Arthur he makes his way, sideways, over to the inner gate.

'Why are you walking like that, Dennis?' Arthur points to his truncheon. 'Just the thing for the old piles, you know. Yum-phyumph!' He ambles over and opens the inner wicket. Dennis exits, backwards.

* * *

1963: My early years of doing 'Prison Officer impersonations'.

Just a few yards from the inner gate, steps lead up to tall double doors. An officer opens one and pops his head out. 'Have you got a new chap there, Arthur?'

'Yeah, I'll pass him through.' He beckons to me. 'Here y'are, me laddo.'

As he opens the small gate I keep half an eye on him. We're obviously not yet well enough acquainted; I emerge unscathed.

My escort, a ginger-headed officer about my own age, twenty-three, lets me through, then locks the door behind us. We walk up a long corridor towards identical doors at the far end. To our left and right are various offices. A brass plate on one states: Governor.

'So, what sort of jail is it to work in?'

'Oh, it ain't too bad. Like all nicks, it has its moments.'

'You been here long?'

'About fifteen months. I'm Barry Palmer, by the way. Usually get called "Ginger".'

I introduce myself. We shake hands.

He opens one of the two doors and we walk onto the tiled, circular Centre.

Just like Preston and Wakefield, the only two I've seen during my three months' training, the prison is Victorian. 'The Green', as it's usually called, is built on the Spoke System – a circular Centre off which the cathedral-like wings run, like spokes from the hub of a wheel. It has been designed so that one officer can stand on the Centre and, with just a slight turn of his head, can see along three wings. To the left is A Wing, straight in front is B Wing and to the right, C Wing.

As I step through the door I'm surrounded by that prison smell. A mixture of unwashed bodies and disinfectant mingles with the permanent odour from the recesses – which contain urinals, toilets and the large sinks into which prisoners empty their chamber-pots every morning when they 'slop out'. Mixed in with this is the ever-present aroma of cooking drifting up from the kitchen; past meals vying with the one being prepared at the moment.

Each wing has four landings. The topmost is known as the 'fours', descending to the 'threes' then the 'twos' – which is on the same level as the Centre. A short flight of stairs takes you down to the 'ones'. To pinpoint a specific landing, they are further identified by putting the wing as a prefix, e.g. A4 is the topmost landing on A Wing, B3 is one from the top on B Wing and so on.

A and C Wings are medium sized, perhaps 60 yards long. B Wing is the largest in the prison at maybe 100 yards long. Each of the landings consist of narrow walkways which run the entire length of both sides of a wing, giving access to the long rows of cells on either side. Outside every cell door is a numbered tally, like a small metal flag. If a prisoner rings his bell the tally drops forward. An officer now knows which cell needs attention. Hanging on the wall by each cell is a board, reminiscent of those used in church to show which hymns are to be sung. Cards are slotted into these boards, one for each inmate in that cell. There will either be one, or three. Two men aren't allowed to share in case of any homosexual activity. This rule will be scrapped a few years later when the Wolfenden Act legalises homosexual practices between males in private. Each cell card gives a prisoner's name, number and sentence. Its colour shows his religion; white for Church of England, red for Catholic and blue for Jewish. If he is of some other religion, or none at all, this will be written in ink across a white card.

I stand on the Centre and try to take it all in. Across the wide space between landings, from the fours down to the twos, wire 'suicide netting' spans the width of the wings from side to side. Metal stairways lead up through gaps in this netting, giving access to the threes and fours. Halfway along each of the upper landings or walkways there is always a short bridge from one side to the other, which saves having to walk the long way round. The decor is a dingy brown and pale buff, the upper walls a dirty white. A paint job is long overdue. High overhead, parallel rows of skylights run either side of the apex of each wing's roof, allowing the sun to penetrate a few feet into the upper reaches. At the far end of B Wing a tall iron-framed window, about 30 feet high, runs down from the fours almost to the twos. It enhances the church-like impression. Except they forgot the stained glass.

Many years later, long after I've left Birmingham, whenever the brilliant *Porridge* comes on TV it instantly transports me back to The Green. The run-down appearance of the wings, the mix of cons – mainly Midlanders sprinkled with Cockneys, Jocks and Taffs. The disparate bunch of screws. Winson Green IS Slade Prison.

As it's mid-afternoon, the cons are still in workshops. A few cleaners amble about the empty wings, sweeping or mopping their designated landings with undiminished lethargy. Occasionally an officer can be glimpsed high up on a wing, probably, as the cons would say, up to no good. The sun blazes in through the skylights but doesn't get very far. Sounds echo down to the Centre; someone whistling, a burst of laughter, a galvanised bucket scraping on a slate landing, a cell door banged shut. There's a feeling of indolence.

Over to one side of the Centre stands the P.O.'s box. Constructed from wood, painted yellow with windows on every side, it's about twice the size of a phone box. Inside it is a sloping desk, high stool and a telephone. This is the domain of the Centre P.O. (Principal Officer). He supervises the daily movement inside the prison; when the landings are unlocked for meals, workshops and exercise and in what order they are called down. Before taking me in to see the Chief Officer, Ginger Palmer walks across to speak to the P.O. who is perched on his stool. He calls me over to introduce me. 'This is P.O. Appleton.' We shake hands.

'Ah, so you're a Jock, are you?'

' 'Fraid so. And by the sound of your accent you're no' very far away.'

'Aye. Ah'm a Newcastle man . . .' Our conversation ends abruptly as a large fire station-type bell, fixed to the wall above our heads, begins an ear-splitting ring. The P.O. and Ginger Palmer immediately look up at the indicator board placed underneath the clammering bell. A red disc has dropped down into one of a row of squares. It says 'Mat Shop'. The bell stops ringing as suddenly as it started. I can now hear pounding feet as officers appear from all directions – landings, wing offices, the censor office, the Chief's office, the library, the punishment landing . . .

'IT'S THE MAT SHOP!' shouts the P.O. They all head down C Wing at speed and stream out of the far door, onto the yard, and up to the workshops area.

'Will I go?' I say.

'No. You're not in uniform. The officers wouldn't know who you are.' As he speaks he's dialling a number on the phone. I listen to one side of the conversation. 'Johnny Appleton. Staff'll be there any second. What's the problem?' I watch his face as he listens. 'Yeah. There's a surprise. I could've took a bet it would be that shitbag! Well I know where he's going in a minute. Right. Tell Tony to put him on report 'cause I'll be putting him straight down the block. The Governor can sort that fuckpig out in the morning. Fine.' He puts the phone back in its cradle, then reaches up and presses a button on the side of the indicator board. The red disc slips silently out of sight.

As Ginger has gone off with the stampede of officers, I have nothing to do but stand and wait. Minutes later the door and gate at the end of C Wing are thrown open again. There is the sound of many feet walking quickly, purposefully, towards the Centre. The P.O. emerges from his box and stands, legs apart, facing them. In the midst of twenty or more officers is a prisoner, grey battledress-type jacket unbuttoned; the front of his blue and white striped prison shirt is torn and hangs out of his trousers. His tie hangs loose. He looks pale, on edge, somewhat defiant. The P.O. holds up his hand to stop the group. 'Take him up to his cell for his kit – then straight down A1 with him.' He points to the con. 'You don't lift your hand to one of my officers, boy. You've made a bad mistake!' The prisoner doesn't reply. 'Just four of you see to him,' says P.O. Appleton, 'the rest of you can go back to your jobs. Thanks lads.'

Less than ten minutes later I come out of the Chief's office. Ginger Palmer is standing at the top of the stairs leading to A1, the punishment landing. He calls me over. The offending con arrived a couple of minutes ago with his kit. His bedding and personal items lie scattered on the floor of the small, isolated downstairs landing. There's no one to be seen. Ginger holds an open hand to his ear. 'Hark!' he says.

I can hear the movement of feet. Grunts. Officers' keys chink together like wind chimes as they take turns giving the miscreant a working-over inside an empty cell.

To lift a hand to an officer entitles a con to a mandatory good hiding. It's an unwritten law.

Ginger and I turn away, walk back over to the P.O.'s box. He and the P.O. seem quite pleased at the con getting his come-uppance. I certainly don't disapprove, but as they talk and laugh about it my thoughts begin to wander. I'm not five minutes in the place before alarm bells are ringing and some con's getting a hiding. Welcome to Winson Green!

Once again I wonder if I'm going to be able to hack it as a prison officer. Folk think because you've grown up in Glasgow, that's you already qualified to be a screw – or a criminal. Huh! Most of my formative years were spent sitting in the back stalls of the local cinemas, or with my nose buried in a book. The games played round the streets with my pals hardly ever led to fights; and if they did I usually made sure I wasn't involved.

I'll have to give it a go. Not only do I need the money, but a house comes with it. If I stay with Nancy's mum and dad in West Lothian, it'll be at least three years, maybe longer, before we'll get a council house. I want Nancy, wee Scott – our son – and me to have our own place; be a family. And anyway, I like being down in England again. Especially the Midlands. I loved my two years in the army, stationed in Nottingham. The best years of my life!

Crack with a Spy

'Did you know we've got Gordon Lonsdale, the Russian spy, here?' Tony Mountford drops it casually into the conversation. We're on 'visits' and he's showing me the ropes. Every twenty-eight days a convicted man is allowed a visit lasting thirty minutes. He applies for, then sends out, a Visiting Order to family or friends.

I'm immediately intrigued. Jeez! Imagine that. A real-life Soviet secret agent. I think back to the trial, just last year. The papers were full of it. 'The Portland Spy Ring.'

'He's doing a helluva sentence if ah mind right.'

'Twenty-five years!' Tony opens the gate and we pass through into the main exercise yard. I lock it behind us. We stop beside the officer who's in charge of the yard. 'What shops are on at the minute, Roy?' asks Tony.

'Mailbags and Mat Shop.'

Tony looks at the three visiting passes he holds. 'Two of them should be on here. EXERCISE HALT!' he bellows. The cons within hearing distance halt first. Those at the furthest reaches of the yard are oblivious. They continue for a few more paces until they realise the majority have stopped circling. Tony waits until the 120-plus inmates are still. All heads are turned in our direction; you could hear a condemned man drop. Visits are important. Even more than letters.

'365221 WAYNE! 364838 JENKINS!' Two guys detach themselves from the rest and come over to us. 'I'm going up to the Mattress Shop for a lad,' says Tony, 'just walk up and down this stretch and I'll tip you the wink when I come back. Okay?'

'Right, boss.' 'Yeah, fine.' The two set off to walk up and down the concrete pathway at the bottom of the yard. Tony and I head for the Mattress Shop.

'So, what sort of guy is he? Lonsdale?'

'Oh, he's all right. Not a bit of bother. He's in patches.'

To make him easy to spot, a prisoner who has tried to escape – or is considered an escape risk – has to wear a prison uniform with a large, bright yellow square patch on the left breast of the jacket and two long yellow stripes on the trousers; one on the front of one leg, one on the back of the other. When he is out of his cell he always has an escort. He is handed over from officer to officer, workshop to exercise to visits to cell. Passed over with him is a hard-cover notebook. As each officer takes charge of an E-man, as they're called, he has to fill in and sign the book with the time, date and place. At night, in his single cell, when it comes to 'lights out' the main bulb is switched off – and a red 'dim' bulb is switched on. Every thirty minutes during the hours of darkness a night patrol (night watchman) comes padding along, silently moves the cover on the door's spyhole, and looks through to check all is well.

'Why is he in patches, did he try to escape?'

'No. It's just that there's never been anybody doing such a long, fixed sentence. So the Prison Department are shittin' themselves. With him being a Russian spy they don't quite know what to do with him. To be on the safe side they've put him in patches. There'd be such a bloody hoo-hah if he was to get away.'

'Do they let him work? Or is he locked up aw' day?'

'No, he works. He's in the Brush Shop.' Tony laughs. 'Would you believe it, he's the shop clerk! There's about forty cons in there, all English, but they've made a fuckin' Russian the clerk!'

I'm really fascinated to find out Lonsdale's here. Since my childhood, starting not long after 1945 when the Iron Curtain began to come down, the Cold War has been a hot topic. In fact and fiction the public has been regularly bombarded with stories of secret agents, spies and traitors. From the late forties, on through the fifties, right to the present day, at regular intervals there will be headlines in the press as yet another Soviet spy ring is uncovered. They are always followed by a lengthy trial. I remember the furore when a married couple, the Rosenbergs, were executed in the United States in 1951 for passing secrets to the Russians. A few years later, over here, we had Klaus Fuchs sent to prison for the same offence. The next big spy scandal, still in the fifties, was the defection of two British intelligence agents, Burgess and McLean. About to be arrested, they skipped to Russia. They were soon followed by 'the Third Man', their fellow traitor, Kim Philby. The next big event, in the late fifties, was the arrest and trial in the United States of undercover KGB man, Col. Abel. He has recently been exchanged – at the famous Checkpoint Charlie border crossing in Berlin – for shot-down American U2 spy plane pilot, Gary Powers.

What Western intelligence didn't know at the time of Abel's arrest was that Lonsdale, also a KGB colonel, was his number two in New York. As their spy ring collapsed, Lonsdale escaped detection and made his way to London. There, he set up his own organisation, which eventually led to the Portland Spy Ring. It would be years later, in the mid-sixties, before the Abel–Lonsdale connection became known.

Just before going off duty at five thirty p.m., I look at the 'detail board'. Great! I'm allocated to the Brush Shop tomorrow as number two discipline officer. I'll get a look at Lonsdale. After years of reading books and being enthralled by the true stories of escaped POWs and secret agents in France during the Second World War, as we've come into the sixties, books and movies are now reflecting the Cold War between the West and Communist Eastern Europe. One thing ALL these agents, past and present, seem to have in common is single-mindedness.

Tomorrow I should get to see a Soviet agent. Will fact measure up to fiction?

It's just after nine a.m. I watch the forty-plus cons circle one of the smaller exercise yards. My senior officer, Bill Bailey, stands at the far corner. There is nobody in patches on the yard. So where is Lonsdale? Eventually, we line the cons up, ready to march to the shop.

'I thought we had an E-man, Mr Bailey?'

Bill Bailey is a tall, lugubrious man in his late forties. Like many of the senior staff, he sports his Second World War medal ribbons. He speaks slowly, with a heavy Brummie accent.

'He's already in the shop. The instructors take him in first thing of a morning along with a few key workers. Lonsdale just takes the afternoon exercise. He don't bother with the morning.'

We file into the shop. The cons make straight for their allotted tables, take off their jackets and start work. As junior officer, I'm stationed at the bottom end of the workshop, farthest away from the office and stores. Lonsdale, as clerk, will be in the office. I'll get a look at him when he comes out. He'll be easy to recognise as he'll be wearing the yellow patches. The two instructors in the shop are Jim Glossop, the senior, an easy-going man in his late fifties, and Tom McKay, a slim, fiery Scot in his mid-forties. They are great mates. The Brush Shop does contract work for the Harris company who make paintbrushes. The inmates are employed in cutting, sizing and sterilising hair and bristle.

Tom McKay, like a number of senior officers, tends to have little to do with new recruits until he gets to know them and, most importantly, sees how they handle prisoners. If you 'get a grip' when the situation demands it, Tom will eventually unbend enough to engage you in conversation. No doubt part of his reluctance to suffer fools gladly is a result of his experiences during the war. Stationed in Singapore with a Scottish infantry regiment in 1942, Tom and a few of his comrades were appalled at the ignominious surrender of the 120,000-strong British force to a small, aggresive Japanese division numbering just 14,000. They decided they were not going to go meekly 'into the bag'. Disobeying orders to lay down their arms, they melted away into the forest, got off Singapore island, and headed north through the Malayan jungle towards freedom. Eventually, after a few months of hit-and-run warfare, he and his group were captured. He spent the next three years as a POW, and was left with an abiding hatred of all things Japanese.

As in all prison workshops, the instructors are responsible for the prisoners' work and productivity. We discipline officers are there to see they behave themselves. If there is any misbehaviour we give them a warning. If they continue with it, we either phone the Centre and request that a couple of officers be sent round to take the culprit in; or, if things are escalating, we ring the alarm bell and a host of officers will appear to remove the troublemaker.

It's nearly ten a.m. I still haven't had a glimpse of Lonsdale. He just hasn't come out of the office. I look up the length of the shop. The cons are busy, the two instructors wander round the tables checking on the standard of work. Bill Bailey sits on the high stool. I look again at the entrance to the office. Just inside that door sits a real-life Russian agent. What the buggering hell is he doing? Is it not about time he went for a pee?

Sometime after ten, Bill beckons me to come up his end of the shop. 'It's tea break time, kid. You stay up this end by the alarm bell. I'll be back in about fifteen minutes, then you can go.' Great! Now I'll get my chance. The cons are all working away. I begin to walk up and down. I casually stroll past the open door of the office. I look in. A small, stocky man, maybe 5 feet 6 inches tall, sits reading a paperback. Things must be slack. I can see the long yellow stripe on one of his trouser legs. He looks to be in his early forties. At first glance he's not unlike a young Edward G. Robinson. At second glance I decide he looks even more like another, lesser known actor – Luther Adler. I look at the cover of his book; *Casino Royale* by Ian Fleming. I can't help but smile. Jeez-oh! A Russian agent sitting reading a James Bond! He sees me smiling. 'Trying to pick up a few tips?' I say.

He smiles in return. Shakes his head. 'I don't think so.' I'd expected him to speak with a heavy, Slavic accent. Not so. It's a soft, American drawl. Curiouser and curiouser.

'They're good fun,' I say, 'I find I race through them.'

'Yeah, they're certainly good entertainment.'

I decide that's enough. I don't want to push it too much. I give him another smile then move away from the door. He immerses himself in the Bond once more. I go and sit on the high stool. I think back to last year's trial. He'd been arrested early in '61 and charged with 'conspiracy to obtain secrets' from Harry Houghton and Ethel Gee, two civilian employees at Portland Underwater Research Establishment. Anything Lonsdale got from them he passed to his fellow agents, Peter and Helen Kroger. They, in turn, transmitted the material to the Soviet Union. In March 1961, after a ten-day trial, Lonsdale received the then unprecedented sentence of twenty-five years' imprisonment. I glance back at the office. I wonder what he thinks about as he sits there reading a James Bond. Even with the automatic entitlement to one third remission for good behaviour, he'll still do over sixteen years. That's a helluva long time. In almost every book, Bond gets captured – then he escapes. But that's fiction.

The First of Many

The Black Maria makes its way into the city, heading for Victoria Law Courts. I sit in the back with half a dozen officers and ten cons. P.O. Butler sits in the cab with the police driver. I feel the suppressed excitement trying to bubble up again. This is my first time on court duty. We will man the docks and cells at today's sitting of Birmingham Assizes.

This is still the era of the centuries-old quarter sessions and assizes. It will be a few years yet before a newfangled Crown Court will be set up in Birmingham to combine the duties of these two courts. Prison officers man these higher courts. The police look after the magistrates.

I'm really looking forward to today. For years I've seen court scenes portrayed on screen in lots of English movies; stern judges on the bench and oh-so-posh barristers cross-questioning the likes of Richard Attenborough or Stewart Granger. I hope I get the chance to sit in the dock.

Just after nine a.m. we file into the basement area. It seems to be all cell doors and corridors. Overhead pipes run in all directions. Electric lights burn all day; no sunlight reaches down here. We split the remands into two groups and usher them into large 'holding' cells. Reuben Roberts gives them the gypsy's warning: 'We'll let you stay like this to 'ave a natter. But if yer gets TOO noisy we'll split yer up. You'll be getting a cuppa shortly.' He shuts the two heavy doors. I follow him into the kitchen. Two women cleaners, court employees, sit at a table. 'Morning, girls,' he says.

'Morning,' they chorus, in rich Brummie accents.

'You won't have met our latest recruit,' says P.O. 'Rab' Butler. 'This is Jock Douglas. Meet Sylvia and Janet.' Sylvia is heavily built, around forty years of age. Janet is in her fifties, thin, and very much in the mould of my pal Sammy's mother, Lottie Johnston – including the half-smoked Woodbine. They wear washed-out, green wraparound overalls.

'Ohaah!' says Janet to Sylvia. 'I once had a bad experience with a Jock! Or was he Irish?'

'The kettles are on the boil,' says Sylvia.

Rab Butler looks at me. 'Can you brew tea?'

'Certainly can, sir.'

'Grand! Do the cons first, then we'll get peace for ours.'

It's just coming up for ten thirty. I stand at the foot of the stairway leading up to number one court. Next to me is a prisoner called John Wood. He cannot stop trembling. In his late twenties, he is tall and thin. He's accused of stabbing his wife to death.

'Jock! Fetch 'im up.' Alec Cox is already in the dock.

'Right, Wood. Up you go.'

We climb the narrow stairway. For the first time of many, I step into the large, wood-panelled dock with its polished brass handrails. Alec points with his Biro. He's already primed me in advance. I guide Wood along to the middle of the long bench. 'Just stand for the moment. I'll tell you when to sit.'

I stand beside him and look around. In front of the dock, lower down, are rows of wooden benches with desk-like slopes in front of them. These are for barristers and solicitors. Facing me is the bench. Above the judge's chair is a wooden canopy. It frames a carved, painted royal coat of arms. This is to remind all and sundry that the judges – especially the High Court judges – are dispensing the Queen's justice. All around me are the rest of the fixtures which make up a courtroom: jury box, witness box, press benches and public gallery. These law courts were built in the second half of the nineteenth century. I instantly fall in love with their Victorian character.

Ten minutes later we're underway. As this is the assizes, a High Court judge sits on the bench. Bewigged and wearing his ermine-trimmed red robe, Mr Justice Paul's word is, literally, law. The prosecuting counsel, John Owen, rises to his feet. Like all barristers, he wears a black gown and a wig.

As John Owen outlines the case against him, I wonder why Wood bothered to plead 'not guilty'. It really is an open-and-shut case. The trial lasts just two days and, inevitably, ends with the jury finding Wood guilty. Mr Justice Paul gives him the mandatory life sentence. Short though it may be, I find my first foray into the dock lives up to expectations. Judge and barristers all play their parts to perfection and I enjoy sitting in the dock as an 'extra'.

I've now 'done' my first murder trial.

A Big Step

There are no married quarters available, and even if there were, I'm well down the queue. This leaves only two alternatives: rent somewhere, or BUY our own place. That really is some commitment. Just five years ago I was living in the Great Eastern Hotel in Glasgow; the doss-house! I could put everything I owned into two brown paper carrier bags. The thought that, at twenty-three. I'd be considering buying a house wouldn't even have been listed under 'wildest dreams'. The more I think about it, the more I realise this is the only way I'm going to get Nancy and Scott down here so we can start living as a family.

I've been talking to some officers who were in the same position and are now buying their own houses. Seemingly it makes good sense. As the Prison Department can't supply me with quarters, I'm entitled to 'rent allowance in lieu'. This could amount to a third of what my mortgage could be. As long as I stay in the job, there won't be a problem. In fact, it's a good opportunity.

Even so, I'm still quite apprehensive about the whole thing. I come from a tenement single-end (a one-room house) in Maryhill. I thought knives and forks were jewellery. Now I'm thinking about buying a house. Jesusjonny!

I arrange to ring Nancy at a neighbour's house in Seafield so's we can discuss it . . .

'That's the only way I'm gonny get the two of you doon here fairly quickly. What dae ye think?'

'Ah think we should go ahead. We've got nearly four hundred pounds put by, so we'll easily manage the deposit.'

'Right, that's it. We'll dae it! Ah'll start house-hunting on my next day off.'

Meanwhile, I'm enjoying being at Gran Jackson's. She's in her seventies and has been a widow for years. Gray-haired, never without her horn-rimmed specs and wraparound peenie overall, she totters round the house leaving a trail of fag ash in her wake and chattering non-stop, especially when you're watching the telly.

While I'm lodging at Gran's, Nancy forwards a letter to me. It's from my father, and tells me that his mother, my Granny Douglas, has died. She was eighty years of age. For the last twenty years of her life she lived in the Salvation Army Refuge for homeless women down in Clyde Street. She was the only grandparent I knew. All during my childhood, until Ma died in 1954, she'd come up to our house at least once a week. She always sat in the first chair as you came into the house; a wooden one. My father said she had fleas. Ma would always give her a wee bite to eat and she'd usually be away before he came in from his work. If he happened to come in early he'd usually tell her, 'It's time you were away.' Sometimes I'd wonder why she didn't live in a house like my pals' grannies.

Born Jane McCrindle in Girvan in 1882, the daughter of fisherfolk, she came to Glasgow to work as a domestic. She married my grandfather, Robert John Douglas, in 1906. When he died in 1941 she began to drink, and soon lost the tenancy of their tenement house at 50 Northpark Street, Maryhill.

After Ma's funeral, in December 1954, with me joining the RAF Boys' Service and later living out in West Lothian, I didn't see her again until a few days before I went into the army in January '59. All of a sudden she came into my mind. I'd been fifteen when Ma died. I was now a month short of my twentieth birthday. I'd made my way down to the Broomielaw on a rainy winter's night and found the entrance to the Refuge. The door was wide open. I'd looked along the narrow corridor which, after about 20 feet, turned off to left and right. A single electric lamp burned overhead. I gave a knock. Then a louder one. A woman, maybe in her thirties, peered round a corner at the far end of the corridor.

'Ah, does Jean Douglas (she didn't like "Jane") still live here?'

'Aye. Who will ah say it is?'

'Tell her it's her grandson, Robert Douglas, tae see her.'

'Right.'

I stood looking along the corridor. The rain was getting a bit blustery so I took a couple of steps into the shelter of the lobby. All of a sudden my Granny Douglas came running round the corner towards me. All my life I'd never, ever seen her without her coat on, worn old fox-fur round her neck, cloche hat on her head and her hair tucked up under it. All this black clothing, which made her look like the cartoon Grandma Giles, had been bought for her husband's funeral. She'd wear it for the rest of her life. Tonight she was wearing a cardigan and, of course, a black skirt. But her hair was down; it was about 3 feet long and hung down her back and shoulders. I hadn't known she had long hair. There was no mistaking her ruddy red cheeks and almost black, piercing eyes.

'Aw, son, son! Imagine you coming tae see me.' She wrapped her arms round me and gave me a big hug. I put my arms round her and kissed her on her plump cheek with its small broken veins. I didn't remember ever having kissed her before. She still had that smell, familiar from my childhood, of stale sweat and cheap perfume. For an instant I was back in our single-end.

'Ah'm away intae the army in a few days, tae dae ma National Service, Granny. So ah thought ah'd come and see ye.' She looked so little.

'Yer faither telt me ye were back in Glesga. My, whit a big laddie you've turned intae.'

'Diz ma faither write tae ye?'

'Aye. Mibbe wance every nine months or so he draps me a letter.'

We talked about where I'd been and what I'd been doing until, eventually, it was time to go. I took my wallet out. 'Here, Granny, here's ten bob for ye.'

'Eeeh, son. That's awfy nice o'ye.' I watched as she tucked the red ten-shilling note into a pocket in her cardigan. I knew that most of it, if not all, would go on a few glasses of her tipple – the cheap wine known as 'red biddy'. She looked at me. 'Mind, ah don't half miss yer mother. When ah wiz hard up, ah knew if ah went up tae Doncaster Street yer mother would always make me a wee bite. She wiz nae age at all. Poor lassie.'

'Aye. Anywye, Granny, ah'll get maself away.' I gave her another kiss on the cheek and she gave me a long hug like she didn't want to let go. I stepped out onto the dark Broomielaw. After a few steps I turned. She was leaning out of the door. She waved. I waved back 'See yah, Granny.'

I fold up my father's letter. Jeez, all those years living in that home, not feeding herself properly, drinking. Yet she still made it to eighty. They must have been a hardy lot, the McCrindles.

After a few weeks at Gran Jackson's I'm joined by George Davis, another new recruit. A Welshman in his late twenties, George stands 6 feet 3 inches in his socks and weighs around 16 stone. After years of working down the pit none of that is fat. His mere presence usually gives the most aggressive con pause for thought. He won't be long at the Green until he gravitates towards the post he was meant for – running A1, the punishment landing. He's normally a good-natured lad, but it always proves to be a mistake on some con's part if he rouses George.

Never a Dull Moment

I've been allocated to B3 as one of its landing officers. One of the biggest in the jail, with around fifty cells, it holds something like 110 prisoners. The idea of having officers designated to a specific landing is a good one. It makes for continuity; you get to know the cons and they get to know you.

Another aspect of being a prison officer is the fact that a five-day week is out. The staff are divided into two: the Governor's Division and the Deputy Governor's Division. I'm on the 'Dep's Division'. Basically, ALL the staff work Monday to Friday. At the weekend, one division is off while the other works. The following weekend it's the other way around. This means I work a twelve-day fortnight, i.e. I only get every second weekend off. Also, during the week I do at least one evening duty, sometimes two. That means I work all day and don't finish until nine fifteen p.m. I usually also do one, perhaps two, days at court. By the time we get back to the prison with those in custody it's generally somewhere between seven and eight p.m. before I finish. The hours are long and there's always plenty of overtime, sometimes too much. Added to these long hours is the fact that we work in what could be described as a hostile environment. Still, nobody forced me to join.

Fogarty is doing three months for a bit of receiving. An affable Irishman, when he's sober, he's in his fifties and is a long-time resident of Birmingham – and occasional resident of the Green. Jim Higginbotham and I are detailed to 'produce' him (escort him there and back) at a civil hearing down at Victoria Law

Courts. After thirty years of an abusive marriage, Mrs Fogarty has decided to divorce him. The marriage has been blessed with five children. They must have been speaking now and again. Fogarty is not contesting it, but has to be present as matters to do with property, maintenance and so on have to be dealt with.

Known as a 'bit of a wag', Fogarty keeps Jim and me entertained during the short ride down to the courts. Because it's a civil hearing, we're supposed to be incognito. We wear civvy jackets on top of our uniform shirts, ties and trousers. Our long key chains and the leather straps of our truncheons occasionally show. We sit either side of Fogarty. If we hid behind signs saying 'SCREWS' we'd have a better chance of going undiscovered.

The hearing is held in a room instead of at court. Fogarty, fat and red-faced, wears an ill-fitting suit. After a month without regular infusions of Guinness, he has lost a couple of stone. During this same month his suit has been lying in a cardboard box in reception and is rather crumpled. Somehow, it seems to match his personality.

Mrs Fogarty, who also originates from the Emerald Isle, is tearfully giving the judge chapter and verse of the abusive treatment meted out by 'Himself' over the years – especially on Saturday nights. Weighing about 8 stone 'wet through' every word she utters is garnering sympathy from those assembled. I notice them all, from the judge down, give frequent glances at this great hulk of a man, no doubt comparing him with his diminutive soon to be ex-wife. With each new barb Fogarty winces. He speaks out of the side of his mouth to Jim.

'Did youse hear dat? She's not givin' me the lickins of a dog!'

'Shhh!' says Jim. He has his arms folded and stares impassively ahead.

Mrs Fogarty continues her litany.

'Will youse listen to dat!' Fogarty shakes his head, appalled at this character assassination.

'Shhhhhh!' repeats Jim.

Mrs Fogarty's solicitor speaks. 'How early in the marriage did the defenda . . . ahh, your husband, start his mistreatment of you?'

'Jayz! Did youse hear him wit' "the defendant"?' says Fogarty in a stage whisper.

'ShhSHHH!' says Jim.

'We'd only been married about three months when it started, yer honour,' she dabs her eyes, 'and then it just exclavated. It got to be nearly every Saturday night.' I shoot a glance at Jim. He continues to stare fixedly ahead. 'And this last few years, Sur, dayr's hardly a day goes by when I don't get a clip!' She looks accusingly at her spouse.

Fogarty, probably realising he's on a hiding to nothing, decides to play it for laughs. He leans forward and knocks on the table we're sitting at. All eyes turn to him. He points a finger. 'Don't pay any attention to dat woman,' he says, 'she's PUNCH-DRUNK!'

By late afternoon I'm back in the prison. Fogarty has resumed sweeping the floor of the Mattress Shop. In anticipation of the cons coming in from shops and exercise, I'm wending my way round B Wing unlocking cell doors. As I cross over from one side of B3 to the other, I glance down at the Centre. Jimmy Green, the diminutive gatekeeper, comes out of the Chief's office. He walks over to the Centre box and stands talking to P.O. Appleton. There's a loud clang as the gate at the end of A Wing is flung open. Three screws are escorting Wilshaw, supposedly one of the jail's hard men, back into the prison. He has been on a visit with his wife and kids. Mrs Wilshaw was spotted passing something to him. He refused to hand it over, or to be searched, so the visit has been ended. His family have been escorted to the gate and Wilshaw brought back in to be searched.

Just before the group reaches the Centre the situation escalates . . .

'You're not searching me, yah bastards!'

'You're gonna be searched all right,' says 'Jacko' Jackson, 'the easy way or the hard way.'

'Get fucked!' says Wilshaw and aims a punch at Jacko.

A struggle now ensues as the three officers try to restrain this young, well-built con. I run to the stairs and make my way to the Centre. Wilshaw manages to hit another officer before he is forced to the floor. He continues to resist, violently. As I make for the group, Wilshaw is now face down. One officer is trying, with great difficulty, to sit on his legs. The other two are on either side of his upper body, each attempting to pin an arm to the ground. They are barely able to hold him. Wilshaw continues to utter threats. 'Just wait till I get up, yah Cockney bastard!' he says to Jacko.

As Jimmy Green and I approach the melee I hear Jimmy mutter, 'I'll sort this fucker out.' He holds out an arm and stops me joining the attempt to subdue Wilshaw. I watch as Jimmy strides over and halts by the prisoner's head. The con is still face down, struggling violently as he tries to get to his feet. Jimmy leans forward, places a hand on the shoulders of the two officers who are holding Wilshaw's arms, and pushes both men apart. This leaves a space above the con. Without a word, this slight, sixty-year-old man takes a little leap into the air, tucks his legs up behind him and drops, knees first, onto Wilshaw's upper back. There is a distinct crack, and a scream from Wilshaw, as one of his shoulder-blades is fractured. He now lies still, groaning.

Jimmy rises. 'Right, take that fucker down the block. He'll give you no more trouble.' He dusts his trouser legs with his hands. I walk over to the P.O.'s box with him. He turns to watch as the officers assist Wilshaw down the stairs to A1. 'You'd better ring for a hospital officer to attend to that git,' he says to Johnny Appleton. He rubs his chin. 'No, better make it a doctor. Must be losing me touch, I think I've only done one of his scapula!'

The P.O. reaches for the phone. As he does so he purses his lips as though giving a silent whistle. He looks at me, then nods his head in the direction of Jimmy. 'Have you ever seen a bugger like that in yer life?'

Denizens of the Night

I stand on a corner of the large exercise yard and watch the cons circle. Gordon Lonsdale and Donal Murphy go by at a brisk pace, trying to get a bit of good out of it. Murphy is the only one Lonsdale has anything to do with. A few days ago it suddenly occurred to me why they've palled up. Lonsdale doesn't consider himself a criminal. If I look at it without prejudice, I suppose he's right. He was an agent working abroad for his country. He regards Murphy – doing life imprisonment for the IRA raid on Aborfield Barracks in the mid-fifties – to be in the same position. It's 'birds of a feather'. If Murphy's not on exercise, Lonsdale just ploughs round on his own. On a couple of occasions I've watched one or two cons, who no doubt think they are 'somebody', fall into step with Lonsdale and try to engage him in conversation. You can see by his face he's not pleased. Within a couple of minutes he'll extricate himself from their company. He has no time for criminals.

Another thought sometimes enters my head as I watch them go by. Here are two guys, supposedly enemies of Great Britain, yet they get treated well by the staff. Officers, me included, regularly take time to chat with them, have a laugh and a joke. Does that sometimes make them feel a bit guilty? Citizens of the country that they supposedly would be quite happy to blow up, having a blether with them. This must say something about the British psyche. If I was locked up in Moscow's Lubyanka Prison, would I be treated so well?

P.O. 'Sticky' Walker calls me over. He gets his nickname from his habit, if he thinks a prisoner is becoming aggressive, of drawing his truncheon (stick) and giving him a few whacks!

'Ah, Mr Douglas. I'm afraid I'll have to put you on a week's night shift, starting tonight.'

'Right. Fine, sir. I didn't know we did nights.'

'Not as a rule. We have permanent night patrols. But if one of them is sick or on holiday, we have to put a discipline officer on for a week at a time. You'll find it's a nice break. The prison's a different place at night.'

'What's the routine, sir? What time do I start?'

'Ah, yes. Right. I'm forgetting you're new.' He seems a bit bewildered for a moment. He's a plump, homely looking man. 'Right, you go off at half twelve. Try and get a bit of kip this afternoon. You come on at nine fifteen tonight. Bring some snap [food]. And something to read. There's a lot of time to be passed. The P.O. on nights this week is P.O. Arnold. We do a week at a time, too. That's about it.' He begins to turn away. 'Oh! And don't forget your slippers.'

'Slippers?'

'Yes. We don't go thumping about the landings during the night in shoes or boots. Bastards would hear us coming a mile away!'

After sleeping very badly during the afternoon, I come into the prison just after nine p.m. to start my first shift. In my bag I carry a brand new pair of slippers. Gran had kindly offered to loan me hers. Mercifully they were only size 7. I'd never have got away with the blue pom-poms!

I'm barely an hour into my first shift when I arrive at the conclusion that the permanent night patrols at Winson Green were almost certainly recruited from Elstree Studios. They probably failed the auditions for *The Lavender Hill Mob* and decided to look for gainful employment.

Aged in their fifties and sixties, they've been in the job for years. None of them have ever served as a prison officer, they were all recruited solely as night staff. Senior amongst them, and therefore the one with the cushiest job, is Paddy Magee. In his late fifties, overweight, and with a shock of white hair, Paddy is as Irish as the Mountains of Mourne. In the years to come, whenever I do a week's nights, Paddy's soporific Irish brogue always has the same effect on me as six mugs of Horlicks. By three or four in the morning, just five minutes of his 'craic' and my eyelids become heavy as lead.

During the night, the job of the night patrol is to visit one of the various 'pegging points' in the prison every fifteen minutes. There, the patrolman extracts a key from a small metal box fixed to the wall, inserts it into the leather-bound clock he carries and gives it a few turns. Inside the clock, a mark is made on a roll of graph paper. In the morning the Chief opens up all the clocks and checks the rolls of paper to see if the denizens of the night have faithfully pegged the night away. Paddy Magee only pegs until one a.m. He then heads downstairs under the Centre, disappears into the kitchen, and is rarely seen for the rest of the night. He has two tasks to perform. ONE: Keep an eye on the prison's main boiler and TWO: Make the porridge. Paddy spends a lot of time trying to convince those around him that his efforts during the hours of darkness are undervalued, and he doesn't skive half the night away in the kitchen. He always tries to impress any newcomers . . .

'Jock, the oats have to be steeped for quite a while. Then it has to be heated slowly in the big copper – and regularly stirred with a large paddle so's it'll not stick. I'm in constant attendance. I'm making porridge for 700. You'll know about the making o' the porridge. It can't be rushed. And I've got to keep that boiler right. It's an antiquated old ting, ye know. Temperamental.'

'You forgot to mention regularly dozing off,' says P.O. Arnold.

Paddy looks hurt. He turns to me. 'Do ye see what I'm up against, Jock?'

* * *

An hour or so later, Paddy has just retreated to the kitchen. I'm sitting with the P.O. He lights a cigarette. He's one of those folk who always look as if they've just taken up smoking.

'Did you hear about "Lofty" Martin putting the wind up Paddy a few weeks ago?'

'No,' I say.

'Lofty was night P.O. About five in the morning – that's usually when the jail's at its quietest – he's about to start doing his last round. Taking the double locks off the main doors. He's under the Centre. So he tiptoes into the kitchen, and here's old Paddy sitting up on the high stool, leaning on the paddle, dozed off in the middle of stirring the porridge! Lofty sneaks back out under the Centre. And you know that giant aluminium mixing bowl that's kept there? The one that stands on metal wheels?'

'I do.' I begin to smile in anticipation.

'Lofty takes a hold of it – the bugger must weigh a couple of hundredweight – and he starts pushing it round faster and faster. The bloody racket it's making on the granite setts. And with it being like a big cellar down there, with that vaulted roof, it's like the crack o' fuckin' doom! Five o'clock in the morning, and it's all echoing and vibrating through the jail. Wakening up the cons and everything. The night patrols are up on the Centre, they're thinking maybe the roof's collapsing under the Centre or summat. Anyway, after a couple of minutes Lofty stops. Then he just walks up onto the Centre as if nowt's the matter. The three night patrols have fled down to the far end of A Wing, they're all holding onto one another, thinking their time 'as come! He's just about to call down to them to ask "What's up?" when he hears running feet behind him. Here's old Paddy coming up the stairs – two at a time – never moved so fast for years . . . "P.O.!" he shouts. "P.O.! For the love o' Jaysus open the gate an' let us out – THE BOILER'S ABOUT TO BLOW!" '

The next senior amongst the night patrols is 'Robbie' Robertson. Also pushing sixty, Robbie is a thin, round-shouldered old guy with rheumy eyes and a wheezy chest. On this, my first night, he tells me his joke. For the next eight years he'll tell me it every time I'm on nights. I eventually check it out with other officers and find it's the same with them. None of us have ever let on he's already told us – twenty times! The pleasure is in watching and listening to him. Robbie: The One Joke Wonder!

We're sitting having our meal break. Robbie clears his throat, then lubricates it with a mouthful of tea. He turns to me. 'Did you ever hear the one about the vicar and the verger?'

Paddy Magee sighs.

P.O. Arnold lifts his *Daily Express* higher and disappears behind it.

'No, ah don't think I've heard that one, Robbie,' I say.

'The vicar's in his pulpit. The church is full. It's a Sunday.' Robbie gives an extra wheeze as he takes in enough breath for the second stanza. 'So the vicar leans out of his pulpit, nods in the direction of a woman who's sitting in the front pew, then speaks out of the corner of his mouth to the verger. "Is that Fanny Green?"' Robbie now has great difficulty controlling himself. He manages it. 'And the verger says . . . "No, it's just the light from the stained-glass window!"' Wheeze, wheeze, wheeze! Robbie goes into a paroxysm of laughter and has to reach a hand out to the table to prevent himself falling off the chair. I laugh along with him. I will for the next eight years.

It's almost ten past nine as I'm let through the door into the Centre – only the P.O. carries keys at night. I'm more than halfway through my week and well into the swing of things. So far I've been in the main prison, where I have the company of the P.O. and a couple of night patrols. The evening duty officers are gathered by the Centre box. All this evening's receptions, whether convicted or remanded, have been located in the appropriate wings. The numbers have tallied. The prison is locked up until the morning. As soon as all the night staff are in, the evening duties can go off. The last two appear.

'That's all my lads in,' says P.O. Arnold.

'Off you go. Thanks boys.' P.O. Hobbs turns to Arnold. 'Right, I'm away. Have a good night.' He lets himself out of the main door. We hear the muffled jangle of his keys as he locks it, then his footsteps fade as he strides off down the long corridor. All the evening duty staff came on at either seven or eight this morning, did a normal day's work, then, after the bulk of the staff went off at five thirty, spent the evening patrolling the wings – usually in pairs – supervising the privileged few cons who 'dine out in association' and then slopping out the majority, who are locked in their cells. Later in the evening they 'locate' the incoming receptions into any vacant cells on the wings. They are now ready for a well-earned pint, or home. Or both.

I stand for a moment and savour that rare event – a locked up, quiet prison. Well, quiet compared with the daytime. There is the low hum that comes from nearly 500 men talking or moving around in their cells. Like a human beehive. There's nothing to see as you look along the empty wings and their landings, yet you know there are many people around. Now and again the sound of faint laughter drifts down to the Centre. Someone, for a reason known only to himself, shouts out loud. Two or three cons in nearby cells request him to 'Shut the fuck up!'

'Jock, you can have a spell down the remand ward in the hospital, tonight.'

'That's fine, sir.'

'Frank will keep you right. Okay, Frank?'

'Very good, sir. Can some kind soul let us through?'

P.O. Arnold takes his keys off the chain attached to his belt. He hands them to Robbie. 'Let them through to the hospital and bring the keys straight back, Robbie.'

Frank and I walk along the twos of the quiet hospital wing and on through to the annexe, which is the main hospital building. It consists of various offices and consulting rooms for the prison's own staff of doctors. There is also a dispensary and a couple of padded cells. Upstairs are a few more isolation cells and the remand ward.

Frank is another night patrol who's been recruited from the Home For The Incurably Eccentric. He's in his early sixties and suffers from alopecia, so he's completely bald. Like the rest of the resident night wanderers, at heart he's a canny old stick.

'Do you know about the remand ward, young 'un?'

'No, I don't, Frank.'

'You're locked in there all night.'

'Oh!' I'm going to have to ask, 'Eh, why's that, Frank?'

'Why's what, kid?' enquires Frank in his rich Brummie accent.

'Why am I locked in all night? What's the remand ward?'

Frank smiles. I get the feeling he's warming to his task. 'It's a secure ward where prisoners who've been remanded for S.O.M. reports are located.' He anticipates my next question. 'S.O.M. stands for State Of Mind. There's always an officer on duty in there, twenty-four hours a day. They have to be kept under constant observation to see how they behave. You'll find a ledger on the desk with their name, number and bed order so's you'll know who's who.'

'So, eh, how many are there in the ward?' I try to sound casual.

'There were eighteen last night. Probably be the same again tonight.'

The thought occurs to me . . . that's unless maybe one of them killed a fellow patient today! 'So, what sort of things are they charged with Frank?' Something tells me it's no' gonny be stealing milk aff doorsteps. I'm needing to clear my suddenly dry throat. That'll probably make me sound nervous. Mibbe that's 'cause I AM fuckin' nervous!

'Mmm,' says Frank, 'if I remember rightly, I think there were ten . . . no, I tell a lie, eleven charged with murder.'

'Oh, really!' is what I TRY to say. But as the number of homicidal maniacs I'm about to spend the night with sinks in, it comes out as 'Hoak, eeky!'

Frank throws me a straw to clutch. 'One of the lads in the ward is the cleaner. His bed is near to your desk. They always pick a good lad. If there WAS any bother, until they fetch somebody with a key, he'd give you a hand. So they say.'

While Frank speaks, I'm trying to muster up a bit of saliva. We've climbed the stairs and are now walking along a corridor. 'Here y'are, kid.' We stop outside a pair of double doors. A flap hangs down and I can see part of the ward through the square grille. There are a row of beds. Inmates in various stages of undress sit on some of them. Others just mill about. One, just one, is already in bed under the covers, head on pillow, eyes shut in spite of the hubbub. That's not natural. I'll keep an eye on that bugger! Frank looks through the grille.

'Come in number nine, your time's up!'

A hospital officer rises into view. He has his keys on him, so unlocks the door. 'In you go, Jock,' says Frank. The officer steps out, I step in.

'Anything I should know?' I ask as we pass.

'No. No problems. All been behaving themselves. For a change.' As he speaks, he's locking the door behind him. Locking me in! I'm standing looking through the grille, my back to the ward. Almost certainly, at this very moment some wild-eyed nutter is sneaking up behind me, pillowcase twisted into a garrotte! I resist the urge to turn round.

As the hospital officer speeds off, Frank's face appears at the grille. 'I'll be looking in on you regularly. Any time you want a mug of tea or coffee, just call. I'm along the corridor in the office. I'll hear you. Okay?'

'Yeah, fine. See you later.' Nice to know my screams will be heard. I turn round. How can I make it appear as if I've done it all before? I sit down at the desk and slowly look around the ward. It's time to start playing 'Spot The Axe Murderer'!

I look at my watch. Just coming up for eleven. It's an hour since I put the lights out. At the right hand edge of the desk is a table lamp. The light from it creates a glare, making the darkness beyond seem even darker. Impenetrable. I can dimly see the first few beds on either side of the ward, then the rest fade out of sight. They could be having a union meeting up the back for all I know. I take another look at the open ledger in front of me. There are eighteen in the ward, as Frank suspected. One is the cleaner, the rest all S.O.M. reports. I've been reading the hospital officers' comments on them . . . 'Doesn't associate much with other patients'; 'Sits staring into space for long periods'; 'Sullen, uncooperative. Can become aggressive'. Jeez-oh! I try to work out what bed that one's in. If there are no problems during the night, all I do in the morning is write against each name: 'Appeared to sleep well'. Seventeen times. If I'm still alive.

Time's not half dragging. It's just after eleven. The ward is quiet; plenty of steady breathing, the occasional snore. I look past the lamp at the few huddled figures I can see. I stretch my legs and arms out in front of me and stifle a yawn. Jeez, what a strange place to be. Locked up in a room with eleven murderers – and a few assorted crazies just tae balance things oot. These last few years I haven't half been in some dodgy gaffs. This is definitely the dodgiest. There's some movement in the darkness. I lean away from the glare so's I can see better. Fuck me! It's that sullen git. He sees me looking. Holds up his hand. 'Toilet, boss,' he whispers. I nod. My mouth has dried, nodding is all I can manage. He has to come right past the desk to get to the toilet. I slip my right hand down my side, hook my thumb round my stick. If this fucker makes a dive at me I'll split him wide open – in mid-air!

It's maybe ten minutes later. All is quiet. I can hear voices; keys jingle. I get up and look through the grille. P.O. Arnold and Frank are approaching. Between them is a prisoner carrying sheets and blankets! He can't have come through reception. They went off hours ago. The P.O. unlocks the ward door. 'Here's a late one for you. His name is David Helbing. It's a murder charge.' Thanks a lot, I think to myself, ah could jist do wi' another wan. 'He was arrested this morning, the police have been questioning him all day. The Governor has okayed taking him so late.'

I step aside. 'Just come through. Stand by the desk for a minute.' Arnold locks the door and he and Frank walk away. I turn and face the prisoner. He's a blond, good-looking young man about twenty-five years old. So THIS is David Helbing. For the last few days I've been reading about the hunt for him, and watching it on the TV news. He looks totally bewildered. Tired. He comes from a good family. Never been in bother until now.

'Could you manage a cup of tea?'

He's been standing by the desk, bedding under his arm. Miles away. 'Oh, yes. Please.'

As expected, he's well spoken. I look through the grille. 'FRANK!' He appears. 'Would you make two mugs o' tea? One for him as well as me.'

'Right, Jock. Be back in a jiff.'

I point to an empty bed. 'Take your bedding over there and make it up. When you see the officer hand the mugs through the grille, come over here and have your tea.'

I sit at the desk and watch as he makes hard work of preparing his bed. I enter his name in the ledger. The murder, then the hunt for him, have been making headlines in the local papers for days. It's almost an exact rerun of my first murder trial, except Helbing has a much better background than Wood. Well-off folks. He'd been courting this girl for a considerable time, she was also from a good family. She'd wanted to end the relationship. He couldn't handle it. Probably always used to getting his own way. Until now. Just as Wood did, he finished up stabbing her and pushing her under the bed. He's been on the run for days. The police arrested him this morning. Never been in trouble in his life – now he's on a murder charge.

* * *

'Pssst! Jock. Tea up.' Frank hands the two mugs through to me. Helbing comes over and I point to the spare chair at the desk. While he drinks his tea he doesn't speak. Just stares into space. I look at him as we sit in this little pool of light. It's nearly midnight. I bet he feels he's in the middle of a bad dream and can't make himself wake up.

I open my piece box. 'Could you manage a cheese sandwich?'

That temporarily brings him back from wherever he was. 'Ah, yes, I could. Thank you.' He tries to smile. 'I haven't eaten for hours.' He takes a large bite.

'You'll have had a busy day, I imagine.'

'Yes. Yes, I have.' He almost hangs his head. 'It's been a very long day.'

By two a.m. all is quiet. Helbing appears to be sleeping. I suppose it's a tragedy all round. From what I read in the paper his family are distraught – for the girl and her folks as well as for their son. It's a good job for him they changed the law a few years back. He might have hanged for this. Since the new Criminal Justice Act came into force you're only liable for the rope if you kill to further a robbery, kill for the second time, or murder a policeman or prison officer. All he'll get is the mandatory life sentence – he'll be out in eight if he keeps his nose clean.

A Day in the Life of . . .

It's just coming up for seven a.m. Having picked their keys up at the gate, the staff stream up the long corridor, through the open door and onto the Centre. Every time someone is about to lock the door, another tail-end Charlie hoves into view down the far end. The screws begin to line up in an untidy four ranks for roll-call. 'Screws' was originally a derogatory name for prison officers, used by cons. Over the years officers have adopted it, so it's lost its bite. Like many things in the Prison Service it has come down from the Victorian era. An early form of lock on cell doors was an iron screw, or 'worm', which was turned by a metal bar to make the door fast. Soon the warders were being nick-named 'screws'. Around 1929 the term 'warder' was itself replaced by the title 'prison officer'. The nation's newspapers, however, have never taken to that. 'Warder Attacked!' or 'Warder "anything"' makes for a better headline. I look along the ranks. The majority of those officers who are in their late thirties and forties sport their medal ribbons – 'fruit salad' as they call them. Almost all the younger screws, like me, have done their two years' National Service. Nine out of ten are ex-service-men.

The parade of officers are just beginning to settle down when there is an 'OHYAH!' followed by 'Yumphyumphyumph!' Arthur Mosely has just reached through with his truncheon and goosed someone two ranks in front. There's an outburst of laughter. I look along the line. His best mate, Don Midgely, stands beside him shaking his head, as if to say 'What can you do with him?' Arthur, pipe clenched between his teeth, smiles broadly.

Bill Frew, who is Centre P.O. today, looks at Arthur. 'I'll take that bloody stick off you one of these days!' He clears his throat. 'Right, lads, roll-call.' Frew has a bristly, turned-up-at-the-ends moustache that gives him the air of one of those Victorian screws. As he calls the roll, every minute or so another latecomer will try to slip quietly through the door and tiptoe over to the ranks. Frew always gives them a black look.

'Right, DISMISS!' We break ranks and head noisily to our landings.

I progress along one side of B3, from B3-1 upwards, counting the numbers. Directly opposite, on the other side, Percy Thompson, a Welshman, has started from the highest number on the landing and we go from cell to cell in parallel. As I come to each cell I slip the spyhole cover to the side, look in, and add the number of inmates to my growing tally; it's either one or three. Some cons are already up, dressed, bed made. The majority are still abed. If they are, I take off the outside 'night bolt' and rattle it briskly back and forth. 'C'MON, LET'S BE HAVING YOU!' Since the large bell hanging on the Centre was rung at around six forty a.m. to waken the prison, many have dozed off again.

Eventually Percy and I meet. He's senior to me so I tell him my tally. 'Fifty-three, Perce.' He adds it to his number then calls the grand total over to Stan Ireland. 'Hundred and twelve!' Stan is on the short bridge which spans the width of the landing. 'B3, ONE HUNDRED AND TWELVE!' he shouts down to the Centre. P.O. Frew raises his hand to acknowledge that's correct. Perce and I go back to where we started our count, on either side of the landing. In a mirror image of one another we lean on the top rail and rest a foot on a lower rail. We watch the activity on the Centre. At last, all the numbers are in.

'UNLOCK!' shouts Frew.

Keys in hand, Perce and I move swiftly along our rows of doors, unlocking them and opening them wide. We frequently come across cons still in bed. 'HEY! Out of it, NOW!' As we progress, cons stream out of their cells behind us carrying their piss-pot in one hand and aluminium water jug in the other, heading for the recess to slop out. Already queues are forming at the two recesses, one on each side of the landing. They empty their pot down the large china Belfast sink, then rinse it under the strong flow of cold water from the tap. Then they line up at the wash-basin to fill their jug with hot water. Just like the army, it always runs out long before it should. On the other three landings queues of cons also slop out. There is the noise of tramping feet and voices.

From his place on the bridge Stan keeps an eye on our two recesses. If one con wants to assault another, these busy places are a popular choice. Sometimes arguments flare up. Tempers can be short in the morning. As time goes on and I get to know the cons, if a fight breaks out and I find a well-known trouble-maker is getting the worst of it, I often walk the other way. There is also the situation where a con will start a fight, with the expectation that a screw will jump in and stop it, thereby saving his face. Sometimes I'll disappoint him. I always intervene if I come across one of the bully-boys picking on someone. That never fails to get my back up. I regularly remind new inmates, 'When you're in jail, you'll find it's not the screws you have to worry about. If you behave yourself you'll get no trouble from us. It's your fellow prisoners, especially those who fancy themselves as hard men. They're the ones who'll pick on you, rob you and threaten you – not the screws.'

A general rule of thumb when two cons start to fight is don't break it up too quickly. If it's between two guys who think they are hard cases and it starts off quite viciously, let them punch themselves out. Intervene too early, when tempers are up and they're still fresh, and you're liable to get a clout. It doesn't take long until they are knackered – then they're only too pleased when you jump in and separate them.

After slopping out, Perce and I go along our sides of the landing carrying the stout, canvas razor-blade holders and dish out the '7 O'Clock' brand blades. The holders have numbered slots for each cell to make sure cons get the same blade each morning. The blades are always replaced in their wrappers to try and avoid cut fingers. Most cons now stand at their doors, mugs in hand, waiting for the call to breakfast. From all over the wing, and the neighbouring wings, comes the sound of feet as landings are called down. Those already served climb back up the metal stairs, balancing mug and stainless steel tray. Breakfast this morning is porridge – a staple – or cornflakes, accompanied by two thin rashers of bacon on a slice of fried bread plus three or four slices of bread and a small pat of margarine. The bread is baked in the prison kitchen. When they return to their landing, many of the old lags step into their cells and without waiting for the screws to bang them up, immediately back-heel the door shut themselves. After all the clamour of slopping out and trekking down to the hotplate and back, they now want a bit of peace and quiet in which to have their breakfast, followed by a shave.

P.O. Frew gives a shout. 'LEAD ON, B3!'

'Right, LEAD ON!' shouts Stan. They need no second bidding. I watch as they troop down the stairway past B2 then further down onto B1 where they vanish through the door taking them to the cellar-like area under the Centre where the hotplates are. With its low, vaulted roof, cobbled floor and whitewashed walls and ceiling it always reminds me of the pit-bottom at Polkemmet Colliery where I worked for a time.

Once the cons are back in their cells the numbers are checked yet again. The bulk of the staff head to the officers' mess for breakfast. It's always busy in the morning so I share a table. Like most of my fellow officers I rose around six a.m. and only had a cup of tea before leaving for work. It's now gone eight and I'm ready for something to eat. I have the full English and a mug of tea. There is a catering officer in charge, but all the cooking and serving of food is carried out by prisoners. They consider it a cushy job. When I'm finished I go through to the lounge and relax in one of the well-worn armchairs. I begin to read the *Daily Express* I bought on my way to work. Officers sit at some of the tables and play cards; usually solo whist. As accents from all over the country wash over me, it's almost like being back in my National Service days. Somewhere near the foot of page three I doze off.

By nine a.m. I'm back on B3, slopping them out preparatory to heading for the workshops. I'm in the Mailbag Shop today. We'll be on the exercise yard for thirty minutes before going into the shop. The cons who are going straight to work are called down first. They will have their exercise at the end of the morning, before coming in for the midday meal.

I take up a position at a corner of the large yard. Cons from three workshops stroll round. The screws who man the yard are the discipline officers allocated to those shops. The instructors and a few key inmates are already inside, getting things ready for the day's work. The cons are all dressed in prison uniform – gray battledress jacket and trousers, and blue and white striped shirts. They amble around in pairs. The concrete circular paths are just wide enough for two to walk side by side and are surrounded by grass, which it's forbidden to walk on, so if a few cons want to walk and talk as a group, they have to walk close behind one another in their pairs. They should all have their jackets buttoned up, but some of those walking on the smaller inner paths occasionally try it on by having their jackets unbuttoned. They hope the officers won't be bothered to cut through the outer rings of circling cons and grassed areas to confront them. I always do. It's all part of making a name for myself. The most persistent offenders at this game are a small group of West Indians. They are all from the notorious red-light district of Balsall Heath and all five of them are in for 'living on immoral earnings'. I watch them go round; three of them have their jackets undone. I cut through the exercise and stand astride the small inner path. As they approach, I point to the three offenders. 'Do your jackets up.' Sutherland, a heavily-built guy, mutters, 'Always pickin' on us, man.'

I give him a nice smile. 'Look around the yard, Sutherland. You're the only three with your jackets undone. Nuthin' to do wi' colour, all aboot jackets undone.'

Being the junior officer, I'm at the bottom end of the shop. Norman Thomas, another Welshman, is sitting on the high stool at the top end, by the alarm bell. Now and again some of the cons working at a nearby table try to engage me in conversation. When you're new it's a regular occurrence for some of them to 'try you out', see if they can – without going TOO far – embarrass you, put you on the defensive. But all the while keeping just within the bounds of civility.

Turvey is a Londoner in his late thirties. All London cons think they are superior to not only cons from elsewhere, but also the screws. He sits at a table with three 'provincials'. They are engaged in cutting lengths of strong thick thread for use by those hand-sewing mailbags. Turvey is their self-appointed spokesman.

'So how do you like this job, guv?'

As the man from 221b Baker Street would say, 'The game's afoot!' I walk over to the table.

'What job's that? Yours or mine?'

'Well, yours, guv. If you don't mind me asking. You know, locking people up. I don't think I could do that, lock up me fellow man.' He gives me a smile. I'm now supposed to go on the defensive, try and justify my job.

'Well, you'll be pleased to know, you won't ever have that problem. Nobody wi' a record can get a job as a screw. And, tae answer your question, it doesn't bother me in the least locking folk up, especially folk who quite happily rob and assault their fellow man. In fact, tae be honest . . .' I look around, as though about to impart something of great importance. I lean forward. '. . . Ah quite enjoy it!' I give the four of them a big smile.

Things aren't going to plan. By now I should be trying to justify my job – without saying I like locking guys up. The thread cutters should be enjoying my discomfort. 'Well,' says Turvey lamely, 'I couldn't do it.' He mustn't have a Plan B to fall back on.

'Well, don't worry aboot it. It's a case of horses for courses. Ah like tae think that ah'm making crime pay. You guys do the crime – ah make it pay! Never made so much money in ma life. Best job ah've ever had.' I lean forward again. 'If there's anything else you boys want tae ask, I'll just be over there.' I wander off.

A few years later I hear that Turvey has been shot dead in a turf war between some London gangs. My first reaction is to assume that he won't want his killer locked up!

I relieve Norman while he goes for his tea break. I sit myself on the high stool. The first few rows of wooden chairs are occupied by old lags, hand-sewing mailbags. They are all over forty and have done plenty of 'porridge' between them. Further back in the shop, younger cons sit at large industrial sewing-machines, also turning out mailbags for the GPO. The lags at the front sit with their feet inside the bag they are working on, knees apart to keep it stretched, rhythmically hand-sewing at a rate of twelve stitches to the inch. They all wear a thick leather 'stall' on the finger used to push the large needle through the tough canvas. Heads down, the only interruption to their work comes when they stop for a moment to turn the bag round to a new bit. A hundred years ago, screws sat where I am now watching convicts with broad arrows on their uniforms sewing mailbags for Queen Victoria's Post Office. Charles Dickens is alive and well in Britain's prisons. Now and again one of the lags will raise a hand. 'Fall out, boss?' I nod. I know they are going to the toilet for a quick few draws at a roll-up. A blind eye is turned to this. Further back in the shop, the younger cons laugh and chatter as they work. The contrast with the first few rows is striking.

Norman returns from the mess. 'Right y'are, Jock. Off you go.'

I climb down from the stool. 'I've just been noticing, Norman. There's such a difference between the older cons down here and the younger ones at the back. There's hardly a cheep from this lot.'

'Don't you know why?' He pauses. 'Well, I s'pose you wouldn't. It's less than two years since talking was allowed in the workshops. The lags have never got used to it. You should've seen the shops the first few weeks after it was brought in. They were still whispering to one another. Couldn't get used to it at all.'

Man of Property

'Ah've found us a house!'

'Oh, that's smashing! What's it like?

'It's what they call a "red brick terrace" doon here. Upstairs there's two bedrooms and a bathroom–toilet. Doonstairs there's two living-rooms and the kitchen. It has a wee backyard wi' a coal-house and an ootside toilet. The toilet still works. It's a nice wee house, ah think you'll like it. The street is nice and quiet, tae.' The pips start going so I insert the three pennies I have ready on top of the cash box. 'Are you still there?'

'Aye.' There's a pause. 'How much is it?'

'£1,650.'

'My God! How much is the mortgage gonny be?'

'Well, they were quite happy wi' the £250 deposit. Ah've taken the mortgage over ten years. With the extra insurance for the house it's gonny be about £17 a month.'

I hear Nancy draw in her breath. 'Can we afford aw' that?'

'Nae bother. Even though you'll no' be working, I'm making more than enough. At the minute ah'm coming oot wi' around £24 a week, clear. Ah'll no' even have tae do any extra overtime. And remember, because they could'nae supply us wi' quarters they've granted me permission to buy ma own, so ah'll be getting about £7 a month rent allowance. We'll manage nae bother.'

'So what's gonny be oor new address?'

'Number 10 Southfield Road, Rotton Park. It's about a mile from the prison. It should'nae be long till the two of ye can come doon. It'll be great, oor ain place!'

'Oh, ah'm really lookin' forward tae it. Not only having oor ain place, but ah really like the idea of living in England. My ma says ah can take my bed, and there's yin or two other . . .' She's interrupted by the pips. In the last few seconds before we get cut off, I tell her, 'Ah've got no more change, ah'll write tonight—' The phone goes dead and I hear the continuous melancholy wail that means we've been disconnected. I've come to hate that sound these last few months. I put the handset back in the cradle and push the heavy kiosk door open.

As I walk back to Gran's the thought of buying a house is uppermost in my mind. I think about the miserable journey I made down south to join the RAF Boys' Service after Ma died. As the train slowed on entering Wolverhampton I'd looked out on row after row of red brick terraces. Four years later it had been the same again when I'd been called up into the army. This time the city was Nottingham. They all seemed so English to me. Since childhood I'd sat in the Blythswood with Ma watching all those English pictures – *This Happy Breed* and *It Always Rains On Sundays*. Everybody seemed to live in houses like that. It wouldn't have surprised me to find the King lived in a red brick terrace. A four-bedroom one. Jeez, now it won't be long until I own one! My own little bit of England.

My mind takes that thought and runs with it. Just eight years ago I was living in oor single-end. As long as there was Ma and me I was as happy as the day was long. I loved oor house. It was only when that wee bastard was in residence, knocking the two of us about when he felt like it. That was what spoiled it. Then Ma took cancer. She'd have been forty-four now. It would have been really great if she'd still been alive, bringing her down to see our house in Birmingham.

I'm sitting in the officers' club. It's midweek, so it isn't busy. Jimmy Green and a few of the senior officers are having a drink. I watch them now and again. There's George Whatmore, 'Jacko' Jackson, Charlie Tipper and Billy Goode. It's quite marked the way they defer to Jimmy. He's in his sixties, small and slim. Definitely not tall enough to be in the service. But he is. I think back a couple of weeks. Dead calm he was when he dropped, knees first, onto Wilshaw. He'd actually intended to break BOTH his shoulder-blades and was quite disappointed when he found he'd only done one. There is definitely something about him. But what?

I find almost all the senior officers, especially those with their medal ribbons up, don't take any shit from the cons. I suppose if you've seen active service during the war you're not going to take any crap from louts or layabouts who can't keep their hands off other folks' property. Nor are you going to be threatened or otherwise bullied by so-called hard men. If they're too big and strong, just call up a few more officers! Even if you've, like me, just done your National Service, it gets your back up when some toerag who'll neither work nor want when he's on the outside starts trying to tell me he's 'entitled' and he's 'got rights'. I take pleasure in telling him that I've got rights. And one of them is that when a con raises his voice to me, he gets nothing! And if he doesn't get back to his cell NOW, he's gonna get nicked! (Put on Governor's report).

I'm on evening duty on A Wing and George Whatmore is my senior officer. I'm getting to like George; he's around fifty, Welsh, has his medal ribbons up – he's been at the Green for years. We're having a 'blow' before we start going round the wing with the suppers. We stand on the bridge on A3, leaning on the rail looking down towards the Centre. It's warm in the jail tonight and George has his peaked hat shoved to the back of his head and the top two buttons on his tunic undone. There's a fag almost permanently sticking out from under his heavy, gray moustache and the side of his tash where the fags hang from has long ago turned yellow from the smoke. Now and again ash falls down his jacket. I decide this is as good a time as any to start making enquiries . . .

'Ah was on the Centre the other week when Jimmy Green broke Wilshaw's shoulder-blade. He just done it no bother at all. Meant it. Where did he get all that stuff from?'

George laughs. He takes a draw, then takes the fag out of his mouth. 'Hah! He's a queer bugger, Jimmy. Goes fuckin' mad, he does, if a con works himself. Just won't put up with it. He was in SOE – you know, Special Operations Executive – during the war. That's where he learned all that stuff. He's getting on now, but if he wanted to do you, boyo, the little fucker could still do it. I've seen 'im lay some big lads out. He's a ruthless little sod when he starts, always aims to hurt, put them out of action before they can start.'

'So, was he an officer? They were usually all officers in that lot, weren't they?'

George takes a cigarette from his packet and lights it from the stub of the one he's smoking. 'He was a staff sergeant. Went into the Royal Engineers the last couple of years of the First World War. He signed on and was just finishing his twenty-two years when the second bugger comes along in '39, so of course he was kept on. He'd been working with plastic explosive – that was fairly new then – and by '42 he was at an SOE training school, teaching agents like Peter Churchill, Odette an' all them how to use it. At the end of '42 the Germans had penetrated a lot of the French groups and they were in a bad way. So Colonel Buckmaster, the head of the French Section – 'ave you 'eard of him?'

'Aye. Maurice Buckmaster. Ah've read most of the books to do with all that.'

'Well, Buckmaster asks Jimmy if he'd drop into France.' George takes a long draw on his cigarette. 'All those agents were young officers, spoke French. Jimmy's in his early forties, he's a Brummie – doesn't even speak proper English! End of '42 Jimmy drops into Brittany. With 'im not speaking French he had to hide deep in the forests with the Maquis, living in tunnels underground. Was there just over a year. Eventually flew 'im out by Lysander.'

'Jeez! Ah'll bet ye he can tell some tales.'

'Huh! Like pulling teeth getting the little bugger to tell you anything. Not so bad if you get a few pints down 'im. Jacko and me went back to his house one night after a session at the club. You should'ave seen the fuckin' stuff he was showin' us. He's got this combination knife-cum-knuckle-duster thing, all these forged French papers. Whenever he 'ad to travel anywhere – with him not 'aving the French – he had to pose as deaf 'n' dumb. Have you noticed he doesn't wear any medal ribbons?'

'Ah have.'

'He's got more medals than any bugger on the staff!' George holds up his fingers to count them off. 'He's got 'is First World War medals. He's got the basic campaign ones from the last do. The French AND the Belgians both gave him their Croix de Guerre – he trained Belgian agents as well as French – the Yanks gave 'im a medal cos he instructed their OSS folks too. He's got three rows of medals. Never wears a ribbon.'

'Yeah, since the first time I saw him I thought he had something about him.'

'Every year Jimmy and 'is wife – they've no kids – are invited down to Buckmaster's estate for a week. Buckmaster thinks there's nobody like 'im. They stay in a cottage in the grounds. Two or three evenings they go up to the big house for a meal. There's usually other guests, a lot of them folk Jimmy trained.'

'Ah suppose with a war record like his, they just waived the height restrictions when he joined the Prison Service?'

'No, that was Buckmaster. Jimmy had told 'im he fancied joining the Prisons, but when he'd gone for 'is medical they'd knocked him back cos he was under the height. Buckmaster said to 'im, "Leave it to me, James." He rang up some mate of 'is at the Home Office, and that was sorted out.' George flicks his fag end over the rail. I watch it send up showers of sparks as it hits the suicide netting a couple of times on the way down. 'C'mon then, Jock. Better get the orderlies unlocked and get round with the suppers. It should be ready by now.'

A Learning Curve

As I come through the door onto the Centre, it's obvious that something's up. The staff aren't lining up for roll-call. Every now and again there's banging and shouting from high up on B Wing. P.O. Appleton motions for us to come closer so he won't have to raise his voice.

'Right, lads. I'm sure most of you will be acquainted with Ferguson up on B3. Nice lad, doing a 'four'. Good to his mother. Also fancies himself as a bit of a hard lad. He's due to be transferred to Strangeways today. BUT, he's barricaded himself in – he likes it so much here, he doesn't want to go.'

There's a collective 'Ahhhh!' from quite a few screws.

'But he's going. The easy way or the hard way! He's in B3-30. Hands up the B3 landing officers.'

I put my hand up along with Stan Ireland, Roy Humphries and Percy Thompson.

'Oh, I think you four will manage all right, won't you?'

'No problem,' says Roy.

'I'm leaving the jail locked up till we get the bugger winkled out,' says Appleton. 'There's a works' officer waiting up there with a pinch-bar to force the door. Oh, and try not to damage him too much, otherwise he won't be fit to travel. Okay?'

As we troop up onto the landing the rest of the staff wait on the Centre. A few wander along B2 and stand so they can look up and watch the fun.

'You won't have done one of these, Jock, will you?' enquires Roy.

'No.' I feel a little frisson of . . . what? It's a mixture of excitement to come – and nervousness. Not so much about being involved in some violence; it's wanting to acquit myself well. Not letting my mates down.

We stop outside cell number 30. The brown boiler suited works' officer, Stan Pearson, leans against the wall. He holds a thick, four feet long, metal pinch-bar. 'Morning, chaps.'

Roy slides back the spyhole cover and looks in. As he does so there are one or two shouts from other cells on the landing: 'LEAVE 'IM ALONE YAH BASTARDS! FUCKIN' SHIT-BAGS!'

Some of the cells have no glass in their spyholes. The cons have slid the metal covers back with their fingers so they can see what's going on. Roy turns round. 'I recognise your voice, Wilson. If there's another peep out of you you'll be straight down the block!' The cover swings shut with a 'clink'.

'I'll get the other bastard,' says Stan. I watch as he tiptoes along the landing, over the bridge, and stands by B3-9. He draws his stick. A minute or so later the metal cover trembles a little, then starts to move. When it's about a third of the way open a fingertip appears and begins to open it wider. Stan gives it a whack with his stick. There's a howl and the finger instantly disappears; the cover swings back and forth like a pendulum, then stops. We can faintly hear: 'Ohyah! Fuckin' bastards!' Stan rejoins us.

Roy looks through the spyhole again. 'It's Mr Humphries, Ferguson. Now, we've been told to get you out. Whether you like it or not, you're going to Manchester. What's it gonna be, easy way or hard way?'

'I ain't fucking going!'

Roy lets the cover swing shut. He motions for us to come closer. 'It's the usual arrangement. He's got the bed, then the table, then the chair, all in a straight line from behind the door to the far wall. He's pulled a leg off the chair and he's waving it about. So,' he drops his voice further, 'never mind what Johnny

Appleton says. Once we get in there, if he starts seriously trying to clout us with that chair leg, split the fucker wide open if you get the chance.' He turns to me. 'Jock, fetch two mattresses from an empty cell. We'll be going in behind them once the door's opened. And remember, when we charge in, shout and bawl at the top of your voices – it unnerves them.'

Five minutes later, the door has had the outside hinges removed and is jemmied open. The barricade has shifted and the bed is now at an angle. 'Right, draw your sticks.'

'AH'M READY FOR YAH, YAH BASTARDS!' shouts Ferguson.

Roy takes a look through the side of the half-open door. 'He's at the back of the cell. The bed's about the only thing between him and us.'

Percy and I are going in behind one mattress, Roy and Stan behind the other. 'Now don't forget, scream like fucking madmen. LET'S GO!' Roy and Stan force the cell door wide open. Holding the thin prison mattress between them, they rush into the cell, brandishing their sticks and screaming like a couple of loonies. Perce and I follow immediately, also shouting and bawling at the tops of our voices. We position ourselves side by side with the other two. Stan reaches down and tips the bed over on its edge so as we can get nearer to Ferguson. The con takes a couple of swings with the chair leg, misses completely with the first and hits Roy and Stan's mattress with the second. Stan times it perfectly. As Ferguson connects with the mattress, Stan takes a vicious swipe with his truncheon and hits him on the back of his knuckles.

'AHHH! Fucking bastard!' The chair leg falls from his hand. He bends down to pick it up and Roy whacks him on the back of the neck. He goes down on one knee. 'OKAY! OKAY! I give up.' He stands up and leans against the wall. He has trouble deciding whether he should tuck his bruised knuckles under his armpit, or use his undamaged hand to rub his neck.

Roy puts his stick away. 'Didn't I tell you it would be a waste o'time? You've now got a sore hand and a bruised neck – and you're STILL fuckin' going to Strangeways. PACK YOUR KIT!'

I sit back in the compartment of the train taking me back to Birmingham. I really enjoyed that week up in Seafield. After four months it was wonderful to be with Nancy again. Just one thing took the shine off it – during the time I've been away, Scott had forgotten who I was. He'd been eight months old when I left. It was to be expected, but even so, it hurt. Still, by the end of the week we'd rebuilt our relationship. It won't be long now, just a few weeks until we move into 10 Southfield Road. Nancy's really looking forward to living in England. I can't wait!

Well, back to the jail tomorrow morning. Before I go down to Gran's, I'll nip into the gate-lodge and ring the Centre; find out what time I start and what job I've been detailed to. I open the *Reader's Digest*. I picked it up at WH Smith in Waverley station. I like the *Digest*; short little stories and articles. Ideal when you're travelling. A little poem catches my eye. I read it, then a few pages later I find its meaning has stayed with me. I turn back and read it again. If you're a screw, or a policeman, you won't go far wrong if you adopt this as your motto . . .

The strength of three
has he who is just.
But the strength of four
has he who is FIRST!

I think back to when I was at secondary school. I must have been about thirteen. It looked like me and a lad called Adamson were about to have a fight; we were sort of squaring up to one another. I felt quite confident I could beat him. Then all of a sudden he let loose with a few good punches, really caught me on the hop. I fought back, but his sudden onslaught had knocked the fight out of me. I read the little verse again. Yeah, I think I should remember this. It reinforces what George Whatmore said to me a month or so back: 'If you think one of them is working himself up to 'aving a go, don't wait for 'im to start, Jock. Get your retaliation in FIRST!'

Studies in Blue: One

Walter Dimmock's talking to me! If I needed proof I'm doing all right as an officer, that fact in itself is proof positive! Like quite a few of the senior officers, during your first year or so they only talk to you if they have to. All during this period they are weighing you up. If, as happened today, you're working with one of them and he actually starts having a conversation with you, that's it! I passed my official year's probation three months ago, and that was good. But Walter Dimmock all of a sudden chatting to me? Jeez-oh!

I'm in G Wing, the remand wing, for the day. Walter is in charge. For over a century this was the women's wing until it was closed a few months ago and all the women sent to Holloway Prison in London. It's now used to hold unconvicted men who have been remanded in custody. It's ideal for this as it's a single wing, standing on its own. The remands therefore have no contact with the convicted men in the main jail.

The wing office is a wooden construction with windows on all sides which stands on the twos and looks down the length of the wing. It's just gone seven thirty a.m. The seventy or so inmates, spread over four landings, have been unlocked and are just about ready to be served breakfast. Those wanting to make 'applications' are queuing in front of the wing office. Walter sits at the desk. He hasn't yet slid open the window to see what they want because he's been talking to me.

Walter Dimmock is a burly man aged around fifty. There are

quite a few words which MUST be used when trying to describe him: Dour. Irascible. Awkward. Stubborn. He has the bulbous nose and gimlet eye of W.C. Fields – and the same manner. In conversation – with officers or cons – he swears profusely, yet no one ever takes offence. It's just his way. Officers and cons like him. Walter appears not to reciprocate their feelings. He strides around the jail, winter and summer, wearing his extra-long uniform mac which is always open and flowing out behind him. This gives a fair idea how W.C. Fields would've looked if cast as Batman!

Walter joined the Prison Service after the end of the recent unpleasantness with Germany. Like Jimmy Green, he had an 'interesting' war. Also like Jimmy, he can't be bothered to wear his medal ribbons. A sergeant in one of the Midlands' infantry regiments, he was posted to Crete in 1941, arriving in the nick of time to be captured by German paratroopers who'd 'just dropped in'. The next four years were spent as a POW.

During his time in the Prison Service, Walter, a lifelong bachelor, spent four years in Germany at the Generals' Camp. This was where high-ranking officers served the sentences imposed on them at some of the Nuremberg War Trials held after 1945. There, he helped guard such notables as Field Marshals von Rundstedt and von Manstein. In the fifties he also spent a year in Cyprus during the 'emergency', when those suspected, or convicted, of being members of the EOKA 'terrorist' group were locked up in increasing numbers.

Before coming to Birmingham he spent five years at Dartmoor, which he loved. Although on the list for promotion to P.O., Walter feels he is being held back deliberately. For some time he has been engaged in a rancorous exchange of letters with the Prison Department.

Walter finishes telling me of his battles with the Department. He sits at the desk wearing his peaked hat; the long mac trails on the floor. He looks at his watch. 'Better get these fookers dealt with.' There are seven or eight remands in the queue and very few will get what they want – the majority will be bollocked to varying degrees. They all know him, so just take it in their stride.

Five minutes later, he is down to the last one. A face long familiar to Walter appears at the window. 'Mornin' boss.' Farrell is a West Indian, aged about forty. He is a regular.

'Foohk me!' says Walter. 'Ah could've took a foohkin' bet yower face would appear at this window!' He looks at me. 'Allus on the fookhin' mooch, he is.' He turns back to Farrell, who looks quite unperturbed. 'What duss yow foohkin' want this morning?'

'A special letter, Mr Dimmock.'

'Special letter! Special foohkin' letter!' Walter rocks back and forth in his chair. He throws his pen down on the desk. 'Ah gave yow TWO last foohkin' week. You're a remand prisoner. Why dussn't tha buy some foohkin' stamps? If tha buys stamps yow can 'ave all the foohkin' letters you want. Any amount!'

'I ain't got any money, boss.'

'No money! What's the fookhin' point o' being a criminal?' Once again Walter squirms as though in anguish. He picks up the pen then throws it back down again. 'Tha's spent years in the foohkin' jail – and yow haven't got enough money to buy a foohkin' stamp! Dussn't tha think it's time yow foohkin' packed it in? Retired? Yower in the wrong trade.' He leans forward. 'Well, yower not getting a special letter. Go on, foohk off!'

During all this tirade, I've been standing by, ready to jump in if Farrell decides to become aggressive. He doesn't. He just shakes his head and turns away. He gets a few yards when Walter shouts 'FARRELL! Come back 'ere.'

I watch as Farrell comes back to the window.

'What's yower foohkin' number?' Farrell gives him it. Walter writes it on top of the two-page, prison-issue letter. He hands it to Farrell, then wags a finger at him. 'Now ah'm in here all next week. Ah don't want to see yower black face at this window, asking for a letter. All right?'

'Yeah, okay boss. T'anks!'

'Right, now foohk off!'

He watches the departing figure of the applicant, then he turns to me. 'Now let that be a lesson to yow, Jock. They get nothing – unless they're foohkin' civil!'

In 1966, Walter at last gets promoted to P.O. and is posted back to his beloved Dartmoor. The following year, along with two other officers, I escort a prisoner down to, as we call it, the Moor. After handing our charge over to reception, we ask if Walter's around.

'You mean the Russian P.O.?' says the officer.

'*Russian* P.O.?' says one of us.

'Yeah. That's what the cons call him – P.O. Fuckoffski.'

A Real-Life Quare Fellow

There's a guy in the condemned cell at the Green. Oswald Augustus Gray. He's a young West Indian. Armed with a gun, he went to rob a newsagent in one of Birmingham's suburbs and finished up shooting the owner dead. How stupid. Since the law changed, there's not that many people hanged now. But this case fits right into one of the categories still liable for the death penalty – committing murder to further a robbery. We've had six officers sent from other jails to sit with him. Divided into three pairs they do eight-hour shifts round the clock, with no days off. Sometimes, if I'm on late dinner – patrolling a locked-up wing while the main staff are on their break – I'll wander along towards the Centre and watch them bringing Gray out for exercise.

The condemned cell is on C2 landing. The jail is always locked up when a condemned man is on the move; no prisoners ever get to see him. Only screws. I lean on the rail and look down on C2. The P.O. opens the door to the condemned cell and lets them know it's clear. Minutes later, an officer steps briskly out of the cell. He's followed by Gray, then the second officer. I look at the condemned man. He's young and slim; in his early twenties. They head off on a circuitous route to a remote part of the prison's grounds not overlooked by any of the wings.

After three weeks, Gray and his officers travel down to London where his appeal against his sentence will be heard at the Old Bailey. A few days later, he's back in the condemned cell; appeal denied. He has just three weeks left to him now – and two chances. He can petition the Home Secretary for a reprieve and, if that goes down, appeal to the Queen for clemency.

Gray has just a week left. During these seven days he'll be given the results of his last two attempts to avoid the rope. Even though we officers rarely see the condemned man, and the cons don't see him at all, everyone is conscious he is THERE. There is an air about the prison – an unseen presence. Whenever I walk along C Wing, maybe four or five times a shift, when I pass the cell I know that just the other side of that wall sits a man who is under sentence of death.

It's Friday afternoon. Gray is due to hang on Tuesday morning. We're unlocking after lunch, ready to go out to exercise and workshops. I'm standing on the bridge on B3. Bernard is a young West Indian; he's a good-natured kid, usually full of fun, and speaks in an accent that's a mixture of Brum and West Indian. He comes and leans on the rail beside me. 'Boss, can I axt you sum'ting?'

'Yeah, course you can.' The wing is noisy. All around us cons are going back and forth between the recesses, in and out of other guys' cells, swapping magazines and comics. Bernard looks slightly embarrassed. He leans nearer . . .

'There's a rumour, Mistah Douglas. You know d' guy in the cell? Folk are saying, the nearer his day come – he done turnin' pale! Is dat true, boss?' Bernard now looks even more embarrassed.

I'm about to say, 'No, it's just a rumour.' I look at him. West Indians are VERY superstitious folk. I can't resist it – the Devil makes me do it! I look to left and right, as though I'm about to disclose some great secret and I don't want to be overheard. I lean nearer to him: 'Gone nearly as white as me!' I have to bite the inside of my bottom lip so as not to laugh.

Bernard's eyes widen, his pupils roll almost out of sight. 'T'anks, boss.' He shoots off along the landing and vanishes into a cell where three black guys are located. He obviously wants to be the first to confirm it's true.

It's Tuesday morning. We gather on the Centre. 'Now then, lads. You know what's on this morning. Get them breakfasted, then locked back up. He'll be going at eight on the dot. No staff goes for breakfast till it's done. Just stay on your landings and patrol.' Sticky Walker looks around our ranks. 'I don't expect there will be any trouble. Most cons won't be bothered. If there is any noise, it'll be from his fellow countrymen. Right, dismiss!'

By ten to eight the main prison is locked up. There are plenty of screws on the landings. All the West Indian cons, twenty or so, have collected their breakfasts then, as a protest, left their trays – with the uneaten meal – lying on the landing outside their doors.

At a few minutes to eight I watch as the public hangman, Harry Allen, and his assistant are let into the condemned cell. Well under five minutes later they re-emerge. It's over.

In with the Bricks

I love my wee house. If I'm on duty in the prison I even come home for lunch. We get an hour and a half so I've plenty of time. It was a bit of a nuisance getting the bus, so I've bought myself an old push-bike. I saw it advertised in a shop window: 'Second-hand bike, drop handlebars. Good condition. £3.' I'm usually quicker than the bus. Whenever I cycle into Southfield Road I look at the house and think, that's mine! Every time.

Nancy has fair taken to living here. She likes being in a city. Just a few hundred yards from us is Dudley Road, the Brummie equivalent of Maryhill Road; plenty of shops and busy with traffic. Nancy likes that kind of street. I do too, but I especially like the city centre with its bookshops and camera shops. I'm toying with the idea of getting myself a movie camera.

Best of all, though, I just love being in our house. If Nancy's off down the street with Scott in the pushchair, I often just sit and . . . well, think. Who owned this house before us, right from the 1880s? If only these walls could speak. I think about all the laughter and heartbreak this silent house will have seen. Husbands or sons going off to the First or Second World Wars, maybe even the Boer War. Someone taking ill and dying long before their time. Just like Ma. Weddings, funerals, births, celebrations. Maybe some poor lass – behind closed doors – having to put up with a bullying husband like Ma did.

I bet every time a new couple would move in here, they'd think it would be for ever. It won't.

With a lovely feeling of anticipation, I wander into WH Smith in

Corporation Street. I make straight for the paperbacks. There might be a new James Bond if I'm lucky. Or maybe something will just catch my eye. I spend ages reading the blurb on the covers, then the quotes from the reviewers. There's a large section of Penguin paperbacks. Normally I don't bother with them, assuming they'll be too highfaluting for my taste. I decide to have a look anyway. There's a whole row of Somerset Maughams. Sometimes I wonder if I should try him. I recall seeing a film in the Blythswood back in the fifties that was a strange sort of thing. It was three of Maugham's short stories, each with a different cast, and Maugham himself introduced it.

I look along the line of Maugham's books. Jeez! There ain't half some amount of them . . . '*The Razor's Edge*; *Of Human Bondage* – what good titles! I slide *Of Human Bondage* out from the rest. I think that was also made into a film. Early forties? Bette Davis was in it. I turn over the first couple of pages and come to the one where they give the book's printing history. Jesusjohnny! It just goes on and on. Every year or two for about the last thirty years it has been reprinted, sometimes twice in the same year. Surely it has GOT to be good? Even I should enjoy it. I close it and look at the red and cream cover with the penguin inside its little oval. Och, I'll give it a try.

During the next couple of years, interspersed with new books, I read most of Maugham's novels and ALL his short stories. Wonderful!

George Whatmore and I are on evening duty on A Wing. I've been at the Green over a year now and I feel pretty well established. George and I get on well and I like working with him. We've just finished 'suppering' the wing, so there's time to stand on the bridge and have a smoke. I've taken to rolling my own with Golden Virginia. George has a fag hanging loosely from his lips, as usual. I'm busy trying to make one with a line of baccy in a Rizla cigarette paper. George – being Welsh – is a great teller of tales. At quiet moments like this he usually takes the opportunity to wax lyrical. Or otherwise.

'Effery time I'm doing suppers on this wing, without fail, when I'm down in that corner of A3,' he points with the Player's he's smoking, 'round about number 16 or 17, I think back to when I wasn't long 'ere. It'd be 1949. We 'ad this prisoner. Williamson by name. Thorough fuckin' nuisance he were.' He turns to me. 'You know that Bulmer on B Wing?'

'Yeah.'

'Exactly the stamp of 'im. Can do the crime, but can't do the fuckin' time. Always moaning, whining, complaining. Petitioning the 'Ome Office. Every month or so somebody would open 'is door and he'd be lying with blood on 'is wrists – just little nicks – or he'd start to climb the protective netting over the Centre. Supposed to be gonna throw 'imself off – always made sure a screw was nearby so's he'd be stopped. Would've shit 'imself if the screw had said "On you go, boyo!"' George laughs. 'Anyway, I'm on evening duty on here one night – I'm sure it were '49 – and I'm on with this queer old cove, Albert Stocks. First World War veteran. Been in the job since the thirties – dry as fuckin' sticks.' George takes out a twenty packet of Player's, extracts one and lights it from the end of the one he's smoking. 'Routine for suppers were just the same as it is now; senior officer in front, just five or six cells unlocked at a time. Let them slop out, back in the cell, orderlies give them their supper, junior screw coming along behind locking up. Old Albert is up in front and I sees 'im reach up and pull down the tally of number 16. I'm sure it were 16. And he calls back to me, "Just leave this one for the moment, Mr Whatmore. We'll do 'im later." So on we go. We finish the whole wing. "Let the orderlies take their supper," he says, "take the trays and urns back down the kitchen, then lock the lads up." I starts to say, "We've still got that one—" Interrupts me he does: "Yes, I know. Later," he says. All sort of mysterious, like.' George takes a deep draw on his Player's. 'Finally we've got the whole wing locked up. "Come along, Mr Whatmore," he says.

We climb the stairs and go along to number 16 and he stops. He puts his key in the door. "Brace yourself!" he says, and unlocks the door. There's Williamson 'anging from the window bars! Used 'is torn-up pillowcase, he 'ad. Face blue, tongue 'anging out. "We'd better get 'im down," I says, "might still be a cha—" He puts a hand against my chest. "He's dead as a doornail, son," he says. "Remember when I put the tally down and said, leave this 'un?" He looks at me. "Yeah. Was he already hanging?" "No. When I looked through the spyhole, he's standing on the chair watching the door. Soon as he sees me look at him, he knows next thing is I'll be opening up – so he kicks off. 'Spects me to dive in and rescue him, doesn't he? He got that wrong! I just reached up and pulled the tally down. He mustn't have known who was on the wing tonight."'

I look at George. 'Jeez-oh! Bit fucking drastic, wasn't it?'

'Oh, I dunno, boyo.' He blows some fallen cigarette ash from off his medal ribbons, then takes a final draw. 'There's two or three in 'ere at the minute who I wouldn't mind giving me the chance. I'd soon reach up and drop their tally!'

Studies in Gray: One

I must admit I really do like Kubey. Reginald Kubey. Occupation: con man. He is a most engaging character. Of course, that's his stock-in-trade. He must be pushing fifty, nearly 6 feet tall, reasonably slim, yet he has a fat man's face – plump, red cheeks; very high colour they are. He looks like a tall Robert Morley. That'll be a help I suppose. You'd trust Robert Morley, wouldn't you? He's a South African, Kubey, though there's not a trace of it in his accent. He's very posh, well-mannered, amusing. Sounds like he's a southerner; Home Counties, maybe. Delightful chap. Such a good listener; hangs on your every word. After five minutes in his company you begin to realise what a fine fellow you are and how sound are your opinions. The thing is, he's not oily – that's perhaps his greatest attribute. He is SO charming. You enjoy his company – and he obviously enjoys yours.

I would think there are many people out there who've handed their cash over to him simply because they didn't want to hurt his feelings. He is such a gentleman, they knew they could trust him. Robert Morley with a dash of George Sanders. Couldn't possibly be a crook.

I sometimes watch him from a distance. He's the library 'red band' (trusty). Come to think of it, that's a laugh, associating Kubey with the word 'trusty'. Whether he's talking to screws or cons, he can't help practising his trade; they get his full attention. In a way it's a shame – he has this gift for handling people and it's just wasted. He'd be a whizz in public relations;

an asset to any company – as long as he didn't have access to any funds.

I'm going round with the suppers. Kubey's on C2. I open his door. He sits at the small cell table poring over the racing pages of two daily newspapers. He and I have developed this Jeeves and Wooster routine between us. Kubey would make an admirable Jeeves. It's a few days since I've seen him . . .

'Ah! Kubey, old chap. How do I find you this evening?'

He beams. 'Sir! All the better for seeing you.'

The two orderlies stand behind me. One holds an urn. It contains the usual lukewarm cocoa made from 95 per cent water, 5 per cent milk. The other holds a tray littered with currant buns which are doing rock-cake impressions. I smile.

'I wonder if one is interested in partaking of this evening's gastronomic extravaganza?'

Kubey rises and comes to the door with his mug. 'Sir is TOO kind. May I enquire what is on offer?'

I point to the urn. 'We have here a rather bold libation of co-co-ah, distilled from beans which were grown on a south-facing hill on an exclusive plantation just outside Pernambuco.'

'Perhaps a half.' The orderly slops some into his mug. 'I am oh-bleeged,' says Kubey, in the manner of a barrister.

I gesture towards the tray. 'Perchance a little something from our patisserie?' That almost gets him; he has trouble keeping his face straight. He coughs. 'A cornucopia of delights – if one may say so.' The orderlies look at one another. Their faces clearly say, 'What the fuck are these two on about?' Kubey reaches out a hand, little finger extended, and selects one.

I nod in the direction of the racing pages. 'Still searching for the mother-lode?'

'Yes. The quest goes on, sir. Sometimes I feel it's within my grasp, then it's dashed from my hand. At the moment it is quite elusive. Never mind, it helps to pass the time.'

I take hold of the door handle. 'Well, Reginald. I'm afraid that rather disagreeable moment is here again . . .'

'Think nothing of it, sir. Do make sure it's firmly locked.' He lowers his voice, glancing along the landing. 'Word has it there are footpads abroad.' He taps his nose with his index finger.

'Have a pleasant night, Kubey.'

He raises his mug. 'Bonne nuit, sir!'

Three weeks later I bump into him on his way to reception. 'What's this I hear, Kubey, off to gentler climes?'

'Indeed, sir. Leyhill Open Prison.'

'And you've still got all the summer in front of you. Couldn't be going at a better time.'

'Yes, things are looking up.' As he speaks, he inclines his head and holds an arm to the side.

For just a moment, he reminds me of the butler on the Craven 'A' cigarette packets.

'Well, enjoy it. If you've got to do time, open prison's the place to be.'

'Thank you very much, sir. I shall miss our tête-à-têtes.'

It's less than a month later and I'm sitting in the officers' mess having a cuppa. Alec Cox makes his usual noisy entrance, all studded boots and jangling keys. He orders a coffee, then sits himself down. 'I see Kubey hasn't lasted long!'

Two or three of us look up. 'What? Is he back?'

Alec takes a sip. 'Naah, but he soon will be! I've just been talking to two Leyhill screws down reception. The dozey buggers put 'im in the canteen, didn't they? He's hardly there a fortnight till they're sending 'im into Chesham – wearing 'is civvies – with a shopping list and twenty-odd quid to buy the special purchases, you know, art materials, hobbies stuff.' Alec takes another mouthful of coffee. 'And that's the last they seen of 'im. Off to Towcester Races he was. Booked into the best hotel in town. Anyway, the Chief at Leyhill knew Kubey of old. Told the police to keep an eye open at the second day of the meeting. Sure enough, he got 'is collar felt in the Silver Ring! Had nearly a hundred quid on 'im! So the canteen got its money back, the hotel got paid, and Kubey's locked up in the cells with nearly fifty quid in 'is property! What a fuckin' bloke!'

Two days later I go down onto A1. I'm on punishment exercise. I open a cell door.

'Kubey! How disappointing.'

He looks up. Sighs. 'Alas, sir. As Wilde said, "I can resist everything – except temptation!" '

Great Expectations

It's quarter to six as I wheel my bike into the backyard and lock it up in the outhouse. As I come into the kitchen, Nancy's preparing dinner.

'Well then?'

Her face breaks into a smile. 'They confirmed it at the hospital this morning. Ah'm expecting!'

'Aw, that's great! Were they able tae tell ye when?'

'Towards the end of August, they think.'

I reach down and pick Scott up. Now eighteen months, he's toddling around everywhere. 'You don't know it, Scott, but you'll soon be havin' a wee brother or sister.'

'Sistuh!' he says.

'He reckons it's gonny be a sister.'

'Well you know mair than us, so ye do.' She tickles him in the ribs.

'Ah'm just thinking,' I say, 'if they're right wi' their date that'll be both their birthdays in August.'

'Aye, that struck me this morning. We can get them both ower in the wan fell swoop.'

'So what are ye hoping for?' I ask.

'Oh, ah'm no' bothered. As long as it's fine and healthy.' She looks at me. 'What about you?'

'If it was possible tae have a choice, ah'd like a wee lassie. Just so as we'd have one of each. It would be nice to have a wee boy AND a lassie. But if we finish up wi' two boys, that'll be good fun, too.'

It's February 1963. Roll on August! As the year slowly unfolds

Nancy and I become totally absorbed in her pregnancy. What will it be? Meanwhile, in the world outside, the Profumo Scandal breaks (War minister John Profumo consorting with call-girls) and the Beatles burst upon the scene and change pop music just as Rock 'n' Roll did. We hardly noticed.

It's a Sunday. I'm on evening duty on A Wing. There are no receptions on Sundays; the courts don't sit. The wing has been suppered and locked up. It's just gone eight thirty. Forty-five minutes from now I'll be finished. I hear the clunk of a cell tally falling, followed instantly by the bell ringing. It's Lonsdale. I open his door.

'I'll have a visit to the recess, Mr Douglas. Save me using my chamber during the night.'

'Of course. Better going now when it's nice and quiet.' I watch as he hurries off to the recess. As he's an E-man, I suppose I should stand on the landing opposite the toilet so's I can see his feet under the half-door. I'll spare him the indignity. I don't think he'll remove the window bars during the next few minutes. With everyone locked up, the wing is quiet. I hear the toilet flush then the tap running as he washes his hands. 'Thank you,' he says as he passes me and enters his cell. He has a chessboard set up on his table and is in the middle of a game – playing both ends.

'Who's winning?'

'Hah! White seems to have the advantage, but . . .' he waves a finger. 'Black is in the middle of working out a complicated attack which might juuust turn the tables.' He looks at me. 'Do you play?'

'Just this last year. Have you heard of these "Teach Yourself" books? Cover all sorts of subjects. Small hardbacks, always have a black and yellow dust-jacket.'

'Yeah, I know the ones you mean. Got quite a few in the library.'

'Aye, they do. Actually, I was surprised to read that chess is

THE national sport of Russia. I would've thought it would be football or athletics, something like that.'

'Oh, yeah. Chess is taken very seriously. It's played everywhere, at all levels, from kids in school to grandmasters.'

'Anyway, I hear you had a major victory last week – and it wasn't at chess.'

He sits back in his chair and laughs. 'I sure did. The Governor wasn't too pleased. It's been going on for the last nine months.' He points to the brown cover of the book of prison rules. There is one in every cell. He gives a shrug; holds both hands out in appeal. 'It's so petty. As you'll know, it states quite clearly in there that every prisoner is entitled to buy a newspaper. For the last two years I've been getting *The Times*. No problem about that. Then I make an application to also have a Russian newspaper. NO! Maybe six months ago I'm looking through the rule book. No reason. I'm bored. Then I spot it . . . "An inmate is entitled to have his *local* newspaper." Ahah! So I make an application to see the Governor. Later that morning I'm marched into his office. "I wish to apply to have my local newspaper sent in, sir." He looks at me. "You could have made this application to your wing P.O. Anyway, what is it?" So I reply, "Pravda!"' Lonsdale doubles over with laughter. 'You should have seen his face. "Out of the question!" he says. "I told you a few months ago, no Russian papers." "But it's in the rule book, sir. It doesn't say it has to be a *British* local newspaper." Anyway, his answer is no, so I finish up petitioning the Home Office. I just got the answer last week. They've ruled in my favour. The Deputy Governor informed me – I don't think the Major could bring himself to tell me.'

'And how goes the other battle?'

Since the day he arrived in prison after being sentenced, Lonsdale has carried on a long-running campaign with the Prison Department because he was put into patches. He maintains he has never tried to escape, has no intention of escaping, and shouldn't have to suffer the indignity of wearing them. He especially hates not being allowed to sleep in the dark and having to put up with the interminable red 'dim' bulb burning all night in his cell, regularly hearing the spyhole cover being slid open every thirty minutes or so as the night patrols check up on him. He turns down the corners of his mouth. 'HAH! I'm certainly no further forward with that.'

'Aye, I suppose it's like chess, eh? Always looking for a move your opponent hasn't thought of.'

'Yeah, but I'm playing against guys who make their own rules as they go along.'

Often, when I have a conversation with Lonsdale and listen to his 'American' accent, I can't help but recall an article by Chapman Pincher in the *Daily Express*. Pincher holds up Lonsdale as a prime example of a 'graduate' from the KGB's School for Spies.

That thought then poses the question – just who am I talking to? There's no doubt he is a Russian agent. He was convicted on overwhelming evidence. But am I in the company of THE Gordon Arnold Lonsdale, born in Canada in 1924 to a Canadian father and Finnish mother? After their marriage broke up in the early thirties, his mother took her son and returned to Finland. Nothing more was heard of Gordon until, some time in the mid-fifties, the man who is now in Birmingham Prison appeared at a passport office in Canada and stated he was Gordon Arnold Lonsdale and wished to apply for a passport.

According to Pincher, the Lonsdale I'm talking to is a KGB man who, after years of intensive training, now speaks fluent North American English and has totally assimilated the culture and history of Canada and, more importantly, assumed the persona of Gordon Arnold Lonsdale. If this is so – and it probably is – there's no doubt that the real Lonsdale will have 'disappeared'.

I drag my thoughts back to the moment. 'Och, you're a terrible man, Gordon. You never give that poor Governor of ours any peace. He's retiring soon – ah would think he'll be glad to see the back of you. Anyway, I'll have to go, it's nearly finishing time. I'll see you around. Goodnight.'

He pulls his chair closer to the table. 'Yeah, goodnight.'

I gently close his door and as it's locking-up time, I slip the outside bolt on. He certainly is an enigma. A real single-minded guy. Yet I like him. He gives the Governor and Home Office a helluva time, but not us officers. He knows we don't make the rules.

I recently found out that now and again special visitors come up to see him. MI5 people from London. They always use an empty office. No prison staff present; not even Governor Grade. Just Lonsdale and two or three guys. Plenty of tea, coffee and biscuits on tap. We're not supposed to know what's going on, but it's obvious. They're making another attempt to turn him. Offering him a new identity, safe location, income for life – if he'll 'come over'. Tell them what he knows about other agents, other operations. Of course they have to try, but they're wasting their time. No matter how long it takes, Lonsdale will sit tight. He knows that eventually the Russians will arrest one of ours. Once that happens, it's only a matter of time until a swap is arranged. He's confident his people will get him back. They always do.

A Busy Month

I come onto the Centre on the morning of 8 August 1963. It's a few minutes to seven so the staff are still milling about, not yet formed into ranks. As soon as I come through the door I know there will be only one topic of conversation – yesterday's Mail Train Robbery. I join the nearest group of officers.

'They reckon it's in the millions,' says Alec Cox.

'Not only that, it's in used notes.' Dennis Slattery looks around. 'They could go out today and start spending it. It's virtually untraceable.'

I decide to contribute. 'Seems to have been a deadly efficient job. They knew how to stop the train, what carriage it was in. It's usually only in the movies you get robberies like that.'

'I'll tell you what,' says Eric Morrell, 'if they catch them, they won't half get some porridge. Not just because it's the biggest robbery ever – but because it's the Royal Mail. You wait and see. They'll hand out some helluva sentences. They have to, to act as a deterrent.'

There's a general murmur of agreement.

'RIGHT! Line up, lads. Roll-call.' Johnny Appleton starts calling out names.

When August had at last arrived the main thing on my mind was that Nancy was due towards the end of it. For a few days the Great Train Robbery, as the media are dubbing it, provides a distraction, as the search for the perpetrators dominates newspapers and TV. As the days go by the full story, or as near to it as possible, begins to unfold . . .

In the early hours of 7 August, the Glasgow to London mail train had been stopped near Ledburn, Buckinghamshire by means of tampered signals, then robbed. Because this journey was being made following a Bank Holiday, the robbers had known there would be extra money aboard. Their haul, in used £1, £5 and £10 notes, amounted to £2.3 million (equal to £40 million today). Because their first hideout after the heist, Leatherslade Farm, wasn't properly 'cleaned' when they left, it isn't long before the police begin making arrests. Within a couple of months most of the gang are in custody awaiting trial. This is set for early next year.

Towards the end of August Nancy's mother and father come down to Birmingham. There have been no complications during her pregnancy, and as it's her second child, it's been arranged that it'll be a home birth. There will be a midwife in attendance and our GP will call in now and again to see all is well. Late morning on Wednesday 28 August, Nancy shows the first signs of going into labour. As the midwife and Nancy's mother, Beenie, are more than capable of taking care of business, it is suggested that Auld Sanny and I take ourselves out of the way for a few hours. I look at him. 'Shall we go doon the toon tae the pictures?'

'Whit's oan?'

'Well, you like your comedy pictures. There's a Charlie Drake one on at the ABC Bristol. It's called *The Cracksman*. Will we go and see it?'

He laughs. 'Aye, that'll dae me.'

Nancy shakes her head. 'Nae matter whit ye take him tae see, he'll be sleepin' within half an hour!'

'Here! Now watch it. Ah'll have a bit o' respect if ye don't mind!' As usual, while he's supposedly complaining, Sanny's chortling away to himself.

'You'll get mair than respect if the two of ye don't buzz off!' says Beenie.

'Okay, ah can take a hint,' I say. I lean forward and kiss

Nancy. 'Well, ah'll leave ye to it. I hope everything goes well. All the time ah'm in the pictures ah'll be dying to know whit it is. Right, we'll get oorselves oot the road.'

Sanny and I walk down to Dudley Road and take a bus into the city. I find out what time the main feature is on, we get ourselves into a café for something to eat, and by two p.m. we're settling into our seats in the ABC. In spite of the fact that I can't fully concentrate, I still enjoy the film. I also have to regularly give Auld Sanny a nudge to waken him up whenever I think a funny sequence is about to start.

At last, some time after five p.m., we return home and I open the door to the back living-room. Nancy's ma sits at the table with a cup of tea.

'Is it all over and done with?'

'Aye,' she smiles.

'Whit did she have?'

She pauses. 'A wee lassie!'

'Aw, great! I was hoping it would be.'

'Ah, that's grand!' says Sanny.

'Will it be aw'right to go up and see them?' Scott's playing on the floor. Just twelve days ago he turned two. I squat down beside him. 'Have ye got a new wee sister, pal?'

'I took him up tae see her,' says Beenie. 'He canny figure oot where she's appeared from.'

'Right. Ah'll away up and see my wee daughter.'

I quietly climb the stairs and push open the bedroom door. Nancy is lying, apparently asleep. I tiptoe over and just as I'm about to try and have a look at the baby's face, Nancy opens her eyes. 'Hiyah!' she says in a tired voice.

I lean forward and kiss her. 'Thanks for a wee daughter.' My eyes fill up.

'Oh, it's aw'right,' she says. The baby lies next to her, all swaddled up. 'Here, have a look at her.' She pulls the covers back from round her face. 'There she is.'

'Well, for a newborn she looks quite bonny, doesn't she? Hasn't got the usual red, scrunched-up wee face.' We both laugh quietly. I sit on the edge of the bed. 'So how was it?'

'It wis'nae bad at all. Once she really started tae come it only took aboot thirty-five minutes.'

'Jeez, that was smashing, eh?'

'Aye. Ah'm a lot less tired than ah was wi' Scott.'

'And we've settled oan Nancy for her name, haven't we?'

'Aye. That's what you want, in't it?'

'Yeah. Well, Nancy Janet. Nancy after you and Janet after my ma. Ah've always said if we ever have a wee lassie I'd like her to be Nancy. Ah've always liked that name.'

And now we are four.

A Strange Old Job

On Saturday 2 November 1963, after a lazy week's leave at home with Nancy and the kids, I start back at work. I'm part of the Deputy Governor's Division and we're 'weekend on'. I'm detailed to the punishment landing, A1. Around eleven a.m. big George Davis and I are exercising a couple of the cons on one of the smaller yards when George Angel approaches. 'I've come out to relieve you, Doug. Chief wants to see you.' He laughs. 'What you been up to, then?'

'Buggered if ah know. Ah just started back this morning after a week's leave, so ah've no' had much time tae get up tae anything. Anywye, ah'll soon find oot!'

'Just knock on the door,' the Chief's clerk nods in its direction.

I knock.

'Come in!' I step inside, come briefly to attention and throw up a salute. 'G'morning, Chief.'

'Ah, Mr Douglas. I want you to stand by for C.C. duty!' (condemned cell duty).

'Jeez-oh! That's a bit of a surprise, Chief.' As far as I know it's usually only the most senior of officers who land this job. It's looked on as a cushy number. I've only been eighteen months in the service. I also know that, whenever someone is remanded on a capital charge – a murder which is still subject to the death penalty – the Prison Department arranges for six officers at various prisons to 'stand by for C.C. duty'. This is usually done a month or two before the trial is held.

'Right, that's fine, Chief. Have you any idea when the case will come up?'

He laughs. 'The jury's out!'

'Eh?' Is he having me on? 'Ah thought officers usually got warned well in advance, sir?'

'They usually do. But what's happened this time is six officers were told to stand by, oh, a couple of months ago. Then, yesterday afternoon somebody at the Department suddenly realised there are two defendants on trial! Twelve officers are needed, not six. So we got a frantic phone call yesterday. "Can you spare an officer for detached duty if these two get sentenced to death?" So you're the one.'

'And the jury's actually out? On a Saturday!'

'Seemingly they got as far as the judge's summing up yesterday afternoon. Rather than prolong things any longer he decided the court would sit today. The last we heard was that the jury went out an hour or so ago.'

'If they do get sentenced to death, do you know where I'll be going?'

'Yes.' He looks at a piece of paper. 'You're earmarked for a guy called Russell Pascoe. If he gets the chop you'll be sitting with him at Bristol.'

'Right. So what happens now?'

'If we get the verdict before you finish at four thirty, I'll send for you. If they aren't back till after then, I'll get somebody to call at your house and let you know. If you are going to Bristol, call in here at eight a.m. tomorrow morning, in civvies, and we'll have your rail warrant and expenses waiting for you. Take your uniform in your luggage. Okay?'

'Yeah, fine, Chief.' I turn to leave.

'If it turns out they just get "life" or maybe a "not guilty", I'll still arrange for somebody to call in and let you know.'

Nancy and I sit watching television. It's coming up for seven p.m. We've had our dinner and Scott and Nancy junior are in their beds. There's a loud knock on the door. My stomach turns a somersault. We look at one another. 'Right! Let's get the verdict.' I head off through the front room. Nancy junior starts to cry; the knock must have wakened her. I open the door. It's George Angel, again. He has to travel up City Road on his way home. It's a rainy, blustery November night.

'Come in a minute, George.' I step back from the door.

'No, it's all right, boyo. Want to get home and get me dinner. They've been sentenced to death, those two. So you're off to Bristol tomorrow. Jammy bugger! Good as six weeks' 'oliday. Chief says he'll see you in the morning.'

'Right. Thanks, George.' I watch him shut the gate. 'Goodnight.'

'G'night, Doug.'

Nancy has turned round and sits looking at the living-room door as I come through it. 'Yeah, it's on. He's been sentenced tae hang. So that's it – you'll probably no' see me for the next six weeks.'

As the express for Bristol makes its way across country, now and again a watery sun shows itself. Magnified by the compartment's window, it's quite pleasant. It won't be long until I'm dozing off. I look again at the news item in the *Sunday Express*. I've already read it three times. 'Dennis Whitty and Russell Pascoe have been sentenced to death for the murder of reclusive Cornish farmer, William Garfield Rowe (64).'

The train is quite busy, the compartment nearly full. There are two girls, probably in their late teens, sitting facing me. They've brought an assortment of newspapers and magazines to help pass the time. The one sitting straight opposite begins to read the *Sunday Pictorial*. I look at a bold headline: 'We Lived In Love Caravan With Killers! Story Inside'. I lean forward and read the blurb underneath. Seemingly three girls had been sharing a caravan with Pascoe and Whitty in the weeks before the murder. One of them has sold the story to the *Pictorial*. It must have been written while the two were on remand. As soon as the jury brought its verdict in yesterday, the presses would have started to roll. When I get off at Bristol I must get a copy.

As the train nears its destination I think about where I'm going to be for the next few weeks. If they are successful with their appeal – they're bound to appeal – I'll be here for just three weeks. They always give a condemned man three clear Sundays before execution, to make his peace with God. If their appeal goes down they'll get another three weeks. Jeez. It's not half going to be a strange job. What was the play that Brendan Behan wrote about a condemned man? *The Quare Fellow* – that was it. I remember laughing at that joke in it: Two convicts, supervised by a screw, are digging the condemned man's grave inside the prison grounds. The officer's out of earshot. 'Tell me,' says one, 'did ye hear about the prison officer that married the prostitute?'

'No, I didn't,' says the other.

'He dragged her down to his own level!'

It's surprising how many screws don't find that funny. Well, I'm now about to sit with a Quare Fellow!

I get to Horfield Prison, to give it its proper name, some time after one p.m. Everything's been laid on. Digs have been fixed up for me with a Mrs Calvert about half a mile from the jail. It's an up-market stone house with bay windows. I'm to start on night shift tonight at ten p.m. As my digs are just bed and breakfast terms, I'm told if I come into the prison tonight around nine fifteen p.m. there will be supper laid on for me in the officers' mess.

I have a cuppa and some biscuits with my landlady, then decide I'll try for a couple of hours shut-eye before I turn out for my first shift. I lie and read Hemingway's *The Old Man and the Sea* until I feel sleepy. I put the book down but find I can't drop off. My mind's too active – it's obviously full of what lies ahead. What *does* lie ahead? Buggered if I know! What will it be like to sit with a guy for six weeks in the condemned cell? Especially if he isn't reprieved?

I come into the jail just before nine fifteen. I don't draw keys. Don't need them. The mess is a wooden hut, much like at Birmingham. The mess caterer is waiting for me. He's a short, stocky guy; Hughes is his name, but his nickname is 'Teddy Bear'. Another officer is sitting at a table and Teddy Bear points to him. 'This is your oppo (partner) for the next few weeks. Ken Russell, from Exeter.'

We shake hands. I like the look of him right away; he's in his mid-thirties, I would think, and is the senior of the two of us. Teddy Bear serves us our supper. Around ten to ten the night duty principal officer enters. His face lights up. 'Hello, Ken! Long time no see.' They shake hands.

'You two know each other, then?' says Teddy Bear.

'Yeah,' says Ken, 'we served down the Moor together.'

I feel very much the junior officer, so I just sit and listen to the craic. After a few minutes, the night P.O. looks at his watch. 'I think we'd better go and relieve them two lads.'

We follow him outside. I expect us to go into the main prison. In all the Victorian prisons the condemned cell is usually located on one of the wings. To my surprise, we walk just 40 feet or so towards a low, square block which stands on its own. In the poorly-lit grounds it looms up as this dark, solid entity. From the direction we are approaching there are no lights to be seen.

'Is this it?' I ask.

'Yeah. Bristol is the only prison with its own purpose-built condemned block. It's all self-contained. Even has a little exercise yard. Once a con's in here he doesn't have to come out for anything – except when he goes to London for his appeal.'

The P.O. opens a door on the end of the dark, red brick building. He leads us along a short corridor, maybe 20 feet, towards another door. He opens it. Two officers stand in a well-lit room. They have their hats and macs on, ready for the off.

'Here y'are, boys. Here's your reliefs.'

We say our hellos. The senior of the two we're relieving steps into the corridor and has a word with Ken. I catch the start of it; he's just telling him how Pascoe has been since they came on. I walk into the cell to have a look. The other officer says, 'I'll away, then,' and steps into the corridor. For the moment I'm alone in the cell, except it isn't really a cell, it's a reasonably sized room, rectangular in shape, maybe 12 feet wide by 25 feet long. To my left, at the far end facing towards me, is a bed. A stocky young lad with dark curly hair sits on it.

He is wearing a dark blue battledress jacket – not the usual gray. He has a pleasant, round face. I give him a smile. 'Hello, how are you doing?'

'Oh, not so bad,' says Russell Pascoe.

Passing Time

The first three weeks have gone well. As we change from night shift to day shift to back shift, Ken and I have built up a good rapport with Russell. We are the youngest of the three pairs of officers. Ken, an ex-Royal Marine, is in his mid-thirties. I'm twenty-four. The other two pairs are in their forties and fifties. We've got ourselves into a fairly relaxed regime. It's also a help that Russell is a sociable kid and laughs easily. He is very much a Cornish farm lad. So far he has not given us any trouble.

The reason why Russell is so relaxed is probably quite simple – he still has all the avenues of appeal open to him. 'Hope springs eternal.' He feels there is no way he's going to hang. We're off down to London this coming weekend, as his appeal against sentence will be heard next Monday at the Court of Criminal Appeal in the Old Bailey. He's quite confident. They're bound to set aside his death sentence and substitute one of life imprisonment – after all, it was Whitty who stabbed the old man. One afternoon, probably to try and boost his confidence for the forthcoming trip to London, he tries out his story on us . . .

'I admits I 'it him with the iron bar. But it weren't very hard. Didn't even knock 'im out. He started to get up off the floor . . .' He stops. 'That was when that stoopid bastard Whitty pulls out the knife.' He looks at both of us in turn. 'Honest to God, I didn't know he 'ad it with him. Next thing he's stabbin' the old lad. It were a bloody shock for me. Over and done with 'fore I could say a word. I wouldn't be 'ere if that bad bastard 'adn't brought that knife.'

* * *

From reading about the trial as I'd travelled by train from Birmingham to Bristol, then hearing about it first hand from Pascoe, there was nothing complicated about the murder they'd committed. Or their reasons. Their victim, William Garfield Rowe, was supposed to have plenty of money lying around the remote farmhouse where he lived alone. They wanted it. Living in a caravan with three girls was great fun, but you needed money. Money for food, for fags, for booze. If none of you are working you've got to get it from somewhere. Pascoe knew where they could get some. He'd told Whitty about this old farmer he'd worked for. Strange old lad – never left the farm, didn't use banks. There was always plenty of money at the house. Easy money.

William G. Rowe had been conscripted into the army in 1917, aged eighteen. A few months later he deserted. From 1917 until 1953 he hid on the family farm. Never left it. During the day he was up in the roof. Only at night would he come down and walk around the yard for some fresh air. Had he been apprehended while the war was still in progress there's a good chance he would have been executed. Over 300 deserters were shot at dawn during the First World War. Even for a few years afterwards, if he'd been arrested, he'd have been sentenced to a lengthy term of imprisonment. Those who deserted and let others do their fighting weren't looked on too kindly. That was the mood of the time – and for many years afterwards. All through the twenties, thirties and forties – including the Second World War – William Rowe remained hidden on his parents' isolated farm. His release came with the coronation of Queen Elizabeth in 1953. As part of the celebrations, in a spirit of reconciliation, an amnesty was declared for all deserters. Suddenly, unexpectedly, he was free. Or was he? After decades of never straying from the environs of the house, he just limited himself to the boundaries of the farm. Was that because he would find it an ordeal to go to town or market? Or was it that he didn't want to be pointed out as the deserter?

By the end of the fifties his parents had died and the farm was now his. Any business to be done at market was dealt with by one of his farmhands. He didn't use banks. All transactions and the paying of employees were cash in hand. During a short period in the late fifties he'd hired a young lad called Russell Pascoe. The few times Pascoe had called at the house he'd noticed there was money lying about in various places; on the sideboard, in tins on the window-sill, on the mantelpiece. Everywhere!

On the night of the robbery which became a murder, Pascoe and Whitty approached the farmhouse late at night. They knocked on the locked door and shouted through to farmer Rowe that they were a helicopter crew who'd been forced down with engine trouble, and one of them was injured. When he opened the door they barged in and Pascoe struck him with an iron bar. As he got back to his feet, Whitty drew a knife and stabbed him. They escaped with just £4. Hidden in the house was another £3,000.

At their trial it had been accepted that Pascoe never struck the fatal blows. Nevertheless, he'd been convicted as an accessory to murder. This offence also carried the death penalty. Anyway, he's quite confident they won't hang him. On Monday he's a cert to have it changed to 'life'.

The days go by fairly easily. It's surprising how busy the condemned cell can be. The Governor comes in every day. So does the M.O. (prison doctor). The padre visits every afternoon. He's a bit of a character. Well into his sixties and an ex-Royal Navy chaplain, he doesn't come too much of the 'holy Joe'. For some reason, he's decided to try and teach Pascoe how to play a complicated card game called Bezique. Maybe he thinks the concentration needed will help take his mind off things for a while. As they sit together he chatters away to Russell non-stop, but as these first three weeks have slipped by Russell has begun to get pretty bored with the padre's Bezique lessons. He admits he'll never master it and, truth be told, he doesn't want to. Then there's the fact that the padre never stays for any less than an hour. Often the three of us will be in the middle of a good game of Monopoly, or cards, then we'll hear somebody coming through the outside door. Ken and I, of course, get ourselves buttoned up, in case it's the Governor. When the padre comes through the inner door you can actually see Russell's face fall. He knows he's in for another hour of complicated boredom. While the card lessons are going on, Ken and I just read, or take the chance to write a letter home.

When you think about it, one of the strange aspects of sitting with someone in the condemned cell is we have to make sure he doesn't try to do away with himself. That's the prerogative of the State. When Russell shaves in the morning he uses a special safety razor that locks, so there is no chance of him cutting his wrists. All the time he's in the bathroom one of us is with him. When he's sitting on the toilet we try to give him a little bit of privacy, but even so, the lavatory door is always ajar. We have to take care of him.

There's a radio in the cell, mostly tuned to the *Light Programme*. Russell's not interested in plays or discussions. *Housewives' Choice* in the morning; *Two-way Family Favourites* followed by *The Billy Cotton Band Show* on a Sunday. If Ken and I are on the two to ten shift we some times tune in to Radio Luxembourg or AFN (American Forces Network) while we sit with Russell playing table games. We were playing Monopoly the other evening, having a good laugh. You have to watch him like a hawk when he's running out of money – the bugger cheats! If he thinks you're not looking he'll jump over a property that carries a big fine . . .

Russell throws the dice. 'Nine!' As he reaches for his token – he always takes the top hat – I have a quick count. Great! He's going to land on Park Lane. I've got three houses on there; that'll wipe him out. I watch as he makes his move. He quickly bounces the piece from square to square – and lands well past Park Lane!

'Hey!' I say. Then I can't resist it: 'This bugger's trying tae get away wi' murder!'

The three of us go into fits of laughter. Definitely gallows humour.

It's Friday morning, 22 November 1963. Ken and I are on day shift, so we're the ones who escort Russell to London. We use a hire car. I sit in the rear with Pascoe handcuffed to me and Ken sits in front with the driver. On the way down we have the same conversations as we do in the cell. Now and again there are long silences as Russell spends time looking out of the window at town and countryside. Is he wondering if he'll ever get to walk in fields or streets again? I find myself hoping that he'll win his appeal and finish up doing life. We left Bristol at eight forty-five a.m. and arrive at Pentonville a few minutes before one p.m. The prison is locked up for the midday meal, so it's no problem getting him into the condemned cell without other prisoners seeing him. After the 'comforts' of Bristol, the cell at Pentonville is quite depressing. Like most old jails the condemned cell is located on the twos of one of the wings. It is really just four cells or so knocked into one. For a start, this makes it a lot smaller than Bristol. The windows are the normal, small cell type. In Bristol's cell we have half a dozen much larger ones. But it's the decor that really does it: the walls are a dark green, the upper walls a muddy brown. The few bulbs are maybe 40-watt. What a dull, gloomy place. I turn to Ken. 'Ah would'nae be surprised if there's been people in here who withdrew their appeal – so as they could get tae the scaffold early! Could'nae face another three weeks o' this.'

He looks around. 'What a fuckin' place. Probably been the occasional screw topped himself in here over the years, never mind a prisoner!'

* * *

There are two condemned cells, separated by the toilet/bathroom which is in the middle. Whitty is lodged on the other side – his appeal will be heard at the same time. During the weekend we will have to make sure the bathroom is vacant, then inform our opposite numbers that our man is about to use it. They will do the same. Pascoe and Whitty catch neither sight nor sound of one another. Pascoe says he doesn't want to see him, anyway. I have a brief conversation in the officers' mess with one of Whitty's team. He tells me Whitty is surly and uncooperative.

When we arrive on the Friday, Ken and I finish at two p.m. The other four officers in our team have travelled to London by train. Ken is staying with another old Dartmoor mate. I've got lodgings with a Scots officer called Jimmy Gardner. After having a meal in the mess I get settled into my room at Gardner's. Ken and I meet up later that evening and go for a few pints. Just before eleven p.m. we head back to the married quarters, say our goodnights and I make for my digs. I knock on the door and Jimmy Gardner answers it. His wife stands behind him, in the hall.

'Did ye hear the news?' he says. I'm still standing on the step.

'No. What news?'

'President Kennedy's been assassinated!'

I look at him. I smile. This'll be one of those jokes: 'Did ye hear, Bing Crosby's dead!' 'Oh! What happened?' 'He was singing "Pennies From Heaven" – and the gas meter fell on him!'

'Away, then. I'll buy it. What happened?'

'Naw, honestly. It's no' a joke. He's been assassinated while visiting Dallas. It's been oan the telly non-stop.'

'JeeSUS!' I spend the next forty minutes watching the frequent news reports.

Next morning Ken and I come in for our last day shift. The assassination is our main topic of conversation. Russell is barely interested. I suppose his own plight, and forthcoming appeal, are dominating his thoughts.

After finishing at two p.m. on the Saturday afternoon, I take myself off to the cinema to see Jack Lemmon in *Days of Wine and Roses*. Brilliant! Ken and I go out again at night for a few pints. We're off until we start night shift on the Sunday night.

We come into the drab, depressing cell at five to ten. The prison library has put a selection of books on the table. I while away most of the hours reading *Panzer Leader* by General Heinz Guderian. In the wee small hours, while Pascoe sleeps and Ken half dozes, I sometimes look around me. Just as at Bristol, we have a table lamp as our only source of light during the night. A green cloth, about the size of a napkin, is draped over the shade to cut the light falling on Pascoe even further. I look at the painted brickwork, the small iron-bound windows. Jeez! If these walls could talk. I was sitting with one of the senior Pentonville screws in the mess earlier today. I'd asked him which famous, or infamous, murderers had been topped in here. It was like a bloody Who's Who? of British criminals: Dr Crippen, John Christie, John George Haig . . . The list was endless. I remember reading about the Christie and Haig trials when I was a kid. When they were hanged, the newsreels showed an officer putting the official notices on the prison gates on the mornings of their executions – the gates I just stepped through to come on duty tonight. As Ma and I sat in the Blythswood Cinema back in Maryhill, watching those newsreels, little did I know that one day I'd be sitting in the condemned cell at Pentonville where those two spent their last weeks.

When we finish in the morning, at seven, we'll have to get some breakfast then catch a train back to Bristol. The day shift officers will take Pascoe to the Old Bailey for his appeal hearing. If he is successful, and his sentence commuted to life, that will be us finished. He'll just become an ordinary prisoner. We six will all head off back to our own prisons.

The train journey back to Bristol is uneventful. As Ken and I have come off night shift this morning, we're quite tired and doze for most of the trip. I get back to my digs just after noon and have a cup of tea with Mrs Calvert, then head straight for bed. Before I drop off I wonder what's happening at the Court of Appeal. I hope he wins.

During the latter part of Monday, no word comes that there has been a reprieve. I come in to the prison about nine twenty p.m. and head for the mess. Teddy Bear has my supper waiting.

'So he didn't get his reprieve, then?' I say.

'Nahh!' He puts a plate down in front of me. 'They got back from London late afternoon. All three judges threw it out.'

'Oh well,' I say, 'he's still got a petition to the Home Secretary to come. And if that fails, a plea to the Queen for clemency.'

Teddy Bear laughs. 'And if those go down, he'll be shaking hands with Harry Allen!'

To a Place of Lawful Execution

The Bristol officer stands, key in hand, ready to open the door. This is it! For Ken and me it's our last shift. It's Russell's last night.

I turn to Ken. 'I'm no' lookin' forward tae this one.'

'Me neither,' he says, in his soft Devon accent. 'What the fuck can we talk about, Bob?'

He nods to our escort. The door is unlocked and we enter the condemned cell for the last time. As usual, it's warm and stuffy. Russell lies on his bed at the far end of the long, rectangular room. He doesn't look up. Ken steps back into the corridor for a moment with the senior of the two we're relieving. 'How's he been?'

'Well, he was all right when we came on at two. But since he got 'is final knock-back this afternoon he ain't said much. Quite depressed now his last chance has gone.'

'Can't blame the poor bastard.'

Ken and I exchange a last few words with the officers, being careful all the while what we say. We won't see them again, but don't want to shake hands or say goodbye. Not in front of Russell. Too much of a reminder for him as to why we're saying goodbye.

The two we've relieved just nod to Russell and exit without another word. What could they say? The door is locked behind them. There is some conversation as they walk along the corridor with their escort. We hear the outside door shut, the key turning. Their footsteps fade into the night. The silence becomes solid. Powerful.

* * *

We take off our hats and start unbuttoning our tunics. I look down to the end of the cell.

'Fancy a cuppa, Russell?' God, it's hard to sound casual.

'No thanks.'

'Ah've got ye a cream doughnut.'

He looks up. He had his twenty-third birthday not long after we came back from Pentonville. As a treat, I fetched him in a cream cake. He really enjoyed it. I've brought one in every day since.

'Go on, then,' he says. He lays aside the book he hasn't been reading and comes down and joins us at the table.

'Good lad!' says Ken. 'I'll put the kettle on.'

Immediately the atmosphere has lightened. We sit together drinking our tea and coffee and watch Russell devour his cream doughnut with relish. All the while Ken and I try hard to think of lightweight things to talk about. Up until last night we hadn't had a problem. But last night isn't tonight. When Russell isn't looking, I glance at my watch. Jeez! Is that all it is? Twenty-five past ten. I thought it would've been at least eleven.

A key rattles in the outside door. Ken takes his feet off the table, I put my mug down and we both hurriedly button up our tunics. 'Who the bloody hell is this?' mouths Ken.

The inner door opens and the Governor enters, accompanied by another man. The three of us stand up.

'All correct, sir,' Ken states.

'Thank you.' The Governor smiles and turns to Russell. 'How are you, Pascoe?'

'All right, sir.'

The man with the Governor suddenly steps forward towards Russell and sticks his hand out.

'How do you do, son?' Russell's automatic reaction is to take it. They shake hands.

'I'm not so bad,' he murmurs. I glance at Ken.

'Right! We'll be going now,' says the Governor. Immediately

he and the man turn on their heels and leave. As the sound of them is lost in the night, Ken and I unbutton again, then sit down. The mood has changed. Russell sits quietly for a minute, then says, 'Who were that with the Governor?'

I know. I've just had supper with him and his assistant in the officers' mess. To avoid the expected anti-capital punishment demo tomorrow morning, the public hangman and his assistant arrived at the prison this afternoon. Just walked in like any other visitors. They'll spend the night inside the jail.

'Ahhh, I'm not very sure,' mumbles Ken.

'I bloody knows,' says Russell. 'That were the fucking hangman, weren't it?'

I look at Ken. He shrugs his shoulders.

'Aye, it was,' I admit.

'I knew it. What's he want to shake hands with me for?'

'It's just a thing Pierrepoint always did,' I say, 'and Harry Allen has carried it on. They always come in with the Governor and just stick their hand out. Probably makes them feel better or something.'

'If I'd caught on quicker who the bugger was I wouldn't 'ave took 'is hand. Fucker! Caught me on the hop, he did.' He gets up, goes to the far end of the cell and throws himself on his bed. A few minutes later he raises his head. 'Hospital officer came in this afternoon and weighed me, you know. That's so as they can work out how far I'll drop!'

Fuck me! What can we say? As he lies on his bed staring at the ceiling, we try to read the papers.

The three weeks since we came back from London have gone well. The day after our return Pascoe had been told the new date of his execution: Tuesday 17 December. That had depressed him for the rest of the day, but by the next morning his spirits had revived. His attitude seemed to be: Okay, my appeal has gone down. But I still have two chances. I'll be all right. I didn't do it. It was Whitty. I'm just an accessory.

Soon we were back into the old routine. Playing table games; listening to the radio; talking. Lots of talking. Ken and I must have dredged up every joke and story we'd ever heard, all to keep him amused, diverted, occupied. Then it got buggered up on Saturday. Saturday the 14th. Ken and I were on our last day shift. It was some time after eleven a.m. The Governor came in and told Pascoe that the Home Secretary, Henry Brooke, had decided he could find no reason for rescinding the death penalty. His petition had been denied. Now that really got to him. Only three days left and just one more chance – an appeal to the Queen for clemency.

This afternoon, Monday 16 December, he was told the Queen had refused his plea for clemency. That was his last hope. There is nothing left. He'll hang at eight o'clock in the morning. While he was on exercise today, unknown to him, the two hangmen came into the block. Entering the execution chamber they secured the new rope to the beam above the trapdoors. The Home Office always supplies a new rope. The traps were tested a few times to make sure they'll open easily.

* * *

WILLIAMS ★ FIREPLACES

EVENING POST

incorporating the Evening World

No. 9,779—3d. The paper all Bristol asked for and helped to create Sat., Dec. 14 1963

Vanden Plas Princess
DISTRIBUTORS
BRISTOL MOTOR CO. LTD.
ASHTON GATE

Protest march starts as Brooke decides...

NO REPRIEVE FOR KILLERS

THEY DIE

Russell Pascoe

ON TUESDAY

Dennis Whitty

A TRENCH AT THE BOTTOM OF HIS GARDEN

Norman Mountford's home is no longer his castle.

Three months ago a man entered his garden at Nore Road, Portishead, hacked through his hedge and dug up rose bushes and other plants.

The Christmas executions at Horfield and Winchester Gaols are to take place. The Home Secretary announced this afternoon that there is to be no reprieve for the two Cornish killers.

Soon after Mr. Henry Brooke's terse statement, Bristol protesters against the hangings began their silent procession through the city centre streets parked with shoppers and traffic.

They will mount a vigil outside Horfield Prison walls until 8 a.m. on Tuesday, when Russell Pascoe (23) will become the first man to be executed in Bristol for 10 years.

At the same hour, Dennis Whitty, the second man convicted of the capital murder of a 64 year-old Cornish farmer, will die at Winchester.

SHOPPERS

December 1963. The headline says it all.

The sound of the outer door being opened again echoes through to us. 'Jesus Christ! Who is it now?' I look at my watch. Ten past eleven. Ken and I are buttoned up as the inner door opens. The face of the duty P.O. appears.

'Sorry, lads. Pascoe's brother and a mate have just arrived at the gate. They've came all the way up from Cornwall on a motor scooter. Should've been here this afternoon, but the bloody thing's broken down three times. Under the circumstances, the Governor's going to let them have a visit.'

I take Russell through to the small visitors' cubicle. As far as I know he hasn't had a visit during the whole six weeks. He sits down on the prisoner's side, facing the reinforced glass. A couple of minutes later the door opens on the other side and an officer ushers in the two young men. They look cold and tired. It's mid-December and they've been on the road for fourteen hours or more on a motor scooter.

No doubt it's a comfort to Russell that his brother and a friend have made such a dogged effort to come and see him, but right from the start the conversation is desultory. What can you talk about when your brother is to be hanged in the morning? After forty minutes, the silences are becoming longer and more uncomfortable as all three struggle to find something to say. Finally, I decide they've all had enough. I stand behind Russell and put both my hands on his shoulders; I want his brother to see he isn't friendless, even in here. 'It's up to you, Russell, but do you think it's time?'

He looks at his brother, who nods. They all stand up and make their stilted, sad farewells through the glass. Without a final touch. I try to smile to the two on the other side as I lead him away. I have a lump in my throat and cannot trust myself to speak. When we return to the cell Russell goes straight to his bed and lies there, silent.

'How did it go?' Ken asks, quietly.

'Fuckin' awful.'

* * *

Russell continues to lie on his bed, staring at the ceiling, lost in his thoughts. Just after midnight, as expected, a hospital officer comes in and gives him a sleeping draught. He slowly changes into his pyjamas and climbs into bed. As usual we switch off all the lights except for the table lamp. I drape the piece of cloth over it so Ken and I have enough light to read by. The far end of the long cell, and Russell's bed, are in semi-darkness. I feel I should say something. He had a few words with the hospital officer, but since his visit he hasn't spoken to us. I try to sound casual. 'Is that dark enough for you, Russell?' I move the piece of cloth around.

'Yeah, yeah. Thass fine, tharr is.' His speech is slurred. The sleeping draught must have been strong.

'That was good of your brother and mate to come up to see you,' says Ken. 'It sounds like they must have made a helluva effort.'

'Yeah, they're goo' lads. On the road for hours an' hours.' He is speaking even slower now. There's a pause. I feel he's going to say something else. But it doesn't come. His steady breathing tells us he's fallen asleep. In a way, it's a relief. It makes it easier for all of us. Ken and I read and half doze the remaining hours of the long night. I manage to finish Laurie Lee's *Cider With Rosie*.

At last seven a.m. comes. Russell hasn't stirred; he's still in bed. For the last time we hear the outside door being opened. There are footsteps and voices in the corridor – more than usual. The inner door is unlocked. The chief officer, a hospital officer and two ordinary officers all enter. A welcome breath of cold December air sneaks into the stuffy cell with them. All of a sudden Ken and I are finished. Russell has one hour left.

'How has he been?' the hospital officer whispers.

Ken puts his two hands flat together, as if about to pray, then inclines his head to rest on them.

'Slept solid all night,' he mouths.

We have to go. We're not allowed to stay. Tunics buttoned, we put our hats on. Russell hasn't moved; there's nothing we can do.

As Ken and I leave, I take a last glance down the cell. He is still in bed, but is he asleep? Is he lying there trying to deny where he is and what's about to happen to him? I can't see his face, just the dark curly hair and his form under the blankets. There's no point disturbing him. What could we say? We leave without a goodbye.

For the remaining hour of his life, Russell will be surrounded by strangers. With our departure, the last of the six officers who've sat with him night and day are gone. We have formed a personal relationship with him during this intense period. It would be asking too much to expect us to stay this last hour. I look at my watch. It won't be long until they'll be giving Russell a shake, telling him he'll have to get up. He went to bed last night with just Ken and me in the cell. Any minute now he'll sit up in bed and find the room's full of strangers. Men he doesn't know. But he knows why they're there. He's bound to feel isolated. Powerless. And frightened to death.

Ken and I take breakfast with Harry Allen and his assistant in the mess. Just 40 feet away is the condemned block. Allen is gregarious company. A tall, slim man in his late fifties. His gray hair, short, clipped moustache and smart blue suit give him a distinguished air. He is a publican in Manchester. For around twenty years he was number two to the doyen of British hangmen – Albert Pierrepoint. Together, after the Second World War, they'd hanged many scores of Nazi war criminals condemned to death by numerous Nuremberg war crimes' trials. On their return to Britain, they'd executed William Joyce, Lord Haw-Haw, who'd broadcast Nazi propaganda from wartime Berlin. In postwar Britain, as the forties became the fifties, together they'd hanged all the notorious murderers of the era – Haig, Heath, Christie, Ruth Ellis – and many more not so notorious, or maybe even not guilty . . . Derek Bentley and Timothy Evans?

Their vocation also frequently took them to more exotic locations. Many colonies of the slowly shrinking British Empire didn't have their own executioner. Pierrepoint and Allen were often called on to fly to destinations including Jamaica, the Bahamas, Cyprus and British Honduras to use their expertise.

As I sit opposite Allen, I think back to last night. The normally empty mess had been busy as I'd entered at my usual nine fifteen p.m. As well as the hangmen and Teddy Bear, half a dozen senior officers, who all knew Allen, had come in to renew their acquaintance. A bottle of whisky stood on the table; two crates of beer lay on the floor. Harry Allen, the exact opposite of the taciturn Pierrepoint, was holding court; he was quite happy to regale us with tales of jobs done, most of them when he was assistant to Albert . . .

'You and Albert would have done Ruth Ellis, I would imagine, Harry?'

'Aye. We hoped she'd get a reprieve. We were never happy doing women. She was no bother, mind. Brave as any man. Well!' He laughs. 'Braver than a lot o' men, as it 'appens.'

'What about all those SS camp guards and other Nazi war criminals, Harry? Did they get this "three clear Sundays" business before they were 'anged?'

'No, did they fuck! We'd still be out there if they did. Folk don't realise just how many war crimes' trials there were at Nuremberg. There were thousands of SS and others all prosecuted. The newsreels only showed the major one; you know – Goering, Hess, Speer and all o' them. At the same time, there were dozens of courts sitting with all these other buggers. Ah'll tell ye what else folk forget – it was a "Four Power" thing. Everything was shared equally between the British, Americans, Russians and the French – including the executions.' He took a sip of whisky. 'So there wasn't time for the "three clear Sundays" palaver. You'd maybe get, say, thirty or more camp guards all tried together. All of those found guilty and sentenced to death, their appeal would be heard an hour later. If it went down, they were marched straight off to this big gymnasium. They'd built a scaffold in it. It hung four at a time. So we had them in this anteroom. The soldiers would bring in four: Quick march! Up the stairs, bag and rope over their heads, pull the lever, down they went together.' He stopped and opened a bottle of beer; lit another cigarette. 'Then, the next thing is, Albert and me had to take over the American's quota. They sacked their lads. Making a right arse of it, they were.'

'What were they doing?'

'Well, they'd sent over a couple of executioners all right – but they were electric chair lads. Hadn't a bloody clue about hangin'. They started off dropping them too far – and were pulling the fuckin' heads off them!' He shook his head at the memory. 'So they overcompensated and next thing the buggers aren't dropping far enough, so they're hanging there strangling!' He waved a dismissive hand. 'Gave the Yanks their cards, packed them off home, and Albert and me took over their quota.'

'What's the most you ever done in a session at Nuremberg, Harry?' someone asked.

We were all quiet as we watched him and waited for his answer.

'Mmmm, one afternoon we did twenty-seven in two hours forty minutes.'

'Bloody hell! So they weren't left to hang for very long.'

'No, hadn't the time. As soon as we put four down, the doc would go underneath the scaffold, 'ave a listen with his stethoscope, feel for a pulse. "Right, okay," he'd say. We had these soldier orderlies. They'd go underneath and lift them up, take the weight, we'd take the ropes and bags off, the soldiers would put them onto trolleys and whisk them away to the temporary morgue. A couple of minutes later the next four were marching in.'

That had been the craic last night. As Ken and I sit having breakfast with the hangmen, I can't rid myself of the contradictory feeling that, somehow, I'm letting Russell down by breakfasting with the men who are about to hang him.

'How was he last night?' Allen looks rather bleary-eyed. He's on his second mug of hot, sweet tea. And at least his third cigarette. We tell him. He takes a deep draw. 'I think this lad will go without any bother.' As he speaks, the blue smoke spills out of his mouth.

Just after ten to eight, from the kitchen door at the end of the mess, Ken, the two hangmen, Teddy Bear and I, watch as the Governor, Lord Lieutenant of the County and other official witnesses file quietly into the block. They enter the empty execution chamber. At three minutes to eight, Allen nudges his assistant. 'Right, it's us.' Before he leaves, Allen places a newly-lit cigarette in an ashtray on the mantelpiece. Ken and I move closer to the kitchen door and watch as the Deputy Governor, at Allen's request, silently opens the door to the corridor. They enter the block on tiptoe.

With the entry of the hangmen into the block, the tempo now increases. A procedure, developed over decades and brought to perfection in the twentieth century by Albert Pierrepoint, now swings smoothly, professionally into action. Russell Pascoe will be dead in less than three minutes.

On Allen's previous instructions, Pascoe is already dressed in an open-necked, blue striped prison shirt, gray trousers and soft felt slippers. He sits on a chair near to the cell door. At five to eight he was offered, and drank, a large tot of whisky.

The two hangmen suddenly appear in the cell. Allen walks swiftly over and stands in front of Pascoe. 'Stand up!' he says. The two officers who relieved Ken and me stride over and take up position on either side of Pascoe. Allen looks the condemned man in the eye. 'Do exactly as I say, son, and it will all be very quick and easy.'

While Allen speaks, his assistant has gone behind Pascoe and swiftly secured his arms with a leather strap. Seconds later, high up in its tower, Bristol Prison's clock strikes the first chime of eight o'clock. 'Right, straight through!' commands Allen.

The officers take hold of Pascoe's bound arms and march him, at the double, the 12 feet from the cell, directly across the corridor, and into the now open execution chamber. The witnesses watch. The officers stop with Pascoe on the trapdoors; they stand on wooden planks which span them. As they hold Pascoe with one hand, they reach up with the other and take hold of the braided ropes hanging from the beams. When the trapdoors open, the planks and ropes are all they'll have to save them following the hanged man through the floor. The moment Pascoe and the officers halt on the traps, the assistant immediately squats behind Pascoe and quickly fastens a leather strap round his ankles. At the same instant, Allen is placing a black cloth hood and the noose, together, over the condemned man's head. He turns the rope so the knot is at the side of Pascoe's neck, takes up the slack, and without a word steps off to one side. The executioner now takes hold of the lever which operates the traps and gives a hand signal to the two officers. They let go of the prisoner's arms.

For a second Pascoe stands on the trapdoors; bound, blindfolded, alone. Not a word has been spoken since the group entered the execution chamber. As the officers let go of him, inside the silent darkness of the hood Pascoe knows it is about to happen. It has come at last. The witnesses see him tense himself. As the fifth chime of the prison clock echoes through to them, Harry Allen pulls the lever. Without a sound, Russell Pascoe plummets 5 feet and dies instantly as his neck is broken and the nerves from brain to spinal column are severed by the weight of his body. He is now beyond pain. He is already dead as the remaining three chimes of eight o'clock reverberate through the prison's grounds. From leaving the condemned cell to dropping through the trapdoors, the whole thing has taken fourteen seconds.

Allen and his assistant immediately leave the block without having spoken a word. Their task is done. The official witnesses have watched the proceedings in stunned silence. They now file out and are led to the Governor's office for a reviving drink.

After we watched the hangmen enter the block, Ken, Teddy Bear and I emerged from the kitchen door of the mess and stood, leaning against the hut, facing the block. At the fifth chime of the clock we heard a dull 'wumph' as the trapdoors flew open and bounced once off the leather pads attached to the walls of the cellar below. It was over.

The hangmen come back into the mess via the kitchen door. It's just over three minutes since they left. The cigarette Allen placed in the ashtray still burns. He picks it up, takes an appreciative draw, returns it to the ashtray then rubs his hands briskly together. 'Any tea on the go?'

I have to know. 'Was he any bother?'

'No, good as gold, Jock.'

Somehow, I find this comforting. I'd hate to have been told Russell had to be dragged, terrified, to his death. Allen lights another cigarette from the last. 'I'd dare take a bet that Whitty was dropping at Winchester same time as our lad!'

The two officers who escorted Russell come into the mess. They look pale and shaken. They have a mug of hot, sweet tea, then go home. As is traditional, they are given the rest of the day off.

I stand up. 'Well, ah think ah'd better get away. Got to get my gear together and catch a train back tae Brum.' I'm not in the mood for any more of Harry Allen's stories.

'Nice to have met you, Jock,' says Allen. 'You can't hear it nowadays in me accent, but would you believe I'm a Jock? Born in Kilmarnock.'

'Jeez! Ah'd never have guessed.'

'Aye. If yer ever in Manchester, call in to the pub for a pint.' He takes his wallet out of his jacket and extracts his business card. 'Here y'are.'

'Oh, thanks.' I look at it: H. B. Allen. Woodman Inn. Wood Street, Manchester. MIDdleton 4783.

I put it into the pocket in my wallet meant for such things and thank Teddy Bear for looking after me so well these last six weeks. Ken and I shake hands. We probably won't see each other again. He's taking a later train back to Exeter. We don't say how we feel.

I walk out of Bristol Prison's gates for the last time. It's not yet nine a.m. It's a cold morning with a weak, wintry sun. For a moment I stand on the cobbled setts in front of the gates and watch folk go about their business. Buses lumber past with passengers reading their morning papers. Very few glance at the

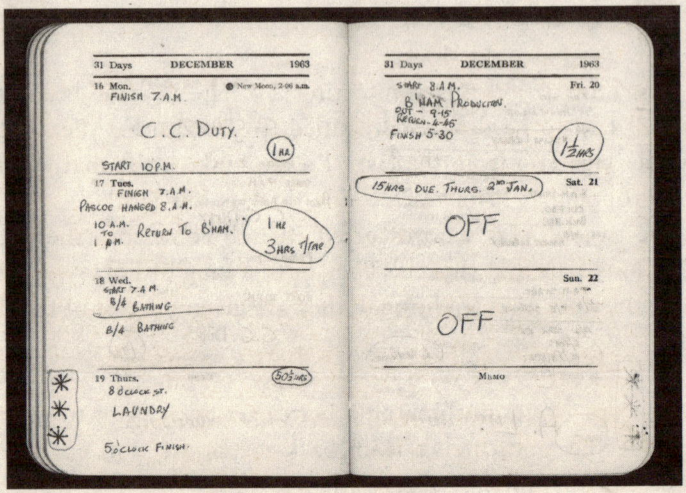

Tuesday 17 December 1963. Pascoe is executed.
Time to return to Birmingham.
I don't forget to record the overtime incurred.

prison. Children pummel one another as they head for school. People walk, cycle and drive by. I take a couple of deep breaths of crisp December air, then set off at a good pace.

In the silent, empty block Russell still hangs through the trap, the hood over his head. It'll be another half hour or so before they take him down. Some time this evening, when the jail is locked up, he'll be buried in an unmarked grave within its walls. It's Tuesday 17 December 1963.

Nine months later, in August 1964, the last judicial hangings are carried out at Liverpool and Manchester Prisons. The following year, in November 1965, the death penalty is abolished. Hanging is consigned to history.

MIDdleton 4783

H. B. Allen

Woodman Inn, Wood St.,
Middleton, Manchester

Less than thirty minutes after executing Pascoe, the hangman gives me his visiting card.

Not For Bending

It's April 1964. Another couple of months and that'll be me two years at the Green. I feel I'm doing all right. All the senior screws who, when I first arrived, reserved judgement on me until they had me weighed up, now treat me as a reliable officer – one of the staff. Things are going well. I have a wife and two kids, we're buying a house, and even though it has its moments now and again, I enjoy my job and consider myself conscientious.

I open Lonsdale's door. 'That Chapman Pincher in the *Daily Express* has been writing about you again.' He looks up. He's hard at work translating one of the Bond novels into Russian. This is the second he's done. 'Pincher says that a recent defector from the Soviet Union has said you are really Colonel Konon Molody of the KGB! Hah hah!'

Lonsdale lays down his pen, leans back in his chair and smiles. 'Is THAT what they're saying?' He's obviously not going to confirm it.

'Anyway, Gordon, *The Bob Hope Show* was on telly last night—' He interrupts me: 'Yeah, I like Bob Hope.'

'He comes out front of stage, gives his usual opening patter. As you'll know, it's always topical. "Have you seen the figures for the amount of money we spend on security?" he says. "Well, I've just written to the President, telling him how we can save all those millions of dollars." Then he pauses and looks round the audience like he always does. "LET the Russians steal our secrets – then they'll be two years behind as well!" '

I've never seen Lonsdale laugh so much since I got to know him.

During these last twenty-plus months, what could almost be called a friendship has grown between this enigmatic man and myself. Its basis is the fact that we like talking to one another. Often, if I'm on evening duty on his wing, I'll stand at his door and blether to him for twenty minutes or so when things are quiet. Now and again I've been the senior of the two discipline officers in the Brush Shop. That means I'm at the top end, next to the office. I'll stand with my back to the door and chat away to Lonsdale while keeping an eye on the workforce at the same time. I've found he enjoys a good joke, especially of that New York Jewish type of humour. Now and again, when he's in the mood, he'll tell me of incidents during the war. A teenage Partisan, he spent almost three years behind German lines in the Pripet Marshes area. No doubt this was when his capabilities were noted and he was earmarked for induction into the KGB after the war, to be trained in other skills.

One evening, he tells me a tale, told to him by one of his instructors, which shows that even espionage can sometimes be done the easy way . . .

'During the 1930s, Soviet agents tried all ways to find out the formula for smokeless cordite. Before its development you could spot a battery of artillery from miles away, there was so much smoke. So we wanted to find out how to produce it. We targeted a French factory which was manufacturing it. Tried all ways to get the formula; offered bribes, infiltrated people into the factory, hoping they'd get access to the laboratories. Nothing doing. Place was sewed up real tight. Then one of our guys has a brainwave. He chooses a nice quiet afternoon, puts an old pair of overalls on and takes a walk along the railway line outside the plant. Goes along tapping the wheels of the freight cars as though testing them. There are always wagons in the sidings waiting to be coupled up and pulled into the factory. As he ambles along the lines of trucks he takes a look at the labels on each of them. They tell you what the contents are *and* in what quantity – 2,000 kilos of saltpetre; 1,200 kilos of sulphur; 1,000 kilos of nitro and so on. Not only does that tell him what materials are used, but also in what percentages! In other words, the formula! So simple. The security department at this factory thought the joint was impregnable. It wasn't!'

Just into the second week in April, Lonsdale gets a new neighbour. The Mail Train Robbers have finally been sentenced and, as expected, dispersed to various jails. We get Charlie Wilson. Considered to be one of the ringleaders, he has been given thirty years. These swingeing sentences are meant to send out a warning: Don't interfere with the Royal Mail! Wilson is located on A2, just a few doors away from Lonsdale. Unlike most London cons, Wilson proves to be fairly quiet and affable.

A couple of weeks later, on the morning of Tuesday 21 April 1964, I come on duty at seven thirty a.m. I'm on the 'farm party', the prison owns a farm just outside the city. It is run by a dozen cons supervised by officers. The prison has been unlocked and gives the usual impression of being in chaos as hundreds of cons flit back and forth along the landings, slopping out, calling across to one another, or making their way noisily down the metal stairways to collect their breakfasts. P.O. Appleton waves for me to come over to the box. He sits on his stool. The bright bulb above his head shines down, making the Centre box seem an oasis of light and warmth in the midst of the drab, gray prison. He leans forward. 'Have you heard the buzz?'

'No. I've just came on, P.O.'

'Three guys arrived at the gate around five a.m. this morning. MI5 types.' He looks around as though checking we're not being overheard. 'Up from London. They've whipped Lonsdale away!'

'Jeez-oh! You know what that'll be, don't you?' At the same

time, I'm thinking to myself, I'm fair going to miss having my craic with him.

'Yeah,' says Appleton, 'I'd dare take a bet they're going to swap him for that, eh, what's his name?'

'Greville Wynne. As soon as the Russians arrested him last year I remember thinking, this could be the one Lonsdale's waiting for. Anyway, we'll soon see.'

Later that evening, I put on the TV News. It's the first item: 'At the Heerstrasse Checkpoint in West Berlin this afternoon, Gordon Lonsdale, convicted Russian spy, was exchanged for British businessman, Greville Wynne . . .'

Well, he knew they'd eventually get him back. So that's him at last on his way home to his long-suffering Polish wife and family. You've got to admire him. If they hadn't arrested someone who could be used as a swap for him, Lonsdale would just have sat tight. He'd have done the whole sentence if necessary.

A couple of days later, Paddy Hutchman, an Irish officer, stops me. 'I was just talking to Lonsdale the day before they spirited him away. He says to me, "Amongst the staff there are only two officers I can have a decent conversation with: you and Officer Douglas. The older officers seem to be a bit wary of me for some reason. The younger ones? All they can talk about is either football or what's going on in the jail." '

'Did he? Oh well, Paddy, I'll definitely take that as a compliment.'

'Yeah, me too.'

Once behind the Iron Curtain, Lonsdale sinks out of sight. But not for long. A couple of years later, for the first time ever, a Russian agent is allowed to publish his memoirs in the West! With the straightforward title *Spy* there's no doubt it is being published for just one reason – to embarrass the Western intelligence services, especially those of Britain and America.

* * *

1966: The Russians allow Lonsdale to publish his memoirs. Their sole aim is to embarrass the West.

After this furore no more is heard of Lonsdale until, some time in the 1980s, it's reported from the Soviet Union that he has died. I felt quite sad when I heard it. I'd found him to be a single-minded, dedicated man who, it must be said, served his country and his cause well. Although our politics were miles apart – at this period in my life I was somewhere to the right of Attila the Hun – he was an interesting, engaging man. And I liked him.

Studies in Blue: Two

You just have to look at George Balche and the first thought that'll hit you is, I bet he's an ex-guardsman. He is. Coldstream Guards. Six feet tall, thick moustache, barrel-chested. What adds to the picture is the fact that he has remodelled his hat by 'propping' the front (inserting a 6-inch rule to force it permanently upwards), then 'slashed' the stitches holding the shiny black skip so he can bend it down to lie almost on his forehead. There is now no mistaking that you're in the presence of an ex-guardsman. He's what I call a real southerner – he originates from somewhere in the Home Counties. In his mid-thirties, George is a good officer who deals with prisoners in a firm, fair, sometimes brusque way. He has a dry sense of humour, tends to talk in a clipped, military manner and often has those around him in stitches without meaning to. Yet it's hard to make *him* laugh. But when something does tickle him . . .

George is dock officer in number one court at Birmingham Assizes. It's a straightforward case: a Jamaican guy is accused of stabbing a fellow countryman at a party. The red-robed High Court judge sits on the bench; the black-robed barristers – for prosecution and defence – are in their places; the jurors sit in their box. It's 1964. When citizens are called for jury service they tend to be a little overawed by it all. They normally turn up wearing their best suits and frocks.

* * *

Yet another West Indian, a guest at the party, is in the witness box. The prosecuting barrister, Mr Farrow, has him under cross-examination . . .

'Now, there were "substances" being smoked at this party, is that correct?'

'Yeah man, ev'body was smoking shit!'

'Smoking shit?' says the barrister, somewhat surprised.

The judge stops writing and peers over the top of his glasses. 'Smoking shit!'

The defence counsel half rises to his feet. 'If it please M'lud, "shit" is one of the many slang names by which hemp or marijuana is known.'

'Ah, thank you, Mr Lawson. I am obleeged. For a moment there I was rather concerned as to what was being smoked.' The judge and the two barristers begin to laugh. The jury, at first surprised to hear these learned men using the word 'shit' so freely, also begin to laugh. George, sitting in the dock with his arms folded, has been so amused by the looks of consternation on the faces of all concerned that he is also dying to laugh. Glad of the opportunity to do so, he takes full advantage: 'HAR HAR HAR HAR HAR!' Unfortunately, George begins to laugh just as the others are stopping. The jury find it comical to see this great bear of a man, every inch the public's idea of a stern prison warder, having such a good laugh to himself – almost a parody of the 'Laughing Policeman' machine on the sea front at Blackpool. The jury break out in laughter again, this time at the warder. George, his mind filled with the thought that both judge and prosecuting counsel had believed for a moment the party guests had actually been smoking shit, is now helpless. 'HAR HAR HAR HAR, SHIT!' The jury are now going into fits of laughter at this incongruous sight in the dock. George is unable to stop. Literally weak with laughter, he manages to struggle to his feet and, supporting himself on the brass rails which surround the dock, makes his way to the stairway and staggers out of sight downstairs to the cells. As he descends, his laughter can be heard, fainter and fainter: 'Har har har, shit! Har har har, shit!' With his departure, order is restored in court.

Five minutes later, somewhat shamefaced, he appears back in the dock. The jury begin to titter. George, who hasn't yet taken his seat, starts to shake with silent mirth. He looks at the judge, tries to apologise, but it comes out as a strangulated 'Murrrgh!' He then points to the dock stairs and once more vanishes down them. It's decided justice would best be served if George didn't appear in the dock for the rest of the day. He swaps duties with the officer in charge of cells.

George comes from an army family. His grandfather was a staff sergeant in the Coldstreams, his father was Regimental Sergeant Major (equivalent to being God) and George joined as a boy and went on to serve twelve years.

I'm at Warwick Assizes with George and Terry Belcher. It's the last day. We've had just one prisoner to deal with and he's been given probation, so we've no one to take back. After repairing to a local hostelry for a bar lunch and a pint, we now sit back in the empty cells area, enjoying a cup of tea before returning to the jail. George, who can be quite shy in a large group is relaxed and at ease with just us two junior officers. He looks at us. 'Do you know the Ceremony of the Keys at the Tower of London?'

Terry and I both say we know of it, saw it on TV, but have never actually been to the Tower.

'Well, it's the guards' regiments who mount the sentries for that,' says George. 'Each regiment, say Scots Guards, does six months, then they might be followed by the Welsh Guards and so on. Anyways, in 1953 it's our turn. This was my first time doing it. They never gave you much time to rehearse, just a couple of days before you relieve the previous lot. It's all ceremonial, of course. Centuries ago it was the actual nightly locking-up of the

Tower; now it's just done for the benefit of the tourists. Any road, there's a sentry on each of the four gates. You've got a Beefeater, in full rig-out, carrying the keys. He's escorted by the sergeant of the guard and two squaddies with rifles on their shoulders. As they approach each of the four gates, the sentries, in turn, 'ave to challenge them – "Halt! Who goes there?" The party then halts and the sergeant says, "The keys." The sentry asks, "Whose keys?" And the sergeant says, "Queen Elizabeth's keys!"' George scratches his big chin. 'That's 'ow it's supposed to go.'

I look at Terry. 'Do ye get the feeling, somehow, this is not gonny go tae plan?'

'Definitely.'

George laughs. 'As I say, we'd 'ad our couple of days rehearsal, and it all would 'ave been fine, except for one thing. Our sergeant 'ad a bit of an impediment in 'is speech and this was making 'im really nervous. In fact, he was shittin' himself! And it was beginning to unsettle the rest of us. Well, comes the evening, and we're on for the first time. You should 'ave seen the crowds of tourists – '53 was coronation year if you remember – the place was heaving! Folk from all over the world come to see the Crown Jewels and the pride of the British Army, the Coldstream Guards. There's loads of people standing at all the four gates, but who's on duty at the first one?' George points to himself. 'Yours truly. I'm trying to look the part, ain't I? Stern, unsmiling guardsman. Immaculate. All these Americans, French, Japs, all clicking away with their cameras. Then I sees the Beefeater and escort approaching, and I'm praying our sergeant will be all right. I lets them get to the designated distance, comes to attention and goes into "the challenge"; one foot forward, rifle pointing at them. "HALT! Who goes there?" They halt, right on the button. But there's no reply. Right away, I know our sergeant's 'aving trouble. I feel the sweat breaking out on me. Finally he gets it out, "The Queez!" he says. The Beefeater gave 'im such a look. So now I've got a second to make me mind up.

Should I correct 'im – or go along with 'im? "Whose Queez?" says I. The Beefeater just shakes 'is head. "The Queez Queez!" says our sergeant.'

Terry and me are totally useless for the next five minutes.

Getting Away From It All

I'm in reception at Wandsworth Prison. Every week we do a 'London run', transferring cons to the various jails in the capital; a few YPs (young prisoners, aged under twenty-one) to Wormwood Scrubs, a remand for Brixton and a few adult cons who are doing sentences transferred to Wandsworth. As I hand over the prisoners' property to an officer, we chat amiably.

'How's Jimmy Bourne settling in?'

'Oh, of course, Jimmy came to us from Brum, didn't he?'

'Aye. Our loss was your loss!'

'He's in the censors today. I'll get one of the lads to take you up if you've time for a word.'

'That would be great.'

As the Wandsworth screw and I go through various doors and along passages, he stops by a window and points. Down below, in a fairly narrow space between what looks like a brick-built boiler house and a stretch of the prison wall, a solitary con exercises. He wears the E-man's bright yellow patches. Two screws stand either end of the designated exercise area.

'Have you got one of them?' says my escort.

'Is that Biggs?' I ask. The Mail Train Robbers have received so much publicity they are probably the most recognisable faces in Britain. With his dark curly hair he isn't hard to identify.

'Yeah, that's Biggsy,' he says. 'Have you got one?'

'Aye, we've got Charlie Wilson. He's in patches, too. They've spread them out all over the shop, haven't they?'

'Yeah. I imagine they'll all be E-men. The Prison Department probably think if they're clever enough to rob a Mail Train, they might be clever enough to escape from the clink.'

It's a late July evening. George Curtis and I are on A Wing. We lean on the rail of the bridge on A3, looking beyond the Centre and into C Wing. The officers on duty there are slopping out C2. Charlie Wilson comes out of his cell, jug and basin in hand, and heads for the recess.

'You know something, George, I cannot see these Mail Train guys settling down to do their time like good lads. Not when they've got all that money just waiting for them.'

'Too bloody right!' George pushes his specs up higher on his nose. 'The sentences are too long for a start. So imagine knowing you've got a couple of hundred thousand quid on the outside. I dare say they know people who'll be willing to come into the jail and get them out – for a price.' He laughs. 'Just hope I ain't on duty when they come!'

On Saturday 1 August 1964, Nancy, the kids and me set off by train for Scotland. It's my two-week main holiday. Not having a car, we go everywhere by bus or train. Our fortnight is always spent with Nancy's parents in Seafield, West Lothian. It lets Nancy see her folks and the folks see their grandkids. I just enjoy a lazy couple of weeks. During that time I might take the bus into Glasgow for a day to see my pal Sammy and his parents Lottie and Frank, up in Maryhill. Otherwise, the furthest I travel is the couple of miles to Blackburn. Two of Ma's brothers have settled there, so I always call on my uncles and aunts, Jim and Jenny, and Bill and Annie. I also usually have a Saturday night in the 'Croon' (the Crown Inn) with Robert Meek, my former workmate from the Gas Board. After the long hours I put in when I'm at the Green, it's great just to laze about, reading and snoozing to my heart's content.

* * *

1965. Nancy's Mum and Dad
in Birmingham with Scott and Nancy.

Just coming up for ten thirty on the morning of 12 August, I turn on the radio inside the radiogram. Nancy is having a long lie-in. Minutes later, I dash up the stairs and waken her.

'Hey! You'll never believe it, Charlie Wilson has escaped from the Green!'

'Eeh, never!' She props herself up in bed. 'Did he saw his bars or something?'

'Well, it's a bit sketchy at the minute, it jist took place during the night. They think people actually came intae the jail and broke him oot!'

'My God! They've got the cheek for anything nooadays!'

'Jist a few weeks ago George Curtis and me were oan evening duty. We were watching Wilson being slopped oot and we actually said, "These buggers will'nae sit still for twenty years, not wi' all the money they've got." Yah boys! Ah did'nae think oor forecast would come true so soon.'

When I start back to work on Monday 17 August, I can hardly wait to find out what has actually happened. Yet again, just like the robbery itself, it seems to have been a fairly simple plan. A night patrol, Mr Nicholl, had been walking along C2 some time after two a.m. All was quiet. As he passed the recess he heard a movement behind him. Before he could turn, he was hit a hard blow on the head and knocked out. Neither P.O. Arnold (the duty P.O.) or either of the other two night patrols heard or saw anything. When Nicholl came to, he staggered along to the Centre and raised the alarm. The first suspicion of the night staff was that an inmate had got out of his cell and was loose in the prison. With the time it took for the officer who 'sleeps in' at the gate to be roused and the police to be informed and allowed into the prison, it was a while before it was discovered that Wilson was missing.

Eventually it became clear that Wilson had been 'sprung'. The media, of course, had a field-day – in fact, more like a 'field-week'! It was, quite rightly, headlined as a 'Daring Escape'. Those in the Prison Service knew it wasn't as difficult as the public supposed. In the early 1960s there were no patrols in the grounds of Britain's jails at night. Prisons were designed to keep people in – not out. Sometime after nine p.m. everyone inside would be locked up, but if someone scaled the walls of a jail they could wander about the grounds all night unmolested.

The crucial point in the escape of Charlie Wilson was that those who came for him had copies of the keys needed to enter the prison and release him. Not the cell and pass keys used during the day by every officer, but the special pass AND Chubb keys used only at night – plus a normal cell key. The night pass and Chubb keys were only used to lock up the prison during the hours of darkness. These keys render the normal pass key inoperative. The only folk with access to these special keys were P.O.s on night duty. As the night P.O. goes off duty in the morning he hands them to the gatekeeper and they are locked up in a special key safe. The only officers other than P.O.s who ever handle them are the few officers who have passed the promotion exam and are waiting to be promoted. These officers regularly take their turn in 'acting up' as a P.O. and often do a week of night shift.

Those who'd freed Wilson had come into the jail with the keys required. They didn't have the original ones – P.O. Arnold had them – therefore, they must have had copies. Presumably these were made from wax impressions. Who supplied them? In my opinion – and the consensus of opinion of my fellow officers on the prison staff, as well as the police who conducted the subsequent investigation – it must have been an inside job, but unfortunately nothing was ever proved.

Why might it have been an inside job? The Mail Train Robbers were 'master criminals', and aristocrats in any prison, and maybe this was enough to turn someone's head.

For some people, it's hard not to get too close to celebrities like this. I certainly don't have a problem with a certain amount of familiarity between officers and prisoners. During my service I had good relationships with many a con. In fact, truth be told, over the years there were some cons whom I got to like as people far more than a few of the anally retentive P.O.s it would be my misfortune to come across at Durham Prison later in my service. Any familiarity I allowed with cons was always on the understanding there was a line they didn't cross. I was still a screw – they were a con.

But Charlie Wilson had been sprung. How did those who got him out get the keys? Did someone succumb to temptation? Could someone have made impressions of the keys when they were on nights? With all the money available to Wilson, there's no doubt anyone tempted could literally name his price. In the forty-plus years since, this has always been my theory. It hasn't changed.

Charlie Wilson would be on the run for four years before he was arrested near Montreal in Canada; his wife's telephone calls to her parents in England had been traced. He was returned to Britain and he served out the rest of his sentence. Sometime in the 1990s, long since released and living in Spain, Wilson was shot dead in a gangland hit.

On 8 July 1965, Ronald Biggs was sprung from Wandsworth Prison in a less sophisticated but nonetheless daring escape. In the middle of the afternoon, while on exercise, associates came over the wall, lowered rope ladders, and the second of the Mail Train Robbers was off and running. It would be May 2001 before Biggs, in failing health, returned from Brazil and gave himself up. He was promptly taken into custody to resume his sentence.

The escapes of Wilson and Biggs, and that of George Blake, a traitor who gave away secrets to the Russians, would lead to the Mountbatten Report on prison security. By 1968 there were dog handlers and officers patrolling the grounds of our prisons night and day. Prisons had to be made secure against those who wanted to come in – as well as those who wished to get out.

Dreams CAN Come True

It's a Saturday evening in March 1966. Scott and Nancy play on the floor. Nancy senior is in the kitchen preparing dinner. *Top of the Pops* is on TV. A guy is singing 'You Were On My Mind'. I'm not into modern pop records. After all, I'm twenty-seven – I was a rock 'n' roll boy. But I've heard this record regularly on the radio and I like it. I glance at the TV just to see what the singer looks like. JEE-SUSS! It's Pete Smith! There were six of us in the billet, all doing our National Service at Chilwell Depot, Nottingham. For twenty-one months we were the best of mates; we went everywhere together.

'NANCY! QUICK! Come and see who's on *Top o' the Pops*. Hurry up!' She runs into the living-room; I'm pointing at the screen.

'Eee, that's Pete thingmy, your army pal, in't it?'

'Yeah. Yah bugger! He always said he'd make it.'

The number finishes. Amidst the mandatory screaming I hear Jimmy Saville say, 'That was "You Were On My Mind" by, of course, Crispian St Peters!'

'Crispian Saint WHO? You mean Pete Smith, Jimmy,' I shout at the screen. I turn to Nancy. 'I couldn't believe it there for a second. I looked up – and there's Pete on the telly! Ah thought ah was hallucinating. Eh, good for him. The big skinny bugger was determined to make it. Always practising his guitar in the billet, playing at the local pubs. Remember that week you were down and we went to see him and Geordie Batey and little Doug whatsisname from Dagenham? On at the White Lion in Beeston they were.'

'Aye, they were really good. They were the main turn that night.'

'Yeah.' All at once my mind is filled with memories from six years ago. My mates. Titch, Butch, Pete, Stan, Hinchie and me. Jeez, we really were good pals. I get on well with lots of guys at the jail, but we're never as close as my army pals. For some reason I feel a bit sad.

It's June. I spot it in the *Birmingham Evening Mail* – 'Radio City '66' for one night only. Live at the Odeon! Dave Berry – Small Faces – Crispian St Peters. Everything's 'Radio' this and 'Radio' that at the moment. All trying to latch on to the publicity the pirate radio stations have been generating. Radio Caroline started the ball rolling by broadcasting, without a licence, from a redundant old ship outside territorial waters. There's a few more set themselves up since then, but they won't last. The government has decided they aren't going to have their monopoly on broadcasting in the UK – or from just outside – challenged.

I determine I'll go down to see him. I don't want to go to the show, my ears wouldn't stand it. From what I see on TV, these pop shows are one long uninterrupted screamfest. Not for me. There are two performances at this city centre cinema. The first starts at seven p.m.

I walk into the foyer just after six fifteen p.m. There's a doorman standing to the side. 'Hi! I'm a friend of Crispian St Peters' – I feel a bit stupid using his showbiz name – 'I'd like to say hello to him.'

'I'd 'ave a word with 'im.' He points to a bespectacled man who's aged around forty, wearing a suit. 'He's the road manager.' I'd have thought he was a bank manager. 'Right, thanks.'

I walk over to him. 'Hi! My name's Robert Douglas. Crispian St Peters, well, I know him as Pete Smith, we did our National Service together. We were good mates. Is it possible to say hello to him? Just for a few minutes.'

'Yeah, of course. I'll take you up to his dressing-room. He's sharing with the Small Faces.'

As we walk backstage, I tell him about the six of us. I finish up with: 'The last few months I'd risen to the dizzy heights of lance corporal, which meant I had to march them all down the depot every morning. Smithy was always playing silly buggers, marching out of step, turning the wrong way. I was always bollocking him!'

'I'll tell you what,' says the best-dressed roadie in the business, 'when we get to the dressing-room, shout something through the door before we open it. You know, sort of thing you'd say in your army days.'

The door is already ajar when we get to it; I can hear voices and laughter inside. I stand by the gap. 'SMITHY! I'm fed-up bloody telling you to keep in step. You're a pain in the ar—'

The door is whipped open. 'DOUG! Bugger me! What a surprise. Man! It's great to see you.'

'I'll leave the two of you to it,' says the roadie.

'Thanks very much,' I say.

'Thanks, John,' says Pete. 'C'mon in,' he says. 'These are the Small Faces. I won't introduce you, not our type of people at all!' He's put on the posh George Sanders voice he'd use in the billet when we were having a laugh. The reaction from the Faces can be summarised as 'Get fucked!'

As Pete and I sit and talk, various members of the group take turns sticking their heads out of the dressing-room window. It overlooks an alley at the side of the theatre. A hundred or more youngsters, mostly girls, are gathered there. Each appearance of a Small Face elicits screams. One of the group reaches for a canister of Vim, the sink and bath cleaner, which stands by the hand-basin. Every now and again he looks out of the window and shakes the tin. As the white powder cascades down it brings even louder screams.

The show starts. 'C'mon down with me,' says Pete. 'When I'm on you can stand in the wings.'

As we watch from the sidelines, the noise from the audience is deafening; a solid wave. We have to shout at one another to be heard. It's Pete's turn. As the MC announces him, the volume increases. He starts straight away with 'You Were On My Mind', followed by his new hit, 'The Pied Piper'. The screaming never lets up all during his performance. When he comes off, we retreat backstage so we can talk.

'Jeez! Pete. You could go out there and sing the phone book and they wouldn't know the difference, would they?'

'Yeah. That's the way it is nowadays.'

'If I went to see Sinatra, I'd want to listen to every word. They like your records, you'd think they'd want to *hear* you singing them.'

'Anyway,' says Pete, 'we've time to nip out for a drink before the second house. Just a few doors along there's a nice little hotel.'

We spend a pleasant forty minutes or so having a couple of pints, talking about our army days, and he tells me of his struggles to make it.

'So what's all this Crispian St Peters carry-on? Where did that come from?'

'Oh, God, I know. My manager chose it. Ah! And another thing – I'm twenty-three years old!'

'Lying hound! You're twenty-seven if you're a day!'

He holds up a finger, 'It's a mortal sin to be old in the pop business. I've got younger!'

'Oh, well. Don't worry. Your secret's safe wi' me, Pete.'

He looks at his watch. 'I think we'd better get back.'

As we leave the hotel we find there's a different scenario outside from forty minutes ago. The first house has come out. A few hundred of them are now packed into the lane which leads to the stage door. 'Bloody hell!' says Pete. He stands in a shop doorway. 'Do me a favour. Go down to the stage door, tell them I'm coming and ask if one or two guys can come out to help me in. I'll give you five minutes, then I'll start coming down the alley.'

I do as instructed. Three guys and myself are making our way back up the alley when Pete appears and starts on his way down. I watch as we get closer. He's maybe a third of the way, when . . . 'EEEEEE! IT'S CRISPIAN ST PETERS!' A pride of screaming young girls descend on him and start pulling at his clothes, hair and anything else that is grabbable. The three guys and me surround him and, after a struggle, eventually get him through the stage door. He tidies himself up. 'Right, that's me safely delivered. Are you coming back up to the dressing-room?'

'No, you're okay, I think I'd better make tracks, Pete.'

'Hey, you can stay if you want. There'll be a bit of a do on at the hotel after the show. You're welcome to come to that, Doug.'

'Honestly, I'm tempted, but I'm up at six in the morning.'

He laughs. 'I'll probably just be going to bed about then!'

'It's been really great tae see you, Pete. If you're back with another show I'll come down again.'

'It's been good.' He laughs. 'When I heard that voice at the door I knew right away who it was. It was a lovely surprise.'

'Jeez! It was the same when I looked up and there you were on *Top o' the Pops*! Anyway, I'm really glad you've made it, Pete. I remember how determined you were. So, all the best, mate.'

'You too, Doug. Best of luck.'

I make my exit via the stage door and get through the fans without any problem. As I travel home on the bus I have a nice glow. Good for Pete. NO, sorry – good for Crispian St Peters!

All in a Day's Work

The coach noses its way through one of the north London suburbs. We're on the weekly run with transfers from Brum to the Smoke. We've got sixteen on board, handcuffed in pairs. Some YPs for the Scrubs, the rest divvied up between Wandsworth and Pentonville. It's just gone eleven thirty a.m. There are four of us: Johnny Bull and Eric Morrell at the front, Mick Murphy and me at the rear. He's a good lad, Murphy. He's twenty-one, still on probation. He seems younger than his years, sometimes.

As we drive further in toward the city the more traffic we're hitting and the slower we're going. I look out the window. This is typical London suburbs. Something or other Broadway, all shops and pavements busy with people. They like that name, 'Broadway', in London. Suddenly there's a noise; movement. Two guys get up from their seats and head quickly down the aisle – they've got out of their cuffs! One pulls on the sliding door, but it doesn't open. Drivers always have them locked. I rise and automatically draw my stick. They'll have to try something else; overpower the officers, then force the driver to unlock the door. Young Mick has also stood up; I turn to him. 'Stay back here, draw your stick. If any of these fuckers move split them wide open!' I set off down the aisle. As I do, I give the others the gypsy's warning: 'DON'T ANY OF YOU FUCKIN' MOVE! STAY IN YOUR SEATS!'

* * *

As I arrive at the front, both officers are involved in wrestling and punching melees with the would-be escapees. They are identical twin brothers called Burns. Twenty years old, they're on their way to Wormwood Scrubs. My first words are to the civvy coach driver, who is more used to taking old folks on trips. 'Just keep driving, mate. Don't stop.'

Johnny and Eric are two screws in their fifties. I weigh up the situation. Johnny was sitting behind the driver. He has wrestled his assailant down onto the double seat and is on top of him. I can hear Johnny is already pretty much out of breath. Eric has been sitting at the front, facing the windscreen, the coach door behind him. The other brother, when he found the door locked, has reached over and tried to get Eric in a stranglehold. He's been only partly successful. Eric aims punches backwards now and again with his right hand; his left is keeping Burns from fully getting the hold on. Now and again Burns throws punches with his left. As I approach, I decide Eric is the one who needs help first. Because they were sitting when attacked, neither officer has had the chance to draw their sticks. Eric's assailant is so involved in trying to get the better of him that he hasn't seen me coming. Mindful of 'Guidelines on using the Truncheon', which state you should only strike the prisoner on the shoulders, arms or legs, I take careful aim – and hit him as hard as I can on the head; it's a beauty! 'OWWW!' He immediately lets go of Eric and starts to turn. I give him another whack on the head, then punch him in the face. This seems to knock the fight out of him. With my left hand I grab the front of his jacket, swing him round and push him onto the seat by the door. 'Don't fucking move or you'll get some more!' I glance up the coach. No one stirs. They sit in silence. Johnny is just managing to keep the other one down. The only target on show is one of the prisoner's hands. I give it a vicious swipe on the back, where all the veins are. There's a yelp and it's immediately whisked out of sight. He stops struggling. Just to make sure, I take aim at the only other part of him available – one of his legs is sticking out, so I belt him right on his shin-bone. 'OHHH! FUCK! OKAY! OKAY!' Johnny, who is quite exhausted by now, gets off him. I put away my stick then grab the con by his lapel. I drag him along the aisle for a few yards then sit him on the third seat from the front. Then I point to the other one. 'C'MERE, YOU!' I sit him level with his brother, but on the other side of the aisle. I stand between them, looking at both in turn. 'So, a couple of hard men, eh? Been watching too many movies ah think.' I throw a left and a right, punching each of them full in the face. I lean forward. 'As you've jist found out, you're no' as fuckin' tough as ye think.'

I make them stand up one at a time and search them. In the second one's trouser pocket I find a 3-inch nail. I hold it up in front of his eyes. 'This what ye used to pick the cuffs?' He nods in affirmation. I walk the few paces to where they'd been sitting and recover the handcuffs. I join them together again. 'Right, sit in that seat.'

I walk down to the front. Eric and Johnny are both rather shook up. I show them the nail.

'Pair o' fucking bastards!' says Eric.

'It's these useless bloody cuffs,' says Johnny, 'the police have had the ratchet type for years. We're still using these Victorian screw-lock things. A bairn could pick them.'

'I'll get the driver to stop when he sees a space,' says Eric, 'and I'll nip into a shop and ring Scrubs.' He nods towards the brothers. 'We'll 'ave a reception committee ready. Need to be put in the picture, these two.'

Trying to escape and assaulting an officer is an offence. Two offences, in fact. Part of the punishment, as far as screws are concerned, is to have a certain amount 'returned in kind'.

In the Bible it is known as 'An eye for an eye'.

Studies in Gray: Two

It's autumn 1966 and I'm on evening duty on G Wing, the remand wing. The inmates have been slopped out, suppered, and I've located the few receptions. Twenty to nine: won't be long until the night patrol comes on. I sit at the table on the twos, legs stretched out, hands in pockets. I look down the length of the cavernous, dimly-lit prison wing. I've let my second officer slip away. I have that feeling that comes at the end of a long day. I came on at seven this morning and I'm ready for the off. There are just over seventy locked up in here. The usual night sounds of a jail drift down to me . . . muffled conversations, a chair leg scraping on a stone floor, a sharp 'chink' as the handle of a galvanised bucket is let go. The heavy sound of a cell tally falling is followed by the bell ringing as the button makes the electrical connection. There it is. The now horizontal tally sticks out from the vertical ones. G2-12. I slide the spyhole cover to the side. 'Yeah?'

'Can I use the recess, boss? Save using me pot.'

'Aye, nae bother.' I unlock, he hurries off. I lean on the wall next to his door. Less than five minutes later, he returns. 'Thanks, boss.'

I've just banged him up again and slid the outside night bolt on when the main door opens, then the inner iron gate. 'Late one for you, Jock.' Ron Percival lets the man through. The remand carries his bedroll under his arm. He holds a plastic bag in his spare hand.

'Yeah, okay Ron. I'll see to him.'

As Ron lets himself out, I wave my hand. 'Just come along

here.' I know there's an empty cell two doors away. The new 'bod' comes slowly along the landing. I open the cell. I've nothing to do but watch him. The fact he's rather portly, plus the added girth of the bedding under his arm, means he has to make his way crabwise along the walkway. The widely-spaced overhead bulbs shine down, casting ever-changing shadows as he progresses. The brush of Edward Hopper could make something of this stark scene. I've even got a title – 'Late-night Reception'.

He's a tall man, with sparse gray hair. He's in his late fifties, I'll discover, but looks ten years older. He's very like the German actor Curt Jurgens. Curt never plays anybody below the rank of colonel. As he comes nearer, I look at the coat he's wearing: extra long, almost to his ankles. Dark navy blue, nearly black. I bet that's alpaca. It's seen better days, heading for shabby. Even so, it's a proper gentleman's topcoat. Although I haven't heard him speak, I'm somehow aware that this man has an air about him. He's different.

He enters the cell, drops the bedding onto the mattress and places the plastic bag beside it. He turns and looks at me. I can tell he's more than tired. Low. I've seen that look before when someone feels they're living through the worst thing that's ever happened to them. It'll be easy enough to confirm.

'This your first time in prison?'

'Yes.'

I take a blank cell card out of my top pocket. On evenings I always carry a selection of the various colours which denote the different religions. 'What's your name? Full name.'

'William Aldritt Squire, sir.'

I get him to spell 'Aldritt'. I point to the recess. 'Fill up your jug with fresh water. I'd use the toilet while you're there. Save using the chamber-pot.' When he comes back I briefly explain what privileges remands have. I lift the rule book. 'Everything you need to know is spelled out in here. When you're unlocked in the morning, first thing you do is slop out. If you want to ask something, or make an application, go along to that box on the centre. The P.O. will be in there. He'll keep you right. It's best to ask an officer if you have a question, not one of the remands. Anything you'd like to ask before I go?'

'No, thank you. That's fine. I'll go through the rule book in the morning.' He has a cultured voice, but without the affected 'cut glass' way of talking that many middle-class people adopt when trying to be something they're not. Those actually born to it don't speak with such strangulated vowels.

I'm about to leave. 'Listen, if you get a good night's sleep you'll feel a bit more able to handle things in the morning. You might not believe me, but you do get used to it. The main thing to remember is, it WILL pass. You won't be locked up for ever. Goodnight.'

'Yes, goodnight. And, ah, thank you, officer.'

The next day's papers carry the story. It's the 'return of the prodigal' – and then some! Our prisoner is a member of the family who own the well-known Midlands lock makers Squire & Sons. William 'Bill' Squire had been quite the playboy back in the thirties and into the forties. Tall, handsome and rich, he was one of the 'sons' in the company's name. He was also a regular on the London nightclub and theatre scene. Then came the war. By late 1940, Britain stood alone; the Germans were bombing every night, and invasion was imminent. Surely only a matter of days away. One morning, young Mr Squire didn't arrive at the office. He seemed to have vanished. It was soon discovered that so had £140,000 of the company's money! (Almost £3 million at today's value.) A few weeks later he surfaced in South America. There he would remain for the next twenty-six years. Until the money ran out . . .

Why had he done it? Almost certainly he'd been convinced, as many people were after the fall of France and the Dunkirk evacuation, that Britain was heading for defeat. So, he'd deserted the sinking ship. Many South American countries had no extradition treaties with Great Britain. He could start anew, go into business, make some investments. He had enough money to last him for life.

I wonder what his thoughts were when he realised he'd got it wrong. Britain survived. Just five years later it was the seemingly all-conquering Germans who were defeated. Now, for him, there was no going back. He'd have to make the best of his life in exile. He didn't.

During the six weeks he spent on remand, no members of the Squire family came to see him. He had long ago been disowned. His sole visitor, surely one of those who'd 'done' the London nightclubs with him in those halcyon days of the thirties, was a former actress, Margaret Beaumont. Perhaps just into her fifties, though looking years younger, the beautiful, classy Miss Beaumont would faithfully make the journey from London twice a week to visit Squire during his six weeks on remand. On each occasion she'd pay for lunch, accompanied by a half-bottle of wine, to be delivered to Squire from a local restaurant; one of the privileges available to an unconvicted man on remand.

During his time in G Wing I'd often be on duty there during the day. I'd see him wander round the exercise yard, usually alone, never without his long alpaca coat. It was now late autumn. After so many years in warmer climes, no doubt he found England colder than he remembered.

At last his case was heard at Birmingham Assizes. He'd pleaded guilty, so there would be no trial. He was appearing to be sentenced. If there had been a trial, no doubt we'd have heard more of his life during his twenty-six years drifting around Latin America. Some of it was disclosed as part of his barrister's 'plea in mitigation'. During his early years there, he'd lived the high life, financed with earnings from the companies he'd created. Eventually, however, bad business deals, even worse partners, gambling debts and his expensive lifestyle all took their toll. At the beginning of this year, 1966, broke and with his health failing, he'd decided to return to England and give himself up. Although his family had disowned him, they'd also decided not to press charges over the theft of the company's money. It was the Inland Revenue who'd brought the case against him, for tax evasion. No tax had been levied on the £140,000 he'd stolen.

As Squire stood in the dock to be sentenced, the judge stated that, had he been apprehended during the war, no doubt he would have received a heavy prison sentence. Now, however, taking into account the passage of time, his penniless state, failing health and his rejection by his family, he felt that a sentence of six months imprisonment would be sufficient.

Squire spent a couple of weeks at the Green as a convicted man. Dressed in the gray prison uniform, his alpaca coat stored somewhere in reception, I'd occasionally glimpse him on the big exercise yard. Without his long overcoat he seemed an even sadder figure. Somehow bereft. Then he was gone. Off to open prison to finish his sentence. I never saw him again.

It would be five years later, the early seventies. I was sitting reading the *Daily Express*. It was just a small news item; four or five lines. My eyes skipped over it and I'd already moved on, then . . . Did I see Aldritt, there? I know that name. I went back to it and read the short piece.

'Man Found Dead in Toilets: Newspaper seller, William Aldritt Squire, was found dead in the gents' toilet at Piccadilly Circus, London, yesterday. Mr Squire, who sold papers next to the public conveniences, had asked a friend to keep an eye on his pitch while he used the gents'. When he failed to emerge after some time, his friend became concerned. Mr Squire was discovered in a collapsed state. It is believed he suffered a heart attack.'

* * *

Into my mind came the image of this tall, forlorn figure, almost certainly still wearing his long alpaca coat, selling papers in the midst of a bustling Piccadilly Circus. How many times had he glanced across the square to the Café de Paris; thought back to his pre-war heyday, just over thirty years ago, when he and his friends would finish the night there, at 'the hottest spot in town'. How often had he stopped to buy a paper from the newspaper seller, probably to check the afternoon's racing results? When he did, he'd hardly give the man a second glance. Why should he? After all, who could possibly have forecast that thirty years into the future, this rich man's son would be the one selling the papers?

I don't think it's too much of a flight of fancy to imagine that, as Bill Squire would hurry off to catch up with his friends – who'd certainly include the delectable Miss Beaumont – the paper-boy would enviously watch him go and mutter to himself, 'Cor! Some people 'ave all the luck!'

Sorting Things Out

As 1967 moves into '68 I feel I'm well established at the Green. With six years' service under my belt I'm now usually in charge whenever I go on an escort with another officer, or I'm on evening duty on a wing. As 90 per cent or more of the cons are regulars, this means that by now they know me – and I know them. I seldom have any trouble. My outlook on how to treat prisoners is very simple. If they behave themselves they don't get any bother from me. Not only that, if they want something extra, say a special letter, I'll usually let them have it. If I'm in charge of visits and we're not too busy, I'll let them go over their time.

At home, when I'm there, life has settled into a comfortable routine. By late 1968 Scott and Nancy are both at school. My relaxation still consists mainly of reading and going to the movies, but I'm becoming increasingly absorbed in photography – movie and colour slides. I've recently started to subscribe to the magazine *Amateur Cine World*, and I've been reading up on how to produce polished, semi-professional little films. To that end, I've bought myself an editing machine and a splicer. I now cut out any badly exposed shots, edit my films, and make my own opening titles and captions. I don't shoot holiday films – I make 'travelogues'.

Within a month of my arrival at Winson Green, I felt certain that, someday, Jack McKue and I would fall out. He'd have been about thirty years of age back in 1962. He's the type who will 'neither work nor want'. He lives by stealing. Whenever he's discharged you know that within a few months, six at most, he'll be back. He is also one of those cons who, because he's a fixture, seems to think that junior officers should give him some leeway, cut him a bit of slack. There are a few cons who think like that. Their attitude seems to be 'I've been here longer than you, I'm entitled to a bit of respect.' Not in my book.

In my early days he'd try it on. I'd be on evening duty. As we were slopping out and suppering he'd go over to the other side of the landing and talk to another con through the spyhole. I'd be standing at his door waiting for him to come back so as I could lock him up. I'd call on him, which he'd totally ignore. I'd then walk over to where he was. 'How long do ye think ah'm gonny stand waiting for you to wander back? Let's have you back in your cell.' Reluctantly, he'd do as I said. In the ensuing years he's long since realised I won't put up with any of his 'old soldier' crap. Many officers will stand and have a conversation with him. I won't. By now he knows I don't like him. All he ever gets when I'm on his wing is what he's entitled to. And I begrudge him even that. I still see him trying it on now and again with junior officers.

He has another annoying habit which never fails to get my back up. If he's involved in one of his regular confrontations with an officer and it happens to be at a mealtime, or on the exercise yard, he'll start shouting and swearing at the screw. Because there are many other cons around, he knows the screws won't grab a hold of him in case it starts a mini-riot. He thinks it makes him look good in front of the other prisoners. In my book it's just a cheap way to try and get the reputation of being a hard man. In reality, he hasn't lifted a hand to anybody – it's all just verbal. On the occasions when he has a confrontation with an officer – with no other cons in the vicinity – he never starts his bawling and shouting carry-on. He knows he might be chinned!

Even though he no longer gives me any bother, years of

watching him maintain this false reputation of being one of the main men in the prison has increasingly made me hope one day I'll get the chance to sort out this gobshite.

I'm going for a tea break. I'm walking with Terry Hopper, a Geordie screw, and as we pass through the narrow gap between A and G Wings, coming towards us is Jack McKue. He's being escorted off the punishment exercise by two officers. At the moment he's doing seven days' cells. When the punishments are on exercise, maybe five or six of them, they're not allowed to talk to one another. The officers keep them well apart, 50 or 60 yards between them as they interminably circle the large yard. I'll find out later that McKue had persistently closed up to the guy in front so as he could hold a conversation with him. Three times he's been stopped by the officer supervising; the other con allowed to get well in front, and three times he's immediately closed the gap. When the officer stops him for the fourth time McKue starts his usual effing and blinding at the top of his voice. Because there are another five punishments on exercise the officer lets him continue his tirade while he presses the alarm bell. Two screws, Bobby Calderhead and Terry Belcher, are now escorting McKue back to the punishment landing.

The officers don't hold McKue. They know it would just finish up with them having to drag him all the way. He walks between them, all the while swearing at them at the top of his voice. As this small party nears the entrance to A Wing, Terry and I are coming towards them. Having left the yard and turned the corner, they are out of sight of the other punishments. There are no other prisoners around. THANK YOU, GOD! As the trio come near me, McKue is directing his spleen at Bobby Calderhead, shouting at him just inches from his face. I can tell Bobby is finding it difficult to control himself. As we're about to pass them, McKue shouts at Calderhead, 'That goes for you as well, yah Scotch bastard!' I get a strong feeling it's also directed at me. 'Excuse me,' I say to Terry. I take a step towards them as McKue and the officers are about to pass. I look at McKue. 'Ah'm sick fed up fuckin' listening tae you!' I punch him once, full force, in the solar plexus. For a split second I'm disappointed; he walks on – but just for two paces – then he topples forward. Out cold. Jeez! I did enjoy that. 'Right, boys. You can take that shitbag in. Ah don't think you'll get another cheep out of him.' I turn to Terry. 'Well, ah think that definitely deserves a cup o' tea. Ah've been wanting tae hit that gobby bastard for years!'

I come back from my tea break, let myself into the prison and walk along towards the Centre. Don Guilliat, an ex-Royal Marine with a booming voice is Centre P.O. There are a few officers with him. As I come along A2 all heads turn towards me; the topic of conversation is obviously my recent encounter with McKue. Guilliat spots me. 'Ah! Mr Douglas. My favourite officer! I'm taking over next week as detail P.O. If ever you want to have a day off at short notice,' he booms, 'just come and see me. Nothing will be too much trouble, dear boy!' He smiles. 'I've longed for the day when someone would chin that git!'

My bursting of Jack McKue's bubble seems to have had a knock-on effect. The news very quickly goes round the jail. Two days after coming off punishment, he asks to be moved out of the main prison. He's now relocated to the hospital wing. The threes and fours in that wing are used for ordinary cons. He's obviously fallen way down the pecking order in the prisoner's hierarchy. A week later I'm on evening duty down there. I have a word with my junior officer. 'When we come to McKue at supper time, just unlock three cells instead of the usual five or six. If he fancies his chances, I don't want too many unlocked.'

When we get to him I deliberately stand by his door as it's opened. He emerges to go to the recess, looks, sees it's me. 'Oh, all right, Jock?'

I nod. 'Top o' the bill!'

I never have a minute's bother with him again. Nor do many other officers.

By 1968, a TV set has been installed on C2 for those who dine out in association. Every evening from six p.m. until eight thirty, around forty cons are allowed to sit, four to a table, and play card games, draughts and so on. Since the TV has appeared, the majority prefer to sit and watch it. One evening, just two months after this new privilege has become available, there are live athletics being broadcast. Switching off time, unfortunately, comes before the end of a 10,000-metre race. As an officer, Joe Ferris, reaches up to switch off the set – with his back to the assembled cons – some 'hero' amongst them kicks one of the metal-framed chairs towards him. It hits him on the back of his legs. Joe, who barely has a year's service, can't do much about it; he didn't see who kicked it. I've heard the noise and come along from the Centre to ask what happened. I stand and look at the bunch of them . . .

'So, who's the hero? Never mind kicking a chair when the screw's got his back turned. Any of ye want tae kick a fuckin' chair at me? From the front!' There are plenty of downcast eyes and, as expected, no takers. We lock them up. When we're finished, I turn to Joe. 'Who do ye think it was?' I know what his answer will be.

'I'm almost certain it was Lark. He was in the second row. It was the chair in front of him that hit me. Could've been somebody reached over and shoved it. But I doubt it.'

'Ah knew you'd say Lark. He's always behind everything, that fuckin' weasel.' Lark is a Cockney. ALL London cons claim to be Cockneys; the sound of Bow Bells must travel a helluva distance. When they're in provincial prisons they always try to dominate the other cons and regularly try it on with the screws. I give it a moment's thought. 'I'll just go and have a word wi' him.' By the time I reach his cell and start to unlock it, I've already worked out what approach I'm going to take. He's in a single cell. I open the door, spring the lock, and enter. He's standing in the middle of the floor. He's slim, blond, maybe twenty-eight years of age and sharp featured, with a hook nose. He looks exactly like what he is – a weasel. He knows he'll be the number one suspect, probably thinks I'm about to accuse him. Trouble is, Joe never caught him in the act. So I'm not going to waste my time. 'You know this incident ten minutes ago, the chair gettin' kicked at the screw?'

'Yeah. Never saw it.'

'Course you didn't. Wouldn't expect you to tell me if you did. No, I've come to see you, Lark, 'cause you are, how can I put it, one of the main men on association. I'd like you tae pass a wee message round the lads. Now I'm gonny tell you straight what I – me personally – intend to do if ever anything like that happens again. There's only you and me here, so if it came to it, it would be my word against yours.' I smile. 'If a chair is ever kicked at a screw again, or something thrown at him by some chickenshit bastard who can't do it tae his face . . .' I watch Lark's face flush; he knows I know it's him '. . . once the prison's locked up ah'm gonny come along and rip all the wires oot the back o' the set, then force the back open and smash it inside wi' my stick. So there'll be no TV for anybody.' I give him another smile. 'You'll know who did it, but just like the chair thing, naebody can prove it. BUT! That will'nae be the end of it. When they eventually put a new set in, I'll wait, ohhhh, maybe a couple of months – then ah'll do the fucker again! Ah would think that after the second time the Governor will probably say, "Bollocks! We can't afford to buy a new TV every few months." Anyway,' I take my keys off the hook on my belt, 'spread the word around, will you?' He doesn't answer. I lean forward. 'You'll spread the word around, won't you?'

'Yeah.' He clears his throat. 'I'll tell them.'

'Good.' I take the lock off, bang his door shut so hard I nearly turn it inside out, then ram the night bolt home.

We never have any more bother at switching off time on C2.

A Stitch in Time

With the kids now at school, Nancy's got fed up being in the house all day. She fancies going back to work and by good luck she's spotted a job that's ideal for her. The Birmingham Sewing Centre, a shop on Soho Road, Handsworth, is looking for someone. The owner, John, sells sewing-machines, but he wants an assistant who can demonstrate them. His luck's in! Who better than Nancy? She's a dressmaker by trade and spent years working at Manclarks clothing factory in Edinburgh, eventually becoming a supervisor, and latterly head supervisor. Over the years she's picked up just about all there is to know about sewing-machines, including how to get them running again if they jam and diagnosing what's wrong when they break down.

Once he realises he has a top class seamstress on his hands, John soon thinks up a scheme to use her skills to the full. He's put a big advert in the window – 'Even if you've never used a sewing-machine-before, buy one from us and we'll teach you how to use it!' For 'we', read Nancy.

Handsworth is an area with a large ethnic population. The majority Asian. With their strong work ethic, lots of Indian and Pakistani women leap at the chance of being taught how to use their new sewing-machine for free. Of course, there is one small problem: communication! Most of these women have no more than a few words of English, but that doesn't seem to hinder Nancy. After all, using a sewing-machine is very much a hands-on occupation. It must also be said that even those who do have a grasp of English usually don't understand a blind word Nancy says in her strong West Lothian accent.

One thing they do all seem to have when they're training, though, is a great time. When we're sitting having our dinner Nancy's for ever saying, 'Eh, what a laugh we had in the shop the day!' She'll then go on to tell me another tale of some sari-clad lady sitting beside her, while Nancy tries to introduce her to the basics of the machine she's just bought. I can always picture it, Nancy in her twin set and skirt, side by side with this exotic woman in a bright silk sari, gold rings and earrings, beautifully made up and with a red bindi on her forehead. I get a detailed description of how Nancy, in words and actions, repeatedly demonstrated some complicated instructions. As she did so, her pupil chattered away in her own language, rocking her head from side to side as she spoke. The end result, according to Nancy, is that they ALWAYS finish up in kinks of laughter, tears running down their faces at the incongruity of it all. Eventually a happy customer will leave the premises with her new machine, anxious to get it home and make a start sewing everything in sight – whether it needs it or not.

1968: Nancy and I on a night out in Birmingham.

Another bit of job satisfaction for Nancy is the number of women who, a few days after their training, will pop into the shop with a little 'thank you' gift for her. Items like a card, sweetmeat, or some scent. Many bring their husbands in for a moment to introduce them to her.

Nancy has another source of income, and has done almost since we first arrived in Birmingham. A couple of weeks after moving into Southfield Road, when Scott was just a baby and Nancy not yet born, she decided to put an advert in a newsagent's window down in Dudley Road, offering her dressmaking and alteration skills. She wrote the details on the blank postcard supplied by the shopkeeper and we paid him eight shillings in advance; four weeks at two shillings per week. We continued doing our Saturday shopping until, maybe half an hour later, laden with carrier bags and pushing Scott in his pram, we trundled our way back home.

We'd barely been back ten minutes, hadn't even put the kettle on, when there was a loud knock on the door. 'Eeeh, who can that be?' said Nancy. It had only been a fortnight since we'd moved in and we only knew our neighbours on either side.

'I'll soon find oot.' I made my way through the front room and opened the front door. A hefty-built woman, maybe in her late fifties, stood there. 'Hello?' I said.

'Is this the house where the lady does alterations?' She had a strong Brummie accent.

I laughed. 'Would you believe we just put that card in the window about forty minutes ago? Come away in.' As she entered, I called through to the back living-room, 'NANCY! You've got your first customer already!'

The lady in question introduced herself as Mrs Wetherall; she lived in nearby Cavendish Street. Over the years she was to become a regular customer and she and Nancy became friends through bingo, attending the local hall two, sometimes three, nights a week.

In spite of being better off than we've ever been, I don't suppose we'll ever have a car. Not now. It would've been different if I'd got my driving licence in the army – with the two of us working we could easily afford to get one on hire purchase, the 'never-never'. But it's getting my licence. At twenty-nine I'm a bit too old now to start lessons. Far too long in the tooth. Anyway, with the hours I work, I don't know when I'd find time to fit lessons in. We're well used to life without a car, so it's not a problem. It's a case of what you've never had, you don't miss. If I've got a week off and we fancy the occasional day out, Nancy just makes sandwiches and a couple of flasks and off we go down to Digbeth bus station. All during the summer they have a large blackboard propped up against the wall near the entrance; on it are the list of day trips available. As soon as we arrive at the depot, carting a holdall containing the picnic and trailing two kids, we make straight for the blackboard to see what's on offer and decide where we'll go. It could be the Vale of Evesham, maybe Stratford-upon-Avon. Then there's that new place, Drayton Manor Park. The kids like that. Plenty of amusements and attractions for them. We tend not to go too far, as they get tired if they're out late. The only thing we miss out on by being in Brum is that we never get to paddle in the sea. You're just about as far away from the coast as it's possible to be in mainland Britain.

Since we came to Birmingham six years ago, each year when I take my fortnight's leave we still go to Seafield for our holiday. Some of these years we'll splash out and go to Blackpool or somewhere. But at the moment we're still quite happy to go to Nancy's parents. I suppose it would be nice to have a car, but we're well used to carting kids and luggage on and off buses and trains. It's second nature by now. Being on the local bus can sometimes have its embarrassing moments, though. Nancy was taking the kids up to Handsworth on the bus one Saturday afternoon and as it wended its way down Winson Green Road and was passing the prison, Scott was kneeling up on the bench seat, looking out of the window.

'Mammy,' he said, pointing to the jail, 'that's where our daddy is, isn't it?'

Odds and Ends

Hickman is around twenty-five years of age. He's doing a 'two'. He's a canny kid, works in the laundry. A good grafter. He's also gayer than a string of bunting. About a year ago the laundry instructor, Ron Ramplin, asked me if I'd like to be trained in the job so I could act as his relief. When he's on his hols, or sick, I run the shop in his absence. I went down to Wandsworth for a couple of weeks, passed the course, and that's another qualification to my name. Ron also had a word with the detail P.O. and arranged it so that when I do my one or two days a week in workshops I'm allocated to the laundry as discipline officer instead of any other shop. When I'm in there I basically combine the two jobs, instructor and discipline officer.

The prison laundry is a place many cons would like to work in. We operate with twenty-two prisoners. It's on a par with any medium-sized laundry; half a dozen large commercial washing machines, three industrial spin-driers, four Hoffman steam presses and a large calender through which, it seems, there passes a never-ending stream of sheets and pillowcases. At the far end of the shop is a drying-room where blankets and such hang from rails, the moisture in them slowly evaporating in a dry heat reminiscent of a Turkish bath. It's also the place where we let the cons go for a quick smoke.

We virtually hand-pick our workforce. It's always busy in there and there's no room for slackers. If we get someone allocated to us and after a few days he's not shaping up, we have him transferred somewhere else. One of the bonuses for our lads is that they can keep themselves smart. The once a week change of shirt, vest and pants doesn't apply to our cons. They can have clean kit whenever they want. They also regularly press their jacket and trousers – especially just before a visit. Another perk, to which Ron and I turn a blind eye, is letting the four Hoffman pressers take a couple of immaculately pressed shirts into the main jail with them at the end of the day. They have a certain number of customers – cons who want to look smart – and they supply them with shirts on a weekly basis. They are paid in tobacco, the prison's real currency. This leaves them free to use most of their earnings, about £2 a week, to buy such extras as sweets, bottles of sauce or jars of jam instead of baccy. Nearly all cons smoke.

Hickman is the best Hoffman presser in the shop. He'll often finish his batch of shirts, look around, and if one of the other guys is lagging, he'll take a dozen or so shirts off his pile and do them as well. Even though he's as camp as Butlins he gets on well with his workmates and no one has a problem with his sexuality. He's very much from the Kenneth Williams mould and often puts it on a bit as he knows he makes me laugh.

It's a Saturday morning. The laundry normally runs on a five-day week, but now and again we'll work on a Saturday, nine till twelve. We bring in seven or eight of the best workers; all volunteers. I unlock Hickman, who's in a single cell. 'Morning, Hickey.'

'Morning, Mr Douglas.' It's said in the breathless manner of Marilyn Monroe. I'm about to move on but I glance at him. He flutters his eyelashes at me. Pouts. I walk on for a few steps, stop, then take the same few steps backwards, appearing in his doorway again. I just stare.

'What? What's the matter?' he says. Unconvincingly.

'You look like Clara fuckin' Bow, that's what's the matter!'

His cheeks are rouged and his lashes are so black it looks like two spiders have taken up residence on his eyelids.

'Well, it's Saturday, Mr Douglas. I like to look nice on a weekend.'

I shake my head, trying not to laugh. 'When we get intae the laundry, Hickman, if you're in that drying-room and you drop something – don't bend down tae pick it up!'

'Oh, Mr Douglas! The things you say.'

'Anyway, what have you been using for make-up?'

'Will you not tell?'

'No. Your secret's safe wi' me.'

'WELL!' He lifts a prison library book. It has red hardboard covers and there's a lighter circle in the centre. 'I wet me fingers and rub them on the cover.' He demonstrates, then holds his fingers up. 'See!' Some of the dye has run; the tips of his fingers are red. 'And that's me rouge.'

I take my diary out and pretend I'm writing on it, speaking as I do . . . 'Defacement of prison property.'

'EEEH! You wouldn't.' He slaps me on my forearm. I don't look up; I continue writing. 'Assault on an officer.'

'EEEH! I didn't.' He has a giggling fit; sits on his bed.

'So what do you use for mascara?'

He stops laughing, goes all businesslike. 'Boot polish thinned with a spot of water. "Cherry Blossom" if I can get it.' He pauses, trying to look coquettish. 'Do you *really* think I look like Clara Bow?'

'Just get yerself doonstairs, ya big girl's blouse!'

He gives a titter and reaches for his jacket.

I'm on evening duty on B Wing and we're serving suppers. I unlock Hickman. 'All right, Hickey?'

'Yeah, fine.' No banter. Not the usual Hickman. When he returns he just gives a quick, on–off smile. I'm about to lock him up for the night.

'Mr Douglas?'

'Yeah?'

'Could I tell you something? Just between you and me?'

'Course you can.'

'It's about an officer.'

'That makes no difference. What's the problem?'

'You know that Mr Coldwell?'

'Yeah.' Coldwell is a big, dour guy. Maybe thirty years of age. Although he's only in the job barely two years I've sometimes noticed him being overbearing and unhelpful to officers junior to him. I find him unlikeable.

'Well, this last month or so, if he's on this wing of an evening, or maybe Sunday afternoon . . .' his voice trails off, his eyes fill up, his chin quivers.

'Hickey, it's me you're talking tae. You know you can tell me. What's the matter?'

He clears his throat, regains some composure. 'He's started opening my door when the wing's locked up. He just stands there, slagging me off. Real nasty things.'

'Oh, does he? What does he say?' Hickman looks at me. 'Hickey, if ye want me to sort this oot I have tae know what he's been up tae.'

He clears his throat. 'He just goes on and on. Things like, "I'll bet you're a real fuckin' fairy, you. Just love suckin' other guy's cocks, or better still, sucking one guy off while another one's fuckin' you up the arse at the same time. Don't yah?" Things like that, Mr Douglas. I've never done anything to him. Why does he have . . .' He stops as he begins to get upset again.

I feel myself getting angry. I hate bullying. It happens often in prison, but it's usually one con onto another. The fact that it's an officer makes no difference. Well, it does. It's fucking worse.

'Right, don't worry, Hickey. Soon as I see him I'll collar him about it. I'll sort it out. Goodnight.' I walk along the landing. Jeez, what a pity that big git's not on tonight. I already know what approach I'm going to take when I see him. Just a few weeks ago I read an article in the *Sunday Times* about exactly this problem. The timing couldn't be better. They have a name for it: Homophobia. I look at the detail board. Coldwell and I are both seven o'clock starts in the morning. Good!

I come onto the Centre a couple of minutes earlier than usual. There he is. 'Bill! Can I have a wee word with you?' I mustn't lose my temper. I walk over to the entrance of C Wing. He follows. 'You know Hickman, works in the laundry? He's been telling me you've recently started opening his door if you're on B Wing and slagging him off for no good reason.'

'Well, he's only a dirty queer. Can't stand them!'

'Hickman's the best worker in the laundry. Never a ha'porth o' bother. In fact, ah wish we had a jail FULL of Hickmans. We'd never have any trouble at all.'

'Huh! Well it wouldn't suit me.'

'There are no other screws give him a hard time because he's queer. You're the only one.' I look him in the eye. 'Now I'm sure it doesn't apply tae you, but I'd be careful in case he makes a complaint. I read an article in the *Sunday Times* a few weeks ago about guys who give queers a hard time for no good reason. They call it homophobia. They reckon that deep down they really fancy them! So, to try and prove to themselves that they don't, they spend a lot of time slagging them off.' I watch as Coldwell goes red in the face.

'I don't bloody fancy him! Poofs don't interest me.'

'Of course.' I'm having a job keeping my face straight. 'But just think how it'll look if he makes a complaint and it all comes out. Hickman hasn't given you any trouble, yet you regularly go to his door and give him a hard time. He doesn't get a bit of bother from other screws – just you. Anyway,' I pat him on the arm, 'leave him alone, will you? Ah don't want his productivity affected.'

A week later it comes into my mind as I'm distributing shirts amongst the Hoffman pressers. I lay Hickman's quota on his table, then sit myself on the edge of it. 'Have you been havin' any more trouble with you know who, Hickey? I had a word with him the day after you told me about it.'

'Never even looks at me, Mr Douglas.' As he speaks he's already starting on his first shirt. He puts a foot on one of the pedals and for a moment I can't see him for steam. It disperses and, like a pantomime dame from a puff of smoke, he's revealed. 'It's as if I've ceased to exist. It's wonderful! Doesn't even give me dirty looks.'

'That's good. Of course, I don't think you need me tae tell you what it was really all about, do ye?'

Hickman tosses his head. 'Fancies me rotten! If he'd carried on, I was thinking of offering to give 'im a J. Arthur Rank if he'd give me peace.' He pouts. 'Could've finished up me sex slave!'

We fall about laughing. 'Anyway, as long as he's not bothering you anymore.' I stand up, about to walk back up the shop to the office.

'Thanks a lot, boss.' He looks at me from lowered eyes. 'If I can ever do anything for you-hoo!'

Going For It

Another of the Mountbatten Report's recommendations has been accepted by the Prison Department. A new rank – senior officer – is to be created. It will now be the first stage on the promotion ladder and will come between officer and principal officer. Officers with at least five years' service are eligible to sit the exam. Those who pass will then go on an 'awaiting promotion' list. The only trouble is, those attaining this new rank will not normally be promoted *in situ*. If I get it, I'll have to move. If I was to be promoted I'd ask for Durham. It's the furthest north of all the English jails. Lots of Jocks gravitate to it because it's handy for Scotland.

It's time to start studying . . .

'STAN!' Stan Horncastle stops in his tracks. A tall, gangly Yorkshireman, he's a rather serious, conscientious type of guy – bit of a jobsworth, truth be told. He's two or three years older than me, but junior in service. We get on well and I've even been known to get a laugh out of him on occasion. He comes over. I look at him. 'Did ye know that one of yer eyebrows has slipped under yer nose?'

'I'm growing a moustache, if tha' doesn't mind.'

'Ahhh!' I peer even closer at it. 'Mmmm, I might grow one of them – tonight!'

'What's tha want?'

'I would imagine you're gonny go for this new rank?'

'Bloody right, I am.'

'What about studying together to a certain extent? You know, bouncing questions off one another. Stuff like that.'

'Good idea, Jock. It's basically the P.O.'s exam. Did tha know it's possible t' buy previous exam papers from the Stationery Office?'

'Can you? That's great! It'll give us a rough idea what sort of subjects we're liable to get.'

'Ah can tell tha already. Billy Goode let me see some he bought when he was studying for the P.O.'s exam a couple of years back. There's allus a "prison paper". It covers history of t' early years of prisons in Britain, then goes on to present-day stuff like rules and regulations – basically what's in the rule book that hangs up in every cell. There's a section on law – statute law and common law . . .' My thoughts immediately flash back to the young army officer trying to give us a lecture on just those subjects at Hilsea Barracks – while the heat of the classroom was sending every man-jack of us to sleep. I tune into Stan again: '. . . the prison section allus has a scenario where you're in charge of the prison on evening duty and suddenly all sorts of things start to 'appen; you've only got six officers, so you have to state in what order you'd deal with them.' Stan's enjoying himself. He always likes it when he's in the know.

'What sort of things are happening?'

'Like, a fight starts between a couple of cons who are on association; a fire breaks out in a storeroom; a con collapses with a heart attack – and somebody rings the prison to say that two cons 'ave got out their cells and they're trying to scale t' wall . . .'

'Fuck me! Jist an ordinary night, then!'

Stan carries on manfully. 'You've only got six staff, remember. What would tha do?'

'Resign!'

He looks heavenwards. 'Will you take it serious? What would tha do?'

'Okay, okay.' I pause for a moment, give it a bit of thought. 'Right, well obviously the first thing is safety of life. So I'd just let them two escape. I can't spare officers to chase them. They can always be recaptured at a later date.'

'Good thinking, Jock.'

'Mmmm. Second thing is send an officer to tend to the guy having the heart attack. Thennn, get two screws to begin tackling the fire. If it proves too big for them I ring for the brigade.'

'Tha's got the right idea.'

'Send another two to break up the fight . . . and have the remaining screw ready to unlock cells in the vicinity of the fire if it looks like getting out of hand.'

'Ah'd say tha'd definitely pass that part of t' paper.'

'Good. THEN I'd resign!'

Stan sighs.

For the next few months, as 1968 turns into '69, Stan and I become hooked on studying. If we're working together, or even just passing in a corridor, we continually shoot questions at one another. If we're at court, we have question and answer sessions as we travel on the coach. When we're in the cells we always find time for some brainstorming . . .

We settle down with freshly-brewed pots of tea in one of the interview rooms. I open my notebook. 'I'm going to ask you questions on prison history AND general knowledge.'

'Okay.' I watch Stan's eyebrows knit together in advance as he starts to concentrate.

'What year's Criminal Justice Act did away with flogging?'

'The 1948. Flogging with the cat-o'-nine-tails was abolished, but birching was retained.'

'Correct!' I ask him a few more, then: 'What colour knickers was Elizabeth Fry wearing the first time she visited Newgate Prison?'

Stan shakes his head; frowns.

'Okay, okay.' I ask a few more, then: 'Tell me – is Mickey Mouse a cat or a dog?'

'Foohk me! Ah wish thou'd take this serious.'

'That's a legitimate question, Stan.'

'So's my arse!'

In April 1969, along with others, Stan and I make our way down to Digbeth Town Hall one afternoon. Here, under the watchful eyes of a couple of Civil Service invigilators, we sit the promotion exam.

'How does tha think tha's done?'

'Oh, ah think ah've done enough to pass, Stan. What about you?'

He shakes his head. 'Ah'm not sure, lad. Ah have me doubts.'

'Stan, man! You'll have pissed it. I bet you have a higher score than me!'

'Wish I 'ad your confidence.'

A couple of months later we get the results. We've both passed – Stan with higher marks than me. The next step will be the call down to London for an interview. That's the biggest hurdle.

All in a Life's Day

Daniels looks like what he is: a nasty piece of work. He's doing a seven. He's also an ugly bastard, with a real Neanderthal look about him – though I suspect he doesn't have as high an IQ as our primitive ancestor. Like many of our residents, he thinks that doing a long sentence makes you a big man.

From the first moment I came across Daniels I didn't like him. Then I came across his file . . . I'm down the records office looking amongst the 'D's for someone else when I spot Daniels' file. Mmmm, might as well have a look and see what the shitbag's in for. When I read his charge sheet I can hardly believe it. Jeez! And this fucker has the brass neck to swagger about the jail as if he's somebody special. I read it again . . .

Late one evening he broke into the home of a couple in their seventies. He bound the two of them hand and foot, left them lying on the carpet in the living-room and proceeded to ransack their house. Before leaving the premises he returned to the living-room, turned the elderly man over onto his face, pulled his trousers down and raped him in front of his wife.

In my seven years' service it's the first time I've come across male rape. I'm appalled. I never knew such a thing happened. Daniels has come to us from another prison. I wonder how many of his fellow cons here at the Green know what he got his seven for? He'll have given them some bullshit story that he's a master burglar or payroll robber.

* * *

It's a couple of weeks later. Now that I've passed the promo exam I sometimes get put in charge of a wing. Today it's A Wing. It's just gone seven thirty a.m. Daniels comes into the office to make an application. He stands there, legs apart, his usual swaggering self.

'What do you want, Daniels?'

'A special letter, guv.'

I look at his letter sheet. 'You're down here just about every week asking for one. Special letters are an occasional privilege, not a weekly thing. So I'm not letting you have one.'

He screws up his face. 'The P.O. always lets me 'ave one. I'm entitled to 'ave one if I think I need it.'

It's the 'entitled' that does it. 'OH! You're entitled, are you? Got rights, have you?' He falls into the trap.

'Yeah I've got fuckin' rights, even in this poxy place.' He's about to try a bit of aggression. I stand up, slam the metal ashtray I've been playing with noisily onto the desk. I lean forward, my weight on my outspread fingers. 'If we're gonny talk aboot rights, what aboot the rights of the old couple whose house ye broke intae? What aboot the rights of the old man whose trousers ye pulled down while he was tied . . .' He knows what I'm about to say; his face goes red. Without another word he turns and stomps out the office.

Alan Mellor is in charge of A2. He appears in the doorway. 'I hope you haven't been upsetting Daniels. He didn't appear to be a happy camper when he left the office.'

I sit down. 'Well, we've got that many of these Labour MPs and assorted do-gooders continually advising these bastards about their "rights". Jist for a wee change ah've been reminding one about his "wrongs". Didn't like it!'

I'm at Coventry Sessions. P.O. Butler calls us all into the kitchen. 'There's a trial starts today. Three Londoners. About eleven a.m. we'll be having a strong police escort arriving, armed with shooters, the lot. They're bringing John McVicar. He's a witness for the defence. I'm sure you'll know the name – he's the one escaped from Durham's top security wing last year. Some of the police will be staying down here with us. When he's up giving evidence, they'll be at the back of the court. At the end of the day they'll be whipping him straight off. All right?'

'Ohhh,' says George Balche, 'got a celebrity coming today, 'ave we?'

I think back to all the furore in the press last year, when McVicar escaped from one of the newly created top security wings. These were another of the recommendations of the Mountbatten Report. They were to be a 'prison within a prison'. Now that twenty-five- and thirty-year sentences are regularly being handed down by the courts, it's felt that to have these long-termers – with nothing to lose – mixed in with the normal prison population is a recipe for trouble.

These 'heavies' always dominate the ordinary cons, often fomenting trouble. The new security wings isolate them. The ratio of officers to inmates is high. Vigilance is the watchword. With all this criminal brain power – and ego – locked up together, it has to be.

Yet, lessons from recent history haven't been learned. During the Second World War, the Germans also thought it would be a good idea to create a top security prison. A place where the cleverest and most persistent escapees could be locked up together. Isolated. It was called Colditz! It became a University of Escaping. By the end of the war, it held the record for the most attempted escapes AND the most 'home runs' (successful escapes).

I come through the wicket-gate at five to seven. It seems quiet this morning. I draw my keys from Tom Semmens, the gatekeeper. He's a big, normally jovial, south-country man. There are around fifty officers milling about between the gates. I walk over and join a nearby group. Roy Humphries speaks. 'You won't have heard the news, Jock?'

'What news?'

'Arthur Mosely took a heart attack at home last night. He's dead!'

'Jesus wept! Arthur. Man! I can't believe it. He was always full o' carry-on. That's awful. I'd think Don Midgely will be taking it badly. They were such great mates.'

Billy Goode smiles sadly. 'Joined at the hip, those two. Their families go on holiday together.'

I stand for a moment, not listening to what's being said. I think back seven years to the day I arrived. Arthur was on that wicket-gate. He was the first member of staff I met. Right from the first instant he was full of fun. I don't think there's a member of staff who hasn't been goosed by that truncheon of his. Well, maybe the Governor.

Hickman comes up to me in the laundry. 'Mr Douglas, is that right about Mr Mosely?'

'I'm afraid so.'

'Eh, war a shame. He was a really nice man.' Two or three other cons chip in: 'Mind, he was';

'Always helpful'.

A few days later comes the funeral. Arthur lived in married quarters round the corner, just off Lodge Road. Jeez, his family will have to vacate the house now. After giving the cons their breakfast, the prison is locked up. A skeleton staff patrol the wings. Around two hundred uniformed officers line the pavements as a mark of respect. Arthur's wife and family are distraught, just about overcome with grief. Don Midgely and his family are with them. Don is ashen-faced. Amongst the many wreaths is one from 'The Lads Inside'. As the prisoners were being 'canteened' this week, there had been a notice on the counter, saying that if anyone wished to contribute – to a maximum of one shilling – they should let the canteen officer know. There was a sizeable response, especially from the old lags who knew and liked Arthur. It was a nice gesture, much appreciated by the staff.

A Late Developer

'Have ye never fancied learning the driving, Robert?' Bunny sits with a glass of Guinness. Nancy and 'Irish' Betty are through in the kitchen talking girls' talk. We're in the living accommodation of the little corner shop they run further down the street.

'Ah'd like tae. But it's finding time tae take lessons. You know the hours I work.'

'Get yourself a provisional and a pair o' L-plates and when we have the toime I'll take ye out now and again.'

'Hey, that would be great, Bunny. Are ye sure ye don't mind?' All at once I feel myself getting a little excited. I'd long ago given up any thought of ever driving. Now, in an instant, my hopes are revived.

'Jayz, not a bit of it. T'wouldn't be any bother.'

'Whit are youse two up tae?' Nancy and Betty come through from the kitchen.

'Bunny says he'll take me oot for lessons in the car. I might have a go at getting my licence.'

'That would be smashing if ye did.' Nancy turns to Betty: 'Whenever we go up hame there's that much stuff tae take. It would be great jist being able tae pile everything intae a car.'

For the remainder of the summer of '69 and on into the autumn, I spend as much time as I can behind the wheel of Bunny's Vauxhall Velox. It's an easy car to drive, helped by the fact it has a column change with just three forward gears. First gets you moving, and that's about all it does. Anything above 10 m.p.h. has it straining. Second is wonderful. You can slip into it at around 7 m.p.h. and, if needs be, accelerate up to 50-plus before having to change into top. I've really got the bug for driving. What a difference from ten years ago in the army when I was trying to learn on that enormous Commer – the tenement on wheels! So much easier in a car. Whenever Bunny has time, he comes and gives me a knock. If they're going to the cash 'n' carry, and I'm free, I drive them. Even if they're just going down the street to the shops, 'Ah'll drive ye! It's not a problem.' I chauffer them back and forth to Dudley and Winson Green Roads and happily sit and wait for them. If there's a chance to get behind the wheel, even for just ten minutes, I take it. When I'm at home – and at work – if I have any spare time it's spent studying the Highway Code. I press those I'm working with to ply me with questions from it. I'm determined to make a major effort. I'm going to get my licence!

At last the great day comes. I take my test today. I'm confident. Even so, my butterflies have scrambled and are doing areobatics in my solar plexus. Bunny stands on the pavement outside the test centre in Ladywood. He gives me a surreptitious wave as I set off, the examiner beside me. A slim, red-headed man in his late thirties, wearing rimless glasses, he's cold, monosyllabic and unemotional. As soon as he walked out of the office and I saw him, I got that feeling in the pit of my stomach – any hopes of passing just faded away. It's not because I'm nervous. It was when he looked at his clipboard and said, 'Mr Douglas?' I knew right away that was it. I'll certainly try my best, I've nothing to lose. But I ain't gonna pass.

Forty minutes later I pull up at the centre and switch off the engine. He shows me some pictures of road signs. I identify them all. 'Right, that's your test finished, Mr Douglas. I'm afraid I have to tell you that you haven't passed on this occasion.'

'Oh, well.' I smile. I don't want the little wazzock to see how disappointed I am. He gets out.

Bunny climbs in. 'No pink slip?'

' 'Fraid not, Bunny.'

'Roight! Afore we leave we'll go back in there and get another test booked. They're not going to bate us.'

'Too bloody right, Bunny.' We re-enter the office and I invest another thirty shillings in a second test.

Six weeks later it's almost *déjà vu*. I return to the centre after my test, park in the same place. But it's a different examiner this time; an affable man in his late forties. He finishes off with the road signs, then reaches into his pocket and places a pad on top of his clipboard. When he opens it, the pages are pink! My heart gives a leap. Jeez, is this me about to pass my test?

'Could I have your provisional licence, Mr Douglas?' He starts to write. 'I'm pleased to be able to tell you, you've passed your driving test.' He smiles.

'And I'm very pleased to hear it! Thanks very much.'

Bunny climbs in and I wave the pink slip. 'Done it!' I offer him my hand. 'Thanks very much for all your time, Bunny. It's been very good of you.'

'Jayz, not a bit of it. It was just I thought it was a shame, you earning enough money to afford a car, but ye didn't have the licence. Well, you've got it now.'

'Right! You and Betty come along tonight about eight, and ah'll fill ye full o' the Guinness.'

He rubs his chin. 'Now dat sounds like a fine idea.'

We're about to pull away when my previous examiner comes out of the centre, escorting a new victim. Bunny peers at him. 'Is dat himself? The fella you had the last time?'

'Yeah. That's him.'

'Jayz! Hasn't he the face on 'im like a well-skelped arse!'

I've been invited to attend a promotion interview at Horseferry House, the London HQ of the Prison Department. Nancy's never been to London, so we decide to make a day of it, taking the kids as well. On the morning of Wednesday 3 December 1969, we catch the train to London from Birmingham's New Street station. Upon arrival we take the tube to the nearest stop within walking distance of the locale. The kids think the underground is great – even better than the train. We all go into Horseferry House and sit together in the waiting-room. Less than an hour later, the interview over, we head for Trafalgar Square then Piccadilly Circus to try and see one or two of the sights.

'How did it go?' asks Nancy.

'Ach, ye never can tell wi' these things. I looked them straight in the eye when I was speaking to them – there were three of them. When they asked me any questions I kept my answers short and to the point. I think I'll have done all right.'

We've been to Trafalgar Square. Now we're in the middle of Piccadilly Circus. It's a damp, blustery afternoon, beginning to get dark. We're all wearing coats, and it's a good job.

'Eros is smaller than ah thocht it would be,' says Nancy. It looks a lot bigger when ye see it in the cinema. We stand for a while, watching the world and the traffic go by. As the sky begins to darken, the famous neon signs shine out brighter. There's a large illuminated advert for the latest hit movie: Dustin Hoffman and Jon Voight in *Midnight Cowboy*. I've brought my 35mm camera with me. The camera magazine I subscribe to says that when you want to take cityscapes at night, don't wait until it's dark. Dusk is best. The lights are on – but you can still see some detail in the shadows. I always take colour slides. I take a few shots, then look around me. It's just ten years since Tommy Watters and I, both in uniform, were standing here. We'd hitched from Blackdown Camp to see the sights with just a pound each in our pockets. Ten years. Now here I am, thirty years of age and married with two kids.

I return to the present. 'We've just about got time tae do Downing Street, Nancy. Then we'd better head for the station.'

* * *

We walk along the short street and stand just yards away from the most famous front door in the land. Maybe the world? It looks just like it should. I recall the times I sat in the Blythswood with Ma, especially during the war, and saw Churchill and Anthony Eden come in and out of this door on the newsreels. I look at my watch.

'Ah think it's time tae make for the station.'

'Will we be going oan the tube again?' asks Scott.

'Aye.'

'Oh, goody!' the two of them chorus.

Just over three hours later, we're back at New Street station. We take a taxi from the rank. The house is cold when we get in, so I switch on the Cannon Gas Miser and turn it up to 'full'. 'Ahah! Soon get the house warmed up, eh?'

'Aye!' they say in unison. It's just gone nine p.m. The pair of them slept quite a bit on the train. Even so, they're still ready for bed. 'Right, c'mon pals. Something tae eat, clean your teeth then up the stairs tae bed.' Nancy's busy in the kitchen. 'Seeing as it's late you can miss your bath the night.'

It's 1970! We manage to get a babysitter, so we see in the New Year at the officers' club. A large wooden hut, it is situated under the shadow of the prison wall on Winson Green Road, a few yards along from the prison's gates. During the last seven years I've gradually been joined by several other Scots officers. We all gather round a couple of tables; Dermot and Betty Fraser, Bobby and Kath Calderhead, Bobby and Jean Brown, and Nancy and me. A good time is had by all.

Well then. Not only a new year. A new decade – the seventies! It sounds dead modern. They reckon it'll be February before I get the result of my interview. Something like three out of ten guys don't pass first time for promotion to P.O. I'd imagine it'll be just about the same for the new S.O. rank. Be nice to do it. Get 'on the list'. Trouble is, it'll mean leaving Brum if I get promoted. I turn thirty-one next month. Plenty of time yet to make S.O. If I don't get on the list this year I won't be too disappointed – another year or two at the Green won't be a hardship. I like Brum.

Studies in Blue AND Gray

George Davis would have been assigned to run the punishment landing of any prison he'd been posted to. At 6 feet 3 inches – and nowadays near 17 stone – where else would you put him? The big Welshman's main attribute is presence. Most of the so-called hard men in prison are, at heart, bullies. They prey on other, weaker cons. Faced with someone bigger and stronger than themselves they lose their aggression. In reality George is a quiet chap, slow to anger. But he looks the part. We've been friends since we lodged at Gran Jackson's together. George is still there. Now and again Nancy and I invite him up to Southfield Road for dinner. Afterwards he and I will have a couple of hard-fought games of chess. We're of the same standard so our encounters are always enjoyable.

During the last seven years A1 has become George's fiefdom. He still does his courts and escorts, but when he's in the jail, which is most of the time, he is always allocated to A1. Down there he runs a tight ship. He always has another officer with him for the day and often the second screw will be senior to George. If he is, they usually defer to the big Welshman. It's his territory.

A1, the smallest landing in the jail, is located just a few yards from the Centre. A flight of around ten stairs leads down to it. If you descend those stairs and stop for a moment, there isn't much to take in. It is a dead end. Eight cell doors on either side and a blank wall faces you at the opposite end of this short landing. The roof above your head is the floor of A2. There is a closed in, austere, isolated feel to the place. Underfoot are smooth, black cobbled setts, which are polished every day. Only screws have free access to A1 – cons don't come wandering down here unescorted.

The numbers on cellular confinement, or 'chokey' as it's called, vary. There are usually between three and six 'down the block'. I've never known it to be empty. Sentences vary from as little as three days to as long as twenty-eight. If a con is violent when he first comes down, the M.O. can order that he be trussed up in a strait-jacket. There is also another, less severe restraint: the 'body belt'. This is a 6-inch wide, thick leather belt which has a single handcuff attached to each side. With this on, the prisoner's arms are pinned to his side. If he decides to start kicking out with his feet, there are leather restraints which can be strapped round his ankles. Cons don't normally spend more than twenty-four hours under restraint. This is usually enough to calm down all but the most violent. While under restraint, the officers regularly check on them and the M.O. is a frequent visitor.

Many cons also get awarded a few days on bread and water as well as chokey. If they are given, say, seven days of this punishment, they don't do more than three consecutive days on the restricted diet. After their first three days they revert to ordinary prison fare for the next three, then follow on with another three days' bread and water. It's very helpful if a con wishes to lose weight!

Just as permanent a fixture on A1 as George is his landing cleaner, 'Pop' Jones. Over the last seven years he has also become a regular sight down there. Pop is another character who has come straight from central casting – but has somehow wandered onto the wrong set. Around seventy-five years old and barely 9 stone, his scraggy neck always makes it seem as though every shirt he wears is too big for him. He potters around most of the day in his blue bib overalls, carrying his stage prop – a large bass broom which is almost as tall as him. It's used mostly for leaning on. Boots always polished, his thin hair combed back and somehow curving away from the back of his head, he wears specs with thick convex lenses which magnify his eyes to twice their size. This gives him a look of permanent amazement. His dentures are only worn at mealtimes. Overall he has the appearance of a rather scraggy old chihuahua. He was really meant to be in a western movie, sitting in a rocking chair on the veranda of the saloon, smoking a corn-cob pipe. There has obviously been a mistake made and he has somehow finished up on the list of extras headed 'prison inmates' instead of 'old timers'. He doesn't seem to mind.

The most important thing to know about Pop is that he does NOT consider himself a criminal. On the contrary, he can't stand them. He was well into his fifties when he entered prison for the first time. A married man, his life was on an even keel until his wife died. With no family to care for him, Pop took refuge in drink. Within a couple of years he'd lost both job and home. Days were now spent drinking; nights sleeping in hostels or the Salvation Army refuge. When the money ran out, he'd sleep rough. Then his luck changed – he was sent to prison for seven days. He took to it like a duck to water. He was able to keep himself clean and he was away from the drink. Soon he was into a routine. During his bouts of enforced freedom he'd drink until his money was done, then – time to go back up the nick! He'd usually get himself arrested for breach of the peace or vagrancy. If it was winter, and he fancied a longer stay than his usual seven or fourteen days, giving the magistrates a mouthful was usually enough to get his sojourn increased to twenty-eight.

That evening the Black Maria delivered him to the familiar surroundings of reception . . .

'Hello, Pop! You're back a bit soon this time?'

'Too bloody cold out there, Mr Bailey. Better off in 'ere.' As if to emphasise his point, Pop rubs his hands briskly together.

'Yeah. Soon 'ave you tucked up in a nice warm cell, Pop. Just 'ave a look at them library books over on the table. Choose three for yourself.'

'Right y'are, boss.' Pop looks disdainfully at his fellow receptions as he makes his way to the table. None of them buggers will ever reach 'favoured customer' status.

Sometime before nine p.m. Pop is sitting up in bed in a single cell. The wooden chair acts as a bedside table. On its seat sits a mug of cocoa, a sticky bun, and his teeth. As he begins to read chapter one of the first book, the sleet throws itself against the cell window. As usual, the cons down reception have given him one of the rich red bed-covers. It seems to add to the cosiness of the cell. He knows that tomorrow the reception board will allocate him to A1 as its cleaner. There will be another con doing the job at the minute, but he will be located elsewhere in the jail. The cleaner's cell on A1 is always kept exclusively for Pop. After greeting his big mate, George, he will immediately take charge of the other con. Ahead of him are twenty-eight days of three square meals a day, total abstinence, and a nice rest. He puts the book down. Long before the night patrol comes round to put the light out, Pop will be sound asleep.

It was towards the end of 1962 when Pop was first allocated to A1 as its cleaner. George had been at the Green less than a year. Pop, who had left Wales over fifty years previously to settle in Birmingham, hit it off immediately with his fellow countryman. Over the years an almost familial relationship has developed between the two of them; the 5-feet 3-inch Pop taking a protective interest in the 6-feet 3-inch George. Pop, it must be remembered, does not consider himself a criminal.

I'm on the Centre, as a spare officer. Things are quiet. P.O. Guilliat is Centre P.O.

'Mr Guilliat, ah'll away down onto A1 for a couple of minutes. Just give me a shout when you need me.'

'Right y'are, Jock.'

It's just gone eleven a.m. when I trot down the stairs. The Governor's already made his daily visit to the punishments. The cobbled setts shine; Pop's been at work. The door of the cell used as an office lies open so as George can hear anyone descending. 'It's just me, George,' I call. I enter the cell. George and Pop sit on their chairs, legs stretched out in front of them. George's hat lies on the small table. 'All right, Jock?' He looks at me. 'Hello, boss,' says Pop. His bass broom leans against the cell wall.

'Not exactly a hive of activity doon here.'

George turns to Pop. 'Have you effer heard of such a cheek?'

'Terrible!' Pop looks up. 'Time for a drink of coffee, boss?'

'Ah'll have a half.'

He rises, reaches for a clean pint pot and puts some coffee into it. 'If you let me through to the kitchen . . .' We go over to the door at the side of the stairs. It leads through to under the Centre. It's always locked. 'I'll wait for you,' I say. Pop hurries off to the kitchen, puts hot water into the mug and returns. I lock the door and we return to the cell. 'How much sugar is it, again?'

'Less than a half, please.'

He stirs it. 'There y'are, guvernor.'

We sit in a companionable silence, just as we've done many times before. Now and again someone will say something. Mostly we contemplate our feet.

'How long are you doing this time, Pop?'

He turns and looks at me with his magnified eyes; I remind myself he's not really surprised. 'I managed twenty-eight days out of 'em.' He takes his baccy tin out of the pocket on the bib part of his overalls and proceeds to roll one of his extremely thin roll-ups.

During the last seven years, Pop has totally identified with A1 landing and his big mate. He considers himself 'staff'. A supernumerary.

Our tête-à-tête is noisily interrupted by the alarm bell ringing upstairs on the Centre. This is usually a sign that George can expect a new customer. I go up the steps. With me being on the Centre, I'd normally be making my way to wherever the bell was rung. There are pounding feet from all directions. I catch the P.O.'s eye. 'George is down here on his own at the moment.'

The P.O. gets my gist. 'Yeah, just stay down there and give 'im a hand.'

George and I remain standing at the foot of the stairs, looking up. Pop loiters at the back of the landing, pretending to sweep. He likes to check out all newcomers.

'Are the empties all ready for occupation, Pop?'

'Number 6, definitely. Just cleaned it this morning.'

George goes over and unlocks it, springing the lock as he does. He comes back beside me. A minute later we hear swift oncoming footsteps, raised voices. I look at George. 'If he's violent, you get stuck intae him. Ah'll hold your jacket.'

'Scotch ratbag!' he murmurs.

The figure of Billy Levert, surrounded by screws, appears at the top of the stairs. 'Just send 'im down. Be all right,' says George. As Levert reaches the foot of the stairs, George grabs him by the scruff of his neck. 'C'mon, you!'

Levert seems more aggressive than usual. 'Fuck off ya Welsh shitbag!' He begins to struggle. I come in close and get his left arm up his back. George continues to hold him by his scrunched-up collar. He still writhes and now and again tries to throw a punch with his free right hand. It always misses. As we slowly edge him towards the empty cell, Pop, who cannot abide badly behaved cons, decides to intervene. We hear the clatter as his bass broom falls to the floor. From stage left he appears – 9 stone of almost knackered fury.

George and I are managing fine, but Pop can't stand by while someone's abusing his mate. He starts trying to kick Levert. 'Why don't you behave thy fuckin' self! Bastard! Can't even behave yer bloody self in't jail!'

'POP! Calm yourself down. We're managing fine.' Pop continues to aim ineffectual kicks at his fellow prisoner. As we propel Levert towards the cell, George is reaching over with his right hand to fend off Pop. At last Pop strikes home. 'OHYAH!' George reaches down to his left leg. 'That's me you've got, you bloody menace!'

'Ger orff yah mad old bastard!' shouts Levert.

By now George and I are becoming helpless with laughter. Levert is so confused he's stopped struggling; in fact he can hardly wait to reach the safety of the cell. We lock him up.

George turns to Pop. 'How many times 'ave I told you, boyo, DON'T get involved. You give me more trouble than the bloody cons, sometimes. You're the cleaner. Gerrit?'

Pop looks shamefaced. 'Sorry, George, eh, boss.' He picks up his broom. We hear laughter coming from above. P.O. Guilliat and three or four screws stand at the top of the stairs just about doubled up. George looks at them, then at Pop. He shakes his head.

A full five years later, when I'm at Durham, Ray Thompson, a fellow officer, stops me. 'There's an escort in from Birmingham, they were asking for you.'

I make my way down to reception. It's Jim Higginbotham and Ron Percival.

'Hello, ratbags!'

'Jock, lad. We were hoping you'd be around.'

After handing over their prisoner, we go to the mess for a cuppa. I spend most of my time asking, 'How is so and so?' They bring me up to date. 'Oh, what about George Davis. Not found himself a wife yet?'

'No. As shy with the lasses as ever. He's still running A1. Do you remember old Pop Jones?'

'Why, of course. George's cleaner. They were a double act, them two.'

'Old Pop died earlier this year. He was gone eighty-five, you know. Died in the prison hospital.'

'Did he? Old soul. He was a canny old stick.'

'Yeah, but wait till you hear this.' Jim shakes his head. 'He'd no family, Pop. So of course he was 'eaded for a pauper's grave. Any road up, George saw the Governor and arranged to pay for the funeral. Bought a new plot down the cemetery. Paid for the hearse and everything. There were three or four dozen screws went.' Jim laughs. 'Didn't 'ave the usual ham tea afterwards, mind!'

'Hey, wasn't that nice,' I say. 'They spent ten years or more down on A1. I'll bet when he went, George wouldn't half miss him. They were great mates, really.'

'Be like losing his grandad,' says Ron.

We go on to talk about other officers; remember events that the three of us were involved in when I was at the Green. But all the time, thoughts of George making sure Pop wouldn't go to a pauper's grave keep coming into my mind. I don't bring the subject up again. But it keeps intruding. Soon, it's time for them to go.

'Well, tell the lads I'm asking for them.' I clear my throat. 'When you see Big George, tell him I thought that was a really nice gesture, paying for Pop's funeral. Don't forget.'

'I won't,' says Ron. He knows I mean it.

Horizons New

Durham Station stands on a hill. As the train draws in, the view can only be described as magnificent. Way below are the roofs of a small town. On the other side of it, another wooded hill rises. On top stands the breathtaking sight of Durham Cathedral and Castle. Built by the Normans, the main intention being to impress, almost a thousand years later it impresses the hell out of me. I try to remember who wrote of Durham Cathedral that it was 'Half church of God, half castle 'gainst the Scots'. Gibbon? Scott?

It also comes to me that because it has a cathedral, the small town below is really a city. The smallest in the land.

A taxi drops me off at the gates of the prison. As I stand facing the gate-lodge, to the left is the grand entrance to the Georgian law courts. They are both built from a honey-coloured sandstone reminiscent of the Cotswolds. I report myself 'in' and a few minutes later I'm escorted up to the Centre and introduced to Chief Officer Wilson. It's Tuesday 3 March 1970. I'm now Senior Officer Douglas and I'm on the staff of Durham Prison.

I come out of the Chief's office and stand for a moment on the Centre. Durham is forty years older than the Green and was built before the spoke system design became the norm. The first wing to be constructed, A Wing, was completed around 1804. Just in time to house French prisoners taken during the recent falling-out with Napoleon. D Wing is the largest in the jail and A Wing butts on at right angles to one end of it. At the other end, B Wing also joins on. There are other wings in the jail, but the one I'm looking forward to seeing is the already notorious E Wing – the top security wing. Created as a result of recommendations by the Mountbatten Report, it houses various 'heavies' who are all doing lengthy sentences. It was from here that John McVicar escaped in 1968. The only prisoner to escape from Durham in all its long history.

Just outside the gate-lodge, on the other side from the courts, is the officers' mess and bachelor quarters. There's a vacancy in the quarters. I dump my case in my newly allocated room and take a walk into town. I'm excited about seeing it. I can unpack later.

The layout of Durham City is medieval – it doesn't have an option. Restricted by the fact that it is built on land contained inside a hairpin loop of the River Wear and constrained by the hills on either side, the city has been unable to grow. The streets still follow the same routes they did in Chaucer's time. The names of streets and bridges evoke centuries long gone: Elvet Bridge, Framwellgate Bridge, Prebends Bridge; Silver Street, Saddler Street, Claypath, Old and New Elvet. Just as I did with Linlithgow Palace twenty years ago, I fall instantly in love with Durham City.

I sit in the café of Crawford's the Bakers and let the local accent wash over me. It's nearer to Scots than English. When I pay my bill I'm delighted to receive Scottish pound notes in my change. During the last eight years I've sometimes inadvertently taken some back to Birmingham with me. They won't accept them down there. I have to take them to the bank where they give me nineteen shillings and sixpence for each pound. The 6d is deducted to defray the cost of sending this 'foreign' money to the clearing banks. From there it's shipped back to whence it came.

* * *

I lie in bed in the bachelor quarters, hands behind my head, staring into the dark. I sure like the look of Durham City. How different from Birmingham. It's too early to make my mind up about the jail. Jeez, that's me finished with the Green. I'm quite sad about that. After eight years I know I'm very much part of the staff – I get on well with my fellow officers, I know the cons – and they know me. What a pity you can't be promoted *in situ*. I'd have been very happy to stay at Brum. It's all happened so quickly. It's only weeks since I was told I'd passed my promotion interview and I was 'on the list'. I expected it would be the best part of a year before I got a post. Just over a fortnight ago I'm called into the Chief's Office . . .

He looks at my file. 'You've expressed a preference to go to Durham as S.O.,'s that right?'

'Yeah, that's right, Chief.'

He flips the file closed. 'When can you take up your post?'

'Pardon?'

'You've got Durham. There's a vacancy.'

'Goodness! That was quick.'

'They're short of an S.O. When can I tell them you'll transfer in?'

'Well, eh, I suppose the sooner the better. Ahhhh, what about a fortnight come Monday?'

'Yeah, that should be fine. It just remains for me to say, Jock, you'll be missed here. If you're as good an S.O. as you are an officer, you'll be all right.'

I feel myself blush. 'Oh, thanks very much, Chief.'

I leave the office and tell two or three of my mates. Harry Gascoigne comes along. I like Harry. He's senior to me and took a bit of getting to know when I first arrived. For the last couple of months he's been learning the laundry job. If I was to get promoted and move away, he'd take over as relief instructor. He has a gruff exterior. On first acquaintance, and second, you could be excused for thinking him a miserable bugger. 'HARRY!'

He comes over. 'What yer want?'

'I've just been told I'm going to Durham in a fortnight as S.O.'

'Hoo Hoo Hoo!' he chortles, showing his irregular teeth. I thought characters only chortled in Billy Bunter stories. 'Foohkin great!' He rubs his hands briskly together. 'I'll foohkin walk straight inter that laundry job of yourn. Hoo Hoo Hoo! Me foohkin luck's in!'

I burst out laughing. He joins me. Officers passing by turn their heads; a couple pop out of the censor's office for a look. In all his twelve years at the Green, nobody has ever witnessed Harry in such a state of merriment. I manage to say, 'Does this mean you're pleased?'

'Tha could say that. A trifle choofed!'

My luck is also in: I know I'll have to put the house up for sale via an estate agent, but I'm saved the trouble of going to see one. A new member of staff, Eddie Headlong, hails me. 'Jock, I believe you'll soon be putting that house of yours up for sale?'

'Yeah. I'm going to Durham.'

'There aren't any married quarters available, so I've just been given permission to buy a house. Would you mind if my wife and I came and had a look?'

As I cycle home, I take a diversion down Dudley Road and look in a couple of estate agents' windows to get an idea on price. I'm pleasantly surprised. Later that evening, Eddie and his wife come up. They like the place. 'What sort of price were you thinking of, Jock?'

'I've had a look at what this type of place is going for, Eddie. How does £4,700 sound?' I feel a bit embarrassed as I say it – we only paid £1,650 for it. But that's the going price.

Eddie doesn't hesitate. 'Yeah, fine. Do we have a deal?'

'Aye, I'm happy with that price, Eddie.' We shake hands. That will save a lot of time and bother.

* * *

Well here I am at Durham. There's another thing I hope will happen with this move – that it will maybe perk up the relationship between Nancy and me. We've been married nearly eleven years. These last two years things have got . . . what? Stale. Yeah, stale is about right. Nancy seems to be quite happy, but that's because she mostly gets her way. As long as she manages at least three nights a week at the bingo, more if possible, that's her satisfied. And if she's not bothered too often for sex. We seem to be settling into a proper rut. I'm quite happy to be in the house, especially after all the hours I work. We have the occasional Saturday night out, usually down the club for a drink. The big problem is sex: I like it. She doesn't. But it's not just the sex itself, it's everything else, too. I get angry, and when we argue, I regularly point out that not once has she ever, EVER, told me she loves me. I'm the one who shows all the affection. She never spontaneously kisses or hugs me. When we do make love she never shows that she's enjoying it. Never lets herself go. Is this what I have to look forward to? If this is it in our thirties, what the hell is it gonna be like in our forties? Or fifties?

The only great pleasure I get out of being married is romping with Scott and Nancy. Scott loves me playing with his toy soldiers. We have elaborate set piece battles. If we're not doing that, we're fencing with one another . . . 'So, m'sieu', you are zee one who keel my brother! I challenge you to a duel. En garde!' Nancy junior loves me reading to her in bed. The pair of them like plenty of cuddles. At Christmas each one of them gets more presents than I got in all my Christmases put together. I often think, what's gonna happen when the kids are up and away? Just Nancy and me left. We'll be like those couples you see sitting in clubs and pubs who hardly utter a word to one another all night. Except for the kids, we've nothing in common. She hardly ever reads the paper; never reads a book. If I try and interest her in some documentary on TV, her eyes glaze over. The fact that Nancy's seven years older than me might be a factor, but it's not the main one. The older I get, the more I become interested in new things, in bettering myself – playing chess, shooting home movies; I intend to learn a second language. Put simply, I like acquiring knowledge. Nancy's not bothered about things like that. I try to enthuse her but I'm wasting my time. Her only interests are the kids, bingo and her job at the sewing centre. That's about it. We have nothing to talk about nowadays. I used to be SO crazy about her – when I was twenty. Slowly but surely these last couple of years I've started to fall out of love with her. I never thought the day would come when I'd feel like that about Nancy. Will our marriage get a new lease of life when we move to Durham? If we don't something will have to happen. I'm thirty-one years of age. The way things are, and seem to be going, I'm increasingly realising I don't want to grow old with Nancy. It will be a dull existence. She's already set in her ways. I've come to realise I've got a brain. I want to learn things, go travelling . . . 'Ach!' I turn over on my side. Better get some sleep. Nancy and our future will have to be dealt with, but tomorrow I've got to start establishing myself as a Senior Officer at Durham Prison.

E Wing

'I'll put you down for the top security wing tomorrow. A day in there will let you get the feel of the place.' As he speaks, Don Redford, the detail P.O., is already using his 'Chinagraph' pencil to make the entry on tomorrow's board: E Wing.

As I make my way down the spiral staircase to the Centre, I feel a little frisson of anticipation. Tomorrow should be interesting.

I've just drawn my keys. It's gone five to seven. Just as at Birmingham, officers gather in small groups between the gates. I don't know anybody well enough to go and talk to them. I stand on my own. A solidly built S.O. comes towards me. I'd take a bet he's played rugby. He's just drawn his keys and is attaching them to his chain. 'Hi! I'm Eddie Stoker. You're in E Wing today, ain't yer?'

'Aye, that's right.'

'We'll just have a wander over. It's nearly seven.'

Minutes later we approach the tall chain-link fence that surrounds E Wing. I look up. Coils of razor wire run along its top; closed-circuit TV cameras are strategically placed at various points round the small wing. It most certainly is a 'prison within a prison'. How the hell did McVicar get out of here? We stop at the gate in the fence. Eddie has his pass key ready but doesn't insert it into the lock. He presses a button on an intercom at the side of the gate.

A crackle of static is followed by a metallic-sounding voice. 'Hello?'

The Top Security E Wing. On the ground floor, facing you, is the window into the Control Room. From here, all electronic locks and T.V. monitors are run.

'It's S.O.s Stoker and Douglas, on duty in the wing today.' A slight movement catches my eye as a CCTV camera high up on a corner of the building swivels to have a look at us. This is followed by a loud buzzing from the lock, then I hear something move inside it. Eddie inserts his key and opens the gate.

'I take it you couldn't unlock that until somebody inside did something?'

'Yeah. It's all done from the control room. All the gates in the wing and fence have an electronic lock. Your pass key is no good until the electronic lock is taken off.'

We walk the few yards from the gate to the main entrance of the wing. While we go through the same routine with the lock, I ply Eddie with questions. 'I take it, then, that if an officer were overpowered and his keys taken, they wouldn't be able to get out of the wing?'

'Yeah. Even if they said on the speaker that it was officer "so-and-so", the TV camera would show that it ain't an officer.'

We enter the wing. I'm immediately struck by how small it is. A stainless steel hotplate, maybe 6 feet long by 3 feet wide, stands in the middle of the narrow floor space. Heated by steam, most of the meals are served from it. Facing me, perhaps forty feet away, is a glass window which is about a foot square. I can see the head and shoulders of an officer looking at us. Eddie points.

'That's the control room in there. You can't get access to it from inside the wing. The glass is unbreakable of course.'

We stand for a moment. The wing is L-shaped. It turns right at the control room. Eddie points up to the top landing. 'All the sex cases, mostly child murderers, are located up there. The other cons are spread round the threes and twos. There's nobody located on the twos, it's just used for the office, store cells, stuff like that, there are no ones in this wing. Turn right at the corner and the first door is the entrance to the bath-house. Also, there are the stairs leading to the upper landings. The floor space round the corner is where all the tough guys have their weights and fitness equipment.'

I laugh. 'This'll be so as they can keep themselves fit enough to assault a screw now and again?'

'That's about the strength of it.'

I shake my head. 'I've never quite got the logic of this. Why allow long-term cons access to weights, punch-bags, whatever, especially when many of them are in for extremely violent crimes?'

'Ah!' says Eddie, 'but the do-gooders insist they've got to be allowed to exercise, keep themselves fit enough to return to their chosen profession upon discharge—'

I interrupt him. 'Aye, robbing fuckin' security vans and the like! Anyway, better not get me started on my hobby-horse. What about the sex cases on the top landing, do they have to be kept away from other cons?'

'No, not in here. They don't mix, mind you. They exercise separately, don't take part in any activities with the ordinary cons. But for instance, if one of them from up top wants to come down the office for summat, he just comes. None of the others will talk to him, give him a nod, anything like that. But they won't bother him. It's sort of like a truce. 'Cause they're all stuck in here doing loads of bird, the ordinary cons tolerate them. Just.'

I look up at the landings. There are officers everywhere; leaning on the rails, talking to one another, walking around. 'Looks like the place is well manned.'

'Oh, yeah. There's usually about eighteen screws here each day.'

'How many cons at the moment?'

'Twenty-one.'

'Mmmm, not bad. Nearly one on one. Good odds.' I look up at the landings again. A short, plump con ambles along the twos. He carries an aluminium basin and has a towel over his shoulder. I look even more intently. Fuck me! That's Ronnie Kray! He enters a cell. I turn to Eddie. 'Did I just see Ronnie Kray, then?'

'Yeah.'

'Are the two of them here?'

'Used to be, but we shanghaied Reg away to Leicester about a month ago. The pair of them were beginning to get a bit heavy with some of the other London gangsters. Some of the old rivalries startin' to surface. You know, "saaf of the river" and "norf of the river". So Ronnie's not a happy bunny at the moment. Misses his bruv!'

'Aye, ah'll bet he does.' Just as I finish speaking, a con comes round the corner from the direction of the stairs. He smiles at Eddie. 'Morning, guv.'

'G'morning, Bruce.'

The con goes into the wing office. As he does so, I turn my head towards Eddie. I nod in the direction of the office. 'Reynolds, the Mail Train Robber?'

'Yep.'

'Jeeesus! It's a buggering "who's who" of crime in here, ain't it!'

He takes me on a guided tour of the wing. As he does so, he fills me in on the regime of E Wing. 'They're unlocked all day. Free to roam about within the wing. The ordinary cons never go up onto the fours. Most of the meals are brought over from the prison kitchen, but as a perk they often send over the raw ingredients and they cook their evening meal themselves. The kitchen P.O. takes them on classes, shows them how to prepare stuff. Four or five of them really enjoy it, so they cook the evening meal for the ordinary cons now and again. The sex cases have the same privilege, but seldom use it. Might make the occasional dish, but not often. Them on top don't mix with one another as well as the rest do. What would they talk about? The best way to murder a bairn?' He unhooks his keys. 'Anyway, we'll go out into the yard. Let you see the outside of the place.'

As we step out of the door, I'm struck by how closed in it feels. The chain-link fence runs fairly close to the outside of the wing. The fence opens out at one end of the building to form a large loop. This loop is the exercise area. It can't be seen from the main jail. A tennis net stretches between two poles in the middle of the yard. A tall, solitary prisoner is exercising at the moment; striding out. He wears a blue cotton jacket, buttoned up to under his chin. His head is shaved. All he needs are a couple of bolts through his neck and he'd be a dead ringer for Frankenstein's monster. Two officers are supervising him. At regular intervals, one or two sparrows land on top of the razor wire which tops the fence. The prisoner is watching all the time. Whenever he sees them perch he immediately bangs the fence with his clenched fist. They take wing. He does this constantly, every couple of minutes, never allowing the birds to settle. It obviously gives him pleasure. I look at him as he passes close by. He exudes strangeness; menace. I wait until he's out of earshot, then ask, 'Is he on punishment?'

'No. He always exercises on his own.'

'Who is he?'

'Straffen.'

Straffen! Bloody hell! This is a name from my childhood. I would've thought this reptile would have died years ago. Was it

John Thomas Straffen? As I grew up, began to try and read the papers and saw newsreels, now and again there'd be some big murder case. John Christie, Donald Hume. Their trials would dominate the headlines for weeks. Then they'd be hanged. I knew Straffen hadn't been hanged – because he was insane. Criminally insane. Imagine that! Here he is, large as life. Never thought I'd get to see him. It must have been around 1948. He'd been locked up in . . . was it Broadmoor or Rampton? Locked up for murdering two children. Then he'd escaped. He was only out for a few hours before he was recaptured. When the police caught him, he immediately said 'I did not kill the little girl on the bike'. The next morning the body of a five-year-old girl was found near to the prison and Straffen was charged with her murder.

I watch him circling. Banging the fence every couple of minutes. I turn to Eddie, 'Is he as weird as he looks?'

E Wing erercise yard. A prison within a prison.

'Weirder! Never talks unless he has to ask for something. Always on his own. All the time he's done has driven him wayyyy into himself. Doesn't mix with the rest of them. Just listens to his radio, hardly reads. Mad as a fuckin' hatter!'

I smile to myself. Huh, and I thought the first night I spent in the remand ward in Brum was strange. Locked up with all those murderers. Not gonny be a patch on E Wing.

The Key to the Chocolate Factory

'What are ye doing wi' yerself of an evening tae pass the time?' Darren is one of the many Scots officers on the staff. I'm in charge of visits. Darren is engaged in keeping an eye on the cons and their visitors. It's midweek. Quiet. There are only a few tables in use. The cons sit on one side, their wives and kids on the other. I'm at a table at one end of the large open visits room. The visitors hand me the visiting order they've been sent, then I mark it as 'paid' and also make an entry in the visitors' book. Because it's quiet, I'm giving them all a bit of extra time. Darren keeps an eye on the visitors, making sure there's no one trying to slip any contraband – cigarettes, drugs, money – to their con. By the look of the families visiting today, I'd think the poor buggers would be hard put to afford twenty fags.

I look up at Darren. 'I haven't been doing very much. Go for the occasional pint. I went to the pictures the other night. Really living it up while I'm in bachelor quarters.'

'Did ye know it's a great club scene up here in the north east?'

'Is it? Singers, comedians, stuff like that?'

'Oh, aye. There's a lot of that. But if ye like the dancin', maist nights o' the week there's a dance oan somewhere. Plenty of talent available. Ye won't have much trouble getting a "click" if you're so inclined.'

'Ah used tae love the dancin'. Have'nae been for ages.'

'Nathan and me are going tae Houghton Big Club oan Wednesday night. If ye fancy it, ye can come along wi' us.'

'That would be great. But ah have'nae got any transport at the moment. When ah sell my house in Brum ah'll be buying a motor.'

'That's nae bother. The three of us can go in ma car.'

Smartly dressed, wearing jackets and ties, we enter the lobby of Houghton Big Club. It's just a quarter to eight, but already there's a small queue. Darren and Nathan pull identical small leather wallets from inside their jackets and show them to the retired miner acting as doorman. This lets him see they are members of Framwellgate Club and, most important, that they are 'affiliated'.

I stand beside the table for a few minutes until one of the local members appears. Darren approaches him. 'Would you mind signing my mate in?'

'Why aye, nowt's a bother, hinny.' I'm duly signed in.

'We'll go intae the bar first for a wee drink.'

'I'll get these, Nathan. You lads are transporting me about, getting me intae the club – so the least ah can do is get the drinks in.'

We manage to find a table in the large bar and sit ourselves down. Nathan leans towards me.

'This'll be your first time in a northern club, is it?'

'Aye.' I look around. 'I've been in a couple down in Brum, but they were quiet wee places compared wi' this.'

Darren puts down his pint and wipes his top lip with the back of his hand. 'Oh, they're fuckin' magic round Durham. Nathan and me are oot at the jigging a couple o' nights a week. The wives think we're just oot for a drink. You'll never have seen anything like what goes on at these dances. There are a lot of wimmin, married wimmin, who come wi' their pals. Most of them are game for a bit on the side if the right guy comes along.' He takes another drink. 'Ah'm no' talking one-night stands, mind you. If ye click wi' one of them ye can find yerself in a nice wee arrangement. Meet at the club once or twice a week. Have a couple o' drinks, a few dances, then head off in the car to some quiet parking place for a session. And the beauty is, she doesn't want tae get back home late – neither dae you. It's purely for sexual pleasure. Something to look forward to. If ye get the right lass, it can go on for a long time.'

'But mind,' says Nathan, 'you'll have tae get a car. You MUST have a motor.'

Darren interrupts. 'Shaggin' them oan the bus is'nae allowed – you'll get chucked aff!'

We make our way to the concert room. The central dance area is clear. Tables and chairs line three sides of the large hall; a four-piece combo is readying itself for the next number. We find three seats at a long table already occupied by separate groups of men and women. Couples are in the minority in the hall. 'If ye fancy somebody, make sure she's not wi' a guy,' says Nathan. 'Waste of time if she is. In the middle of the evening they have what's called the Bradford Barn Dance. It's what they call a progressive dance. Nearly everybody gets up. It's supposed tae be so you get tae meet most of the wimmin in the hall, and they get tae meet the men. It's hard tae explain. But it's great for getting tae meet all the talent. Make sure ye get up when it's announced. You form a large circle. When it starts you do this sort of set piece few steps, then you change partners. You get about thirty seconds wi' each new partner. So if you've been fancying somebody, you should get the chance tae have a few words wi' her at the Bradford—'

Darren butts in. 'Just ask her if you can have a dance later. If she's no' available she'll say, "Oh, I'm with somebody." If she's just with her pals, she'll soon let you know.'

It's three pints past nine o'clock and I'm really beginning to enjoy myself. I've had quite a few dances with various women, all quite fanciable. The Bradford Barn Dance is announced. Darren and Nathan rise, ready to ask a partner up. 'Just get anybody up,' says Nathan, 'as long you are on that floor. Doesn't matter who you ask, you'll be losing her anyway. You keep changing partners, remember? It's not who you ask up – it's who you meet as you go round.'

'Oh, of course.' I rise and ask a woman further along the table if she'd like to dance.

We stand at the side of the floor. The couples are lining up, the bandleader is encouraging more folk to join the ever-increasing circle round the edge of the dance area.

I smile. 'This is the first time I've ever heard of this barn dance. I hope I don't stand on your feet.'

'Oh, I'll keep you right.'

At last the music starts. As Nathan forecast, I pick up the simple routine within minutes. It is, most definitely, a great way to meet just about all the girls in the hall. As I go from woman to woman I exchange pleasantries with them. I finish my brief little set with the latest one and gently swing her off in the direction of the next guy. I pause for a moment while my next partner spins round, comes towards me and gently slots herself into my arms. She's half smiling. I look at her face, then her eyes. 'JEEZ!' She's a slim blonde; fine featured. She laughs at my involuntary exclamation. The three pints I've drunk have given me such confidence, I'm King of the World, I can do anything. I haven't had such a good time at the dancing for years. I haven't had such a good time at the dancing EVER! There isn't a moment to lose. 'Where are you sitting?'

She points. 'Over there.'

'I've got to have the next dance. Is that okay with you?'

'Of course.'

We're doing the last turn, I have to hand her over to someone else in a few seconds. I lean back a little so as I can look her in the eyes. 'In fact, I think I'll have to have all the dances for the rest of the evening. What do you say to that?'

She gives the sexiest half-smile I've ever seen. Her fine features remind me of Grace Kelly.

'Sounds good to me.' I give her a final twirl and hand her over to the next guy.

Ten minutes later, we're dancing. Her name is Margaret. We dance the rest of the evening away. This is what I never had as a teenager. While other guys were experiencing this I was too shy to show my plooky face in a dance hall. Then when I did, I quickly committed myself to Nancy. I missed out in my teenage years. All I had was poxy acne. Even when I was in the army in Nottingham I was still plagued by it. I'd go to Coleman's Club purely for the dancing – and also because it was dimly lit. Now here I am, thirty-one years of age and at last my skin is clear. And all of a sudden there's tonight. I'm dancing, I'm talking to women – and some of them are finding me attractive. Especially Margaret. Where did all this come from?

It's the last waltz. We've been dancing real close since I headed straight for her after the Bradford. I look at her. 'I'll be coming over here every week, unless I'm on evening duty. It'll probably be a couple of months before I sell the house in Birmingham, move into quarters, and most important of all – get a car. Then we really can start seeing one another.'

She gives me that enigmatic smile which I already can't get enough of. 'We won't have to wait that long. I have a car. I'll come and pick you up. That's if you want me to?'

'Hah! I think all my birthdays and Christmases have come at once tonight. Won't your husband be a problem? I take it there is a husband?'

She shakes her head. 'We've been going our separate ways for the last two years.'

I pull her in tight with both arms. 'I think we're all set for something special.'

As the last dance finishes, we stand in the centre of the floor for a moment. We don't want tonight to end; to go our separate ways.

I thought it was only in books and movies things like this happened, not in real life. She looks up into my face. 'After the Bradford, when you said you'd come over for me, I went back to my table and said to my sister, "I've just met my next lover!"'

I laugh out loud. 'Well, I never put it into words. But as soon as you spun away from your previous partner and came towards me, I just looked at your face – and that was IT. I was gone!'

I lie snug in bed in my bachelor quarters. I've just had the best night out of my life. I'm going to make up for all those fucking rotten teenage years. And for the last few years of 'Oh, are you wanting sex again? Well go on then, hurry up.'

I turn over, pummel my pillow, get comfortable. My thoughts go back to the club. I really enjoyed my dancing tonight; especially the quickstep. Swinging the girls out wide then pulling them back in. They love it. It was great to see how responsive, interested, quite a few of them were. Though once Margaret came along they all took second place. Everything about tonight has been wonderful. It's like all of a sudden I'm a grown man. And Margaret and I are going to be lovers. Jeez! Imagine me having a lover. The folk who know me wouldn't believe it. I never felt like this about Nancy when I first met her. Maybe I was too young. I think about it some more. I don't feel in the least guilty.

I'm like a kid who's found the key to the chocolate factory. I don't intend to give it back.

Studies in Blue: Three

John Bryden is by far the toughest screw I've ever worked with. At over 6 feet tall and maybe 14 stone in weight he is, in the best sense of the word, a 'hard' man. Always fit, with a solid rangy build, even though he's in his early forties he's still not a man to mess with. John has been bald on top from an early age, with hair only at the sides. Not one to let it bother him, he decided years ago he may as well have none at all. He keeps his head shaved. Like Yul Brynner, he is one of the fortunate few who actually suits it. A natural athlete, in his early twenties he was a pro footballer, playing in goal for Clyde. He is also an avid golfer. In spite of the hours we work he still manages to keep his handicap down to three. He is frightened of nobody.

I regularly spend a day or two in charge of the punishment landing. As at Birmingham, it is down on A1. I often have John with me as my officer. He is good company. Like most guys who can look after themselves, he is always relaxed and full of fun – if trouble starts he knows he can handle it. Just like Jimmy Green at Birmingham, John always gets annoyed when he comes across a con who persistently causes trouble. I especially like having him with me when we receive someone who is already on punishment and has been shanghaied to Durham from another jail for continually disruptive behaviour – including assaulting screws. It's always interesting to watch the maestro at work . . .

'Good morning, sir. Five on punishment.' I throw up a salute.

'Thank you, Mr Douglas.' The Governor, Lionel Steinhausen,

accompanied by the Chief, is doing his rounds. John is already standing, key in lock, ready to open the first of the five doors. As the Governor makes for the cell, John opens it. 'On your feet!' The con rises.

The Governor looks in. 'All right?'

'Yes, sir.' As John, Governor and Chief all head for the next cell, I lock up the first. In around two minutes the Governor has seen all five. No complaints. Just before he leaves, he turns to Bryden. 'You know you've got a troublemaker arriving later today from Hull?'

'Yes, so I believe, sir,' says John. He looks from John to me. 'The two of you will manage all right, I assume?'

'Oh, I think so, Governor.' I nod in John's direction. 'When I've got Mr Bryden with me I don't have any worries about taking another jail's tough guys. John specialises in trouble-makers.'

'Yes. Well, I'll leave you to it. Let's go, Chief.' John and I throw up another couple of salutes then stand in the middle of the floor, watching them as they climb the stairs and set off along A2. We go back into the office and sit ourselves down.

'Seen any good pictures lately, Robert?' Like me, John loves the cinema.

'Aye, ah meant tae tell ye, ah finally caught up wi' *The Wild Bunch*. By! It's a helluva movie in't it? Ah reckon it's got tae be one o' the best westerns ever made. Up there wi' *The Magnificent Seven*.'

'Aye. It's got a great cast. And that shoot-out at the end, aw done in slow motion. Pure cinema!' Our in-depth discussion on what the modern cinema has to offer is interrupted by a shout from above. 'HELLO, A1!' John puts his hat on and goes to the office door.

'That guy from Hull will be along in a few minutes.'

'Right, thanks.'

I rise, put on my hat and join John on the landing. We stand side by side, facing the stairs.

We hear the noise of feet, officers' keys jangling as they hurry along. Prisoner and escort hove into view. The con carries his bedroll and a carrier bag. 'Just send him down, boys. Mr Douglas and I will manage.'

The officers halt at the top of the stairs. The con starts to descend. I weigh him up; he's a hefty built young lad, late twenties, maybe 6 feet tall. He swaggers down the stairs. Must be trying to live up to his new-found reputation. John walks over to an empty cell; unlocks it; springs the lock. 'Here ye are, in here.' I half smile; this is just the type Bryden loves.

The con saunters over and turns sideways so as he can pass through the door with the roll of bedding. John enters, I follow. I stand and watch. This will almost certainly be a master-class. I won't be needed.

'What's your name?' asks John.

'Fratton.' He puts his bedroll on the mattress, but still holds the plastic carrier bag.

'What huv ye got in the bag?'

'It's personal stuff.'

'Personal stuff? There's no' such a thing as personal stuff in the jail. Anything you're allowed tae have you get wi' oor permission. That goes double doon here. Gimme the bag!'

Fratton doesn't move. 'It's person . . .' John snatches the bag out of his hand. 'Ah said gie me the fuckin' bag.' He throws it on top of the bed, turns, then in one swift movement he grabs Fratton by the front of his jacket and slams him, full force, against the painted bricks of the cell wall. The speed and violence of it not only takes the prisoner by surprise but also knocks the wind out of him. He can feel the strength of John's grip. Like many before him, he realises he's just come up against an extremely strong man. John continues to hold him firmly against the wall. He has turned his lower body so that his hip and the side of his leg runs across the con's legs; that way Fratton can't attempt to knee him in the groin. John's face is inches from Fratton's. 'So, you've been sent here 'cause ye lift yer hands tae screws now and again. Is that right?' Fratton doesn't answer. 'Whit aboot liftin' yer hands tae me?' Without warning, John swings him round and violently throws him onto the cell bed as though he weighed about half the 15 stone he probably does. There's a crack as his head bounces off the wall. John takes his peaked hat off and throws it onto the bed. He stands in front of Fratton. 'What about it, then? Do ye want tae get off tae a good start at Durham? You want the chance tae assault a Durham screw the day ye arrive?'

There's no answer.

'Yeah, ah fuckin' thought so.' He turns and empties the carrier bag onto the mattress; riffles through its contents: paperback books, a couple of pencils, a Biro. 'Right, ye can huv this stuff.' John puts his hat on. 'Remember what ah've told ye. You assault a screw here, the next one you're gonny have tae take on is me.' He turns. 'Right, that should do for the minute, Mr Douglas.' I let John leave first. As I take off the sprung lock and prepare to leave the cell I pause to look at Fratton. 'You should see him when he turns nasty.' I shake my head as though recalling a terrible memory. I gently close the door.

We go into the office and sit down again. I look at Bryden. 'Well, I don't know about Fratton, but you certainly frighten the crap out of me, John!'

Making the Best of It

It hasn't taken me too long to realise Durham Prison ain't a patch on the Green. I love the city and the area, but there's a whole different ethos at the jail. Cliques. At Winson Green, the staff had been a mix from all over the country with only a slight preponderance of Midlands lads. At Durham there's a high percentage of locals. Next comes a sizeable group of Jocks. The Scots are mostly vociferous and there are occasions in the officers' club when you could be forgiven for thinking they make up the majority of the staff. Both major groups are fairly heavy drinkers. It's a 'northern thing'. The ability to drink to excess, without falling over, is taken as a mark of how macho you are. 'Eeeh, he can't half hold his drink' is the finest compliment you can pay most members of these two factions.

As well as these major groups there are smaller, perhaps more powerful, cliques. The Freemasons for a start. In the Prison Service – and the police – Freemasonry has long been seen as the way to get on, to curry favour. In my eight years at Brum it may have been around, but I don't ever recall it rearing its head. I'm not too long at Durham when I'm asked, 'Are you interested in joining the Masons, Bob?'

Having made my own way since I was sixteen without help from any organisations – social security and social services in particular – my reply is to the point. 'Naw thanks, ah'm afraid my outlook is the same as Groucho Marx: "Any club that would have me – ah don't WANT to join it!" ' No doubt that was my card marked as far as those P.O.s who are Masons were concerned.

Amongst the Scots there is, of course, the Catholic/Protestant divide. It rears its head on a weekly basis as the results from Ibrox and Parkhead are awaited. Amongst the locals this is replicated by how well 'the lads' are performing at St James or Roker Park football grounds. During my first few months at Durham, the occasional probe had been made to try and discover my religion . . . 'Are you a Rangers or Celtic fan, Bob?'

Once again my answer probably fell short of expectations. I smiled. 'Well, if you're trying to find out what religion I am by asking that question, the answer is, Church of Turkey! If you want to discover if I'm a football fan, the short answer is no. The long answer? I think football is a load o' shite! I've got more to do with my time, and my life, than worry aboot eleven men kickin' a ball round a muddy field.' No doubt that would be a few more folk alienated.

Then there are the P.O.s. With the honourable exceptions of Norman Hutcheson and Arthur 'Tiger' Denton, I find the rest are jobsworths. To get a decision out of them, especially if it's to deal firmly with a troublesome con, is almost impossible. I usually let them know how I feel. More enemies made. Then another clique is set up. It's decided to create a security section to be run by a P.O. He, of course, hand picks his staff. Their mandate is to go about the prison on a daily basis trying to find out if the cons are up to anything, carrying out snap searches of cells or workshops when they receive information some of the heavies may be up to something. Within a year, the security section seem to spend as much time trying to unearth any titbits of gossip about their fellow officers. The more salacious the better. I rename it the security sewing circle.

As for the staff in general? There are some very good screws at Durham. There is also a high percentage of lazy buggers who have to be continually chivvied to get them to do their job . . .

It's ten past five, and I'm in charge of A Wing. The wing has been fed and locked up. There are four or five screws in the office killing time until we finish at five thirty. I come in. 'Joe, here's a letter for a guy up on A4-20. He's just been moved from D Wing, take it up to him will you?' I go off to do something else. I come back into the office just after twenty past five.

'Well, time to head down the Centre,' says someone. I notice the letter is still on the desk.

'What about that letter, Joe?'

'Oh, it'll do in the morning, Bob. Finishing time now.'

'No, it won't do in the morning. I gave you it a quarter of an hour ago. So take it up to him.'

'Oh, bloody hell!' He reluctantly takes the letter, makes for the door.

'Here!' I say. He stops. I reach out and take the letter from him. 'I'll do it myself, I wouldn't see you in my fuckin' way!' I make for the door.

'Haway, Bob, I'll take it. I didn't think it would be a problem if it waited till morning. Bob, man!'

I stride off along the landing and up the stairs without answering. Two minutes later the con has his mail. I should now make my way to the Centre and put my wing numbers in so the staff can finish. My officers have all gone along to the Centre, ready for the off. I stand on the bridge on the fours and complete today's entry in my diary. As expected I soon hear calls of 'Mr DOUGLAS!' echoing along D Wing from the Centre. It's gone five thirty as I stride along towards the waiting Centre P.O. The staff are all looking at me; I'm holding everyone up.

'Haway, Mr Douglas. Where have you been? We're waiting for you.'

I stop, maybe 10 yards from the Centre, then say in a loud voice, 'I'll tell you what's kept me. I gave one of my officers a letter to take up to a con at around ten past five. He was too fuckin' idle to climb from the threes to the fours to give the guy his letter – so I took it myself. That's where I've been, P.O.' I look at the lazy bastard in question; he's had the good grace to blush.

'Oh, well. Anyway, we'll have your numbers, Mr Douglas.'

How to win friends and influence people. Not my strong point.

The Goldfish Bowl

I'm sitting in the office in E Wing. I've had a few days in the wing by now, beginning to get the feel of it, getting used to the regime. Bill Burns sits on the corner of the desk. He's worked in here for a while, so he's the ideal man to fill me in on the different personalities of the inmates and how they interact with each other. A con appears at the door. It's Ian Brady, the Moors Murderer. This is the first time I've seen him. 'Could ah huv a lend of the whisk, boss?'

'I'll get it,' says Bill. On the back wall of the office there is a 'shadow board'. All the cooking implements that are available to the cons, including knives, hang on it. The board is painted black. Each implement hangs on a white silhouette of itself. This means officers can tell at a glance if something hasn't been returned as there will be the white outline of what is missing. As soon as he speaks, I realise that I'd forgotten Brady was Scots. It's been two or three years since I read *Beyond Belief* by Emlyn Williams, a brilliant dissection of Brady and Hindley and their crimes. Just for something to say while he waits by the door, I ask, 'What are ye making, scrambled eggs?'

He picks up on my accent. 'Naw, potato scones, would ye believe?'

'It's a long time since ah had a tattie scone.'

'Aw, they're dead easy.'

Billy hands him the whisk; he heads off to the kitchen.

'I forgot that Brady was Scots. With it all happening in the north of England round Saddleworth Moor, it slipped my mind. So what's Brady like?'

'Never causes any trouble. Spends all his time with petitions and appeals to try and get permission to visit Myra. With them not being married we don't have to let them see one another. If they were man and wife they'd be entitled. The Home Office has never allowed it. They ain't seen each other since the day they were sentenced.'

'I imagine he doesn't get any visits, then. Who'd want to come and see him?'

'Well, he has that dozy old sod Lord Longford. He visits her as well, down at Holloway.'

'Oh aye, of course. He's chosen the two most evil bastards in Britain and wants to show that, eventually, Christianity will save them. It's a bit late, ah would have thought.'

'Brady just uses him to try and get visits with Myra. Silly old prat can't see it. He's so full of Christian zeal. He just doesn't accept that the pair of them are, quite simply, two evil bastards. He's no bother, Brady, but he's a devious git. Quite intelligent. His mind's always working – working for Brady.'

It's five minutes later. Bill and I are still in the office and Brady appears at the door.

'Here ye are, boss.' He hands me a piece of lined paper, torn from a notebook. There's writing on it, in pencil. 'That's the recipe for potato scones. Ye can give it a try some time.'

'Oh, right. Ah will.'

Brady heads off, back to his cooking. I read the recipe; look up at Bill. 'Who the fuck wants anything from that reptile?' I tear it up and throw it in the bin.

It's almost thirty years later. I'm reading a piece in a magazine on how certain articles can fetch large sums of money on e-bay. The thought comes into my head: I wonder what a handwritten recipe from Ian Brady would fetch? We'll never know. And nor would we want to.

* * *

It's later in the afternoon. I'm standing watching a group of the E Wing cons having a weightlifting competition amongst themselves. The usual suspects are there. There's Charlie Richardson, leader of the so-called London Torture Gang. Supposedly they weren't averse to connecting the testicles of a rival to the mains. Then there's a guy called Lambrianou – he's a member of some gang or other, too. There's five or six of them, all Londoners. The Prison Department has kindly supplied them with all the gear; broad leather belt to support their stomach muscles, talcum for the hands. One of them is about to attempt to lift the barbell. He walks up and down, trying to psyche himself up for the big lift. He must have been watching it on telly, he's got the routine off to a T. As he walks back and forth he lets out little shouts now and again, glaring at the barbell like it's his mortal enemy. The other four give him encouragement. All, of course, in the London 'tough guy' manner:

'Go on my sahn, you can do it!'

'You're the guv'ner, Mikey, you're gonna do this!'

They all mill about. I have to force myself not to smile. It's all so fucking phony, like they're doing a parody of how gangsters should behave. At last, suitably psyched Mikey stands in front of the weight. Eddie Stoker, the S.O. who showed me round on my first day, is passing by. He stops to watch this major attempt on the E Wing record. Mikey reaches down; grips the bar; stares fixedly ahead, concentrating. The support reaches a crescendo.

'GO ON, my sahn!'

'You're THE MAN! Do it!'

Mikey snatches the barbell and he gets it up to chest level. It rests along his collar-bone for the moment; he's very red in the face. The next bit's the hardest. In one movement he'll have to raise it above his head, lock his arms, and hold it there for a few seconds. His cohorts continue to give encouragement.

'NOW, Mikey!'

'Don't waste any more fahkin' time, you'll lose it my sahn!'

'Huppp!' Mikey goes for it. 'Aaaarghhh!' He can't get it up to where his arms can lock out.

'GO ON MY SAHN!'

It's no good. Red-faced from his exertions, rapidly weakening, he lets the barbell fall with a loud clang onto the thick mat. He sways a little, light-headed from his exertions.

'Hard to bear, Mikey. Next time!'

Eddie Stoker points at the barbell. 'How much you got on it, like?'

'Hundred and twenty pounds.'

'Is that ahl? Me little lad could lift that. In fact our lass could.'

'Get fahked! Let's see you lift it, guv'ner.'

'Why aye,' says Eddie, 'nowt's a bother.' He takes off his peaked hat, hands it to Bill Burns, and walks onto the mat. He stands in front of the weight. He looks every inch the ex-rugby player he is. He reaches down and takes hold of the barbell. In one fell swoop, without bothering to stop at chest level, he raises the weight high above his head, locks out, then stands there looking at the cons, smiling. He puts the weight down gently, then three times in succession raises it again from the floor to the required arm's length. 'There y'are, boys.' He takes his hat from Bill. 'Bye, lads.' Smiling, he goes on his way.

The championship contenders watch him go. 'Flash fahker!' somebody mutters.

Resolutions Not Made

It's about two o'clock on a Saturday afternoon. We come into the lobby of the King's Arms Hotel in Berwick. The guy on reception smiles, 'Good afternoon, sir. Madam.'

'Hello. You should have a double room for us. Mr and Mrs Douglas. For two nights.'

He consults his ledger. 'That's correct, Mr Douglas.' He reaches for a key. 'Number six, on the first floor. Would you like someone to take your luggage?'

'No, not a problem. Just point us in the direction of the stairs.'

I open the room door. We step in, shut it behind us. It's almost straight out of *Homes & Gardens*. The decor is light; pale flowers on a cream background. The bed-cover matches it. The lower windows have been opened 6 inches or so, the net curtains waft in the warm breeze, sunlight slants through onto one wall. I turn the key in the lock and look at Margaret.

'Looks very nice.'

'Yeah, it does.' You could cut the sexual tension with a knife.

'That bed looks even nicer. Shall we?'

She glances down at me. 'By the looks of you, pet, I think we'll have to!'

Minutes later we're in bed. Now that we are, I don't want to rush things, I want to make it last. There's something extra nice about lying in bed with your mistress on a summer afternoon, the room bright as day, the rumble of the traffic and hubbub from

Saturday afternoon shoppers drifting up. Knowing you're about to have great sex. The best ever.

Later, as I'm about to doze off, the scene from the movie *Room at the Top*, where Laurence Harvey and Simone Signoret have gone to the coast for their 'stolen' weekend, comes into my mind. Though I'd had no experience of such a thing, the intensity of their pleasure in one another had been quite explicit. I'd read the book in the army and loved it. When the film had come out I'd been so pleased because it hadn't disappointed. My weekend hadn't either.

Margaret drops me off outside the jail late on Monday afternoon. 'Well, I don't know when we'll get the chance to go to bed again. Nancy and the kids will be moving up in less than a fortnight. It'll be back to the front passenger seat.' I laugh. 'Whoever invented reclining front seats should get a medal as big as a frying pan! Don't you think?'

'Definitely, pet.'

I stand on the platform at Durham station and watch the train steam slowly in. It's hardly halted before most of the carriage doors are opening. I spot Nancy and wave. I can't see the kids yet because of all the adults streaming towards me.

'DADDY!'

'Hello, pals!' There are lots of kisses and hugs. Jeez, I really have missed the kids. I kiss Nancy, give her a hug. There's no elation. It's well over a month since I last saw her. Absence hasn't made the heart grow fonder. I really don't want to be with her. Yet, if we . . . when we split up, it'll mean losing the kids too. I try to put it out of my mind. For the moment.

'Did aw the stuff arrive yesterday?'

'Aye, I just got the removal men to put it in the quarter. You know, beds in the bedrooms, three-piece suite in the living-room, etc. We'll sort oot what goes where once you see the size and shape of the rooms. Anyway, before we get a taxi, come and have a look at this view. Come and see this, kids.' The train is still standing at the platform; I take them along to the end, point to the Cathedral and Castle. 'Ain't THAT something! Eh?'

'WOWWW!' they exclaim in unison. 'Is that a real castle, Daddy?' says Scott.

'Yeah. Hundreds of years ago, soldiers with chain-mail on used tae walk along the walls, and knights in armour used tae ride in and out of the castle gates. And they used tae regularly be fencing with their enemies just like you and me do.'

'Geeee!'

We quickly settle in at 72 Langley Road, Framwellgate Moor. Our neighbours are all prison officers and their families. On that first day I decide to lay the first of many lies on Nancy. I try to sound casual. 'Oh, I'll tell you what I've started doing since I've been here. I've started having a night out once a week with the lads. It's a different way of life, nothing like Birmingham. There's six or seven of us. Usually head out to one of the working men's clubs. There's maybe a comedian on, then a singer or a magician. Sometimes even a stripper. And if we can get a babysitter on a Saturday, there's always a dance on at the officers' club. You and I can start going tae that.' I hope that by including her in the 'going out' she'll accept my solo nights out – believe what I say about Durham's active social scene. The hardest thing for her to get used to will be the change in me. I never used to go out in the evening. Not on my own. Will she smell a rat? If she does, it'll be me.

It doesn't take long. The occasional smear of lipstick or make-up on my collar is a bit of a giveaway. I usually don't bother trying to tidy up before I go home. Maybe I want to get caught, have it all out in the open? When the inevitable row follows, I usually say, 'I told you, if I can't get good sex from you, I'll get it elsewhere. You didn't believe me when we were in Birmingham.

You thought you were safe enough 'cause I didn't go out. It's a different story now!'

When I say things like that to her I always feel really rotten afterwards. She doesn't deserve it, but what can I do? I don't love her anymore. If I apologise that'll be me making up with her. I don't want to make-up. I don't want to live with her. Don't want to be married to her anymore. I also don't want to lose my kids. Jesus wept, even Solomon couldn't solve this.

As I get used to the jail and being an S.O., I also start to become friends with certain officers. Guys with much the same outlook and sense of humour – birds of a feather, in other words. Jack Walton, Alan Briggs, Gerry Paige, John Thomas. Of these, Jack becomes my main mate, perhaps because we are both in marriages that we know won't last. If I'm in charge of a wing and Jack has the time, he'll often come into the office and we'll sit and blether. Without fail the conversation always gets round to how long it will be until the inevitable break-up happens. We both want to see our kids grow up as far as we can, we don't want to lose them, but we know that we will. We also agree that the longer we live with our wives, knowing we don't love them anymore, the more difficult daily life becomes. Regular rows, accusations, made all the worse because it's our fault. We are the cause of it. You can't defend the indefensible. I recall something I read years ago. It was meant to be funny, but I remember thinking, how true . . . 'There's no good trying to put your foot down if you haven't got a leg to stand on!'

HAVEN on Earth

The nearest pub to the prison is the Court Inn. It is well frequented by Durham staff, especially those who have just come off duty after a long day in the prison or are back late from an escort. There's a second influx of screws just after nine fifteen p.m. as the evening duty staff finish. Mine hosts at the Court are Bob and Irene, a couple in their late sixties. It's in their premises, late one evening, when I'm given the golden opportunity to 'adapt' a joke – and tell it as though it were true . . .

It's just gone ten p.m. I'm standing at one end of the long bar with P.O. Arthur Denton, also known as 'Tiger'. Arthur likes a laugh.

Having started at seven a.m. this morning and just finished at nine fifteen p.m., we are relaxing and unwinding. We lean companionably on the bar. There's nothing to do but watch Bob. Short, fat and balding, he always reminds me of the henpecked cartoon character 'The Born Loser'. Arthur speaks out of the corner of his mouth. 'Have you ever noticed, it's Irene's name above the door as licensee? Not Bob's?'

'No, I haven't.'

'I've been told,' he says conspiratorially, 'that's so as Bob can draw the dole. He's drawn it for years, seemingly. Because she's the licensee, he's able to sign on as unemployed.' He pauses for a moment, his glass half raised to his mouth. 'How the bloody 'ell can some folk stay on the dole for years? I thought you had to take a job after a certain time, otherwise they cut off your money.'

Into my mind comes an adapted joke. Its time has come!

'Well, the secret is simple, Arthur. If you're a labourer or something like that, after six months they make you take a job. If you refuse, they stop your dole. But if you're a TRADESMAN you've got them beat, they have to find you a job in your line of work. If not, you can stay on the dole for evermore. Bob's been signing on for the last thirty years. They can't find him a vacancy in his trade.'

'Bugger me! So that's how he does it.' He raises his glass towards his mouth, then pauses again. 'Mind, I never knew Bob was a journeyman. I wonder what he does?' He starts to drink.

My timing is impeccable. 'He's a Zeppelin builder!'

There's a choke followed by an arc of beer. Bob and Irene turn their heads. I slap Arthur on the back. 'Something gone down the wrong way?' I ask. Although I'm a fairly frequent visitor to the Court I also, however, pledge my allegiance to, as far as I'm concerned, the best pub AND landlord in Durham City: Thomas Wilson, Esq.

Bobby Marrs, a Scots officer, is the one who does the honours. We hang up our keys and step out of the prison gates. It's just gone twenty past nine . . .

'Are ye going for a pint?' he enquires.

'Aye, good idea.' I'm about to set off in the direction of the Court.

'Do ye no' fancy the Dun Cow?'

'I've never tried it yet.'

'Oh, ah think you'll like it.' This will prove to be correct.

We walk straight down from the gates, maybe two hundred yards, and into the broad street known as Old Elvet. Facing us is the narrow frontage of the Dun Cow. We enter the tight passage on the left and open the sliding door which is immediately on our right. A small, square bar – about the size of our single-end in Maryhill – is revealed. It's already crowded beyond anything the Department of Health and Safety would recommend. Nobody's bothered. I don't know it yet, but there's already just about a full turn-out of the local suspects. There is nearly always a wonderfully eclectic mix of clientele at the Cow. Durham City is, in reality, a small town. It has an ancient, large, world-renowned university. This means there is already a rich mixture of 'town and gown' and added to that, especially in the Dun Cow, is a pinch of 'in your face' prison screws! It is a heady brew. Discussions, arguments, statements, aspersions and – always – hilarity is usually the order of the day. Never violence.

The locals are strongly represented that first evening: Big Bill Mitchell, the Minnesota Fats of the shove-ha'penny board; Joe Seed, piss-taker extraordinaire and ace domino player; John, caretaker at the Freemason's Hall and, one of my favourites, Mickey Brown – occupation: local character. There is a strong section of undergraduates representing the uni. The majority of these are the lads who have formed themselves into a very good football team which is doing well in one of the Sunday leagues. With old-fashioned courtesy they have named themselves the Durham Boilers in honour of their female supporters – and fellow undergrads. That name topped the poll. A close second was the Durham Slappers.

Bobby Marrs introduces me to Tommy Wilson. We stand at the bar. Just. The sliding door opens, another four or five folk somehow fit in. No one ever seems to leave; there's a constant influx of new customers in dribs and drabs. I look at Bobby.

'This place got elastic walls?'

'Ah sometimes wonder. You should see it oan a Saturday night. Some folk come intae the corridor, they open the sliding door – and there's three or four people fall OOT o' the bar intae the passageway! Then a few minutes later you'll look, and somehow they've got back intae the bar! Ah'm sure that bugger Wilson slips round via the lounge and uses a crowbar tae jemmy them in!'

1974: Senior Officer at Durham.

'It's my turn tae get them in, Bobby.' I manage to catch Tom's eye. 'Could I have two pints o' lager, Tommy, and have one yerself.'

'No, thanks all the same, bonny lad. I don't drink.' He starts pulling our pints.

'There's not many landlords can say that.'

'Aye. Tommy doesn't drink. He reckons ye can be a drinker, or a landlord. Not both.'

Reluctantly, just after half ten, I leave the Cow. Bobby gives me a lift home. He also lives at Framwellgate Moor. He pulls up outside my quarters.

'Well, this'll be just about ma last lift. I'm picking up a new car this Saturday.'

'What are ye getting?'

'A brand new Hillman Hunter – with an overdrive. Cost me an extra £49 for that. All in, it's coming to £1,044. Never ever thought I'd spend that much money on a car. You ever had an overdrive?'

'No.'

'Och, well. Ah suppose ah'll learn how tae use it. Ah'll have to.'

After my introduction to the Dun Cow it immediately becomes my pub of choice. If I'm in the prison during the day, instead of going to the officers' mess for lunch I more often than not nip down to the Cow for a sandwich and a pint.

Talking Shop

I always enjoy talking to Joe Vincenti. A Newcastle lad, mid-thirties, he's doing a five at the moment. He's a professional criminal. Unlike the majority of our residents, who fall into the category of 'gas meter bandits', Joe and his cohorts always attempt to pull off decent jobs – a few thousand quid here, a few thousand there. Of course, that may be the problem. There are so few clever criminals in Newcastle that whenever a half-decent job is pulled, there are only a limited number of possible suspects. Joe is one of them.

One of the things I like about him is the fact he can do his porridge. Prison is an occupational hazard to Joe. There are so many who, when they get a few years, arrive in prison 'full of hell'. You would think they'd been these innocent guys, walking along the street minding their own business when half a dozen hairy-arsed screws had leapt on them, put their arms up their back and press-ganged them into jail for the next seven years. This is not Joe Vincenti's outlook.

I'm on evening duty in C Wing. I've had Joe out giving a hand with the suppers. We've just finished. It's a Sunday evening, so there will be no receptions tonight. Time for a blether. Joe sits in his cell. He has, of course, one of the coveted red bed-covers; family photos are stuck on the cork board on the wall. I stand at his door, leaning against the frame. I enjoy a blether with Joe. He likes to laugh, tell jokes, and is always good craic.

'So what's new, boss?'

'I'll tell you what impressed me this week. I actually came across a con with more than the statutory one brain cell – present company excepted, of course.'

'Oh, thank you guv. You're too kind.'

'I was at Newcastle Sessions on Monday. This kid was up for sentence, a string of burglaries. At first glance ah thought, just gonny be run o' the mill. Nowt special.'

'You took the words right out me mooth, boss.'

'Well, I happened to be up in the dock on the last day. So I heard his brief and the judge giving their speeches. Now what finished up impressing me about this fella was his single-mindedness. And his intelligence. He's twenty-six years of age. Never

Saturday 8 July 1972.
Evening duty Gatekeeper at Durham Prison.

been in trouble wi' the police before. He's unemployed, in debt, so he decides he'll do a bit of burglary.'

Joe interrupts. 'You've not got Eamonn Andrews coming in 'ere any minute wi' the red book, have yee?'

'No, yah daft bat. Now, this kid lives in Ryton. He chooses villages within a 5-mile radius – so he can walk over the fields to them. Always at night, of course. When he gets there he only screws houses on the perimeter of the villages. That means when he's done the job – or if he's disturbed – he's straight out, over the fence, and off home across the fields in the darkness. So, if it's two a.m. and the householder makes a 999 call, the police are flying up and down the few roads in the area, looking for someone to stop. They take it for granted the thief will be making his getaway in a car, don't they? Now I thought that was so simple, yet brilliant.'

Joe grabs hold of a Biro and pretends to write while saying out loud, 'Walk over fields, only screw houses on edge of . . .' When we finish laughing, he puts the pen down. 'Mind, you're right, boss. Simple things can definitely be the best. And another thing that's a help. People can be so gullible. They'll believe owt! Ah knew a couple o' lads – no names, no pack drill – it would be around 1959 – and they thought up this scam. You know the night safes that all the banks have? Businesses that open late use them; restaurants, pubs. They have a little leather bag, put the takings in it, then come along to the night safe with their key and drop the stuff in.' Joe stops for a moment to take a mouthful of cold cocoa. 'Most banks have a flat above the premises. Used to be the manager's house in the old days. You might have noticed, they always paint the woodwork round the door to the flat the same colour as the bank, cos it's all their property. Anyhow, these two had been sussing the job out for weeks. So they come along the street, just coming up for half ten, pubs haven't emptied yet so it's nice and quiet. They've got these two professional looking notices – also in the bank's colours, and with the logo on top – and they stick one over the night safe –

'Safe Out Of Order: Please Use Emergency Night Safe' – with an arrow pointing to the flat door. Above the big letter-box on the door they stick another notice: 'Temporary Night Safe Positioned Behind Door'. They then go round the back of the premises. The flat next door to the bank's flat is also vacant. They break into it, then punch a hole through the wall into the bank flat, to avoid the alarms on the windows. Once in, they go down the stairs and sit behind the outside door. They've brought a home-made metal chute, which they stick to the back of the letter-box, and a black bag which goes on the bottom of the chute. If anyone comes along to put their takings in and are maybe a bit suspicious, if they put their hand in they'll feel a solid metal chute. If they try to look through the letter-box, everything is dark – like it should be. From just after eleven o'clock till about two in the morning, they sit in the dark on the stairs behind the door. Some time before midnight it starts. As the pubs, clubs and restaurants cash up, slowly but surely it gets busier. Every quarter of an hour, twenty minutes, they'll hear footsteps, which then stop. The letter-box rattles open and there's a 'swish' as another leather bag, stuffed with money, slides down to add to the kitty. He was telling me they had a helluva job trying not to giggle every time another bag came down that chute. So, just like we were saying, boss: dead simple – but real clever.'

I look at my watch. 'Well, time to wander along to the Centre and put me numbers in, Joe.' I take hold of the door handle. 'When are you gonny think up your million dollar scam?'

He laughs. 'Believe me, boss, I'm working on it night and day.'

'What about maybe packing it in and going straight?'

He pretends to be surprised. 'Bugger me! Ah never thought o'that, guv!'

Family Ties

I stand and look out of the window of 72 Langley Road. A white Hillman Hunter is parked at the pavement. That's mine! Nancy comes through from the kitchen. 'Are you looking at that car again?'

'I can't help it. I just keep thinking, that's mine! If I feel like it I can take the keys, unlock it, and drive anywhere I want. I never ever thought I'd have a driving licence, never mind a car. Shall I drop a line to my father, suggest we come for a couple of nights so as he can see the kids – and the new car?'

'Aye, ye know me, ah'm always game for a wee trip away somewhere.'

Although my father treated Ma and me badly during my childhood, then got rid of me after Ma died when I was fifteen into the RAF Boys' Service, I've never been out of touch with him. I see him every few years and write the occasional letter, yet I don't have any affection for him. I've long ago given up trying to analyse why I want to keep in contact. The only reason I can think of is that he's my last link with Ma.

It's late afternoon by the time we arrive at the Port (Portpatrick). As we decant ourselves from the car I see my father and Beenie at the living-room window. It's six years or more since we last visited. That was to let him see Nancy junior. Since then it's just been the usual one, or at most two, letters a year. Whenever a letter arrives with his scrawly writing, before I open it I always say to Nancy, 'Here we are! I bet it's the usual . . . "Dear Robert, hope this finds you, Nancy and the kids well. We are okay down here, well, except for the electric bill which has just arrived a couple of days ago. There seems to be nothing but bills . . ." Always on the bloody mooch—'

Nancy interrupts me: 'Well, that's because they know you'll send them a fiver.'

'Not *always*.'

'Naw, jist nearly always.'

As I'm unloading the car, my father comes out of the house. 'So this is the new motor, eh?' He has never had a licence. 'Aye, very nice. Many miles have ye done?'

'Just over 800.' As he's looking at the car I'm thinking – Aye, and I done it all myself. There's no thanks due to you. That makes me feel good. Very good.

'Wiz the journey doon okay?'

'Aye, nae bother.' Whenever we have one of our rare visits I'm always struck by how strong his Glasgow accent is. I look at him. He's very gray now. How short he is! Just over 5 feet 2 inches.

May 1972: Nancy aged eight; Scott aged ten.

Looks smaller. Maybe he's shrinking with age. He'll be sixty next birthday. He doesn't work anymore; he's on the permanent sick. We go into the house and Beenie greets us in her strong Galloway accent. 'How are the two of ye?'

'Fine, Beenie. Are you all right?'

'Och aye.' She's even shorter than my father. I've never had a problem with Beenie. Right from the first time I met her I quickly worked out she'd no idea how my father used to treat Ma and me. Because he'd wisely stopped drinking, she's never got to see that side of him.

After taking the luggage upstairs we gather in the living-room. Our old 'Utility' sideboard from Doncaster Street is still in use. Beenie has made tea and there is plenty of home baking to accompany it. She's made treacle scones.

'Now, I'll bet you've made these specially for me, Beenie. You know I love them.'

She beams. 'Aye, ah thocht ah'd make a few for ye.'

The next couple of days are spent mostly at the harbour or out at the remote Sand Deal Bay. The weather is good and I enjoy the rest. Beenie's son, Billy, calls in with his wife and kids. I'm not surprised to see most of his upper front teeth are gone. When I'd stayed at the Port for a few months fifteen years ago, he was for ever eating sweeties and rarely cleaned his teeth. He works on a farm and they live in a tied cottage. He's obviously quite happy with his lot. Even though he's almost thirty, he's still very much the Billy I remember. He likes to laugh and enjoys company, and he's as pleased to see me as I am to see him.

'You enjoy your few days away?' Jack Walton falls into step with me as we head up to the Centre for roll-call. 'You'll be making up for lost time when you meet Margaret later this week?'

'Ah! You're behind the times, Jack. That's all over! It's time to move on.'

'Never! I thought that was still pretty hot?'

'It was. Until she told me she's gonny split with her man. They've been going their own way for this last couple of years or more. Now all of a sudden she's talking divorce.'

He looks at me. 'And you're lined up to take his place, I'd imagine?'

'That's what ah'm thinking. So I said to her last week that I thought we should see a bit less of one another. Our relationship is supposed to be just for fun. Anyway, she wasn't best pleased. I think I'll give Houghton Big Club a miss for the next month or two.'

Jack puts on his best pious face; holds an admonitory finger up in the air. 'Oh, what a tangled . . .'

'Bullox!'

It doesn't take long to find a replacement for Margaret. I've started going to Hebburn Trades and Labour Club. The concert hall, which is where the dance is held on a Monday night, is the best I've seen. It's like being in a nightclub. Separate tables and chairs, a top-class surface for dancing on, and the stage hung with rich blue curtains which are discreetly lit from below. The music is supplied by a five-piece combo and a girl singer who can't half belt a song out. By my third visit I'm in love again! Yet another married woman who, like myself, is looking for a bit on the side. She's called Jean. This relationship will also last for a few months, until it goes off the boil and we decide, amicably, that it's time to move along.

All this time, of course, Nancy knows I'm at it. But she can't do anything about it. She knows if she threatens to leave me that won't stop me. If it wasn't for the fact I'd lose the kids she could leave tomorrow as far as I'm concerned. I simply don't want to live with her anymore. I don't love her. There are times when I feel so bad about the upset I'm causing her – but what can I do? If I was to give up going out I'd be so bloody miserable. Except for the kids, we don't have anything in common anymore. We regularly get a babysitter in on a Saturday night and go out to the officers' club. The conversation all evening is, at best, desultory. When we come home we hardly talk. I go to bed and read until I fall asleep. She just won't accept it's over. When I'm weekend off and things have been like that, which nowadays is the norm, I'm often relieved when Monday comes and I can get back to the prison.

The Last of Lottie

We've decided to change cars. It's 1973 and the Hillman Hunter is pushing three years old. But what to get? It's a Sunday afternoon. With Nancy and the kids in the car I drive round two or three dealers. We fully intend to get a new one. We park at a showroom in Hebburn. As we approach the premises, I stop.

'Aww! Look at that!' In the window is a beautiful pale blue Volvo 144 saloon. It's second-hand, just 14,000 miles on the clock and £1,495. 'I know we've come for a new one, but I'd quite happily have that if we could afford it. What dae you think?'

'Aye, it's nice. Anywye, you're the one that takes tae dae wi' things like this. Ah'll jist leave it tae you.'

We enter the premises. 'Let's at least have a look at it. Give our minds a treat.' We walk into the open window where the car stands in isolated splendour. 'Jeez! Ain't it beautiful? It's like brand new. And 14,000 miles is nowt on a car like this.'

'Ah love the colour,' says Nancy.

'Yeah, it's gorgeous. And that pale blue upholstery – that's real leather, you know. Och well.'

We turn away, about to start looking round the showroom.

'You like it then, do you?' One of the salesmen has come over.

'Certainly do. But a bit rich for my blood at £1,495.'

'Ah, you never know. We could be a little bit flexible on the price.'

He begins to raise a first glimmer of hope. Nah, c'mon, get real. Me – own a Volvo?

He has a look at the Hillman. I show him its service record. He quotes me a price. I take out a pen and paper and do my sums while conferring with Nancy. 'I could get the maximum on that new Barclaycard whatsit, and that would be it.' I tally up and turn to the guy. 'Now I can assure you we've come in here with the intention of getting a new car, round about the £1,200 mark. We just looked at the Volvo 'cause it was there. The most I can raise, without taking a loan, is £1,410. And I'm not bullshitting you – that would be us cleaned out.'

'I'll just have a word with the boss.'

I watch as he heads for the office. I will the boss to say yes. I turn to Nancy. 'I can't see them knocking £85 off the price. It's too much.' After a long few minutes, he comes over to us and says, 'We can do it for that if you want it.'

Thirty minutes later I drive out of the showroom. King of the World! I can't believe it – I'm driving a Volvo!

On Saturday 6 May 1973, we set off up to Seafield for a week's holiday. It's gone three years since I came to Durham. I still continue to see other women. Nancy, reluctantly, has to put up with it. We hide our problems from the kids as best we can, but have frequent rows and no doubt they know something's going on. We try to keep things going just for Scott and Nancy's sake. I'm sure Nancy senior hopes that eventually I'll feel I've sown my wild oats and I'll be ready to settle down again. I know I won't.

It's the middle of our week's holiday. 'I think I'll take a wee run into Glasgow and go up and see Lottie and Frank. Do you realise it's about five or six years since I last seen them?'

'Is that the man and the lady who had Toby the cat and Sally the dog?' asks Scott.

'That's right. They live in Glasgow where your daddy was brought up when I was a wee boy.'

'Are they your aunty and uncle?'

'No; they're just like an aunty and uncle, but they aren't really. After my Ma died I used to spend a lot of time up in their house. They'd give me something to eat. When I was seventeen I even stayed at their house for a few months. Their son, Sammy, was my best pal when I was growing up. You know how you've got your pal, Andrew, at school?'

'Yeah.'

'Well Sammy and I were just like you and Andrew. We went to school together. Of course we're grown-up now, but we're still pals even though we don't see much of each other nowadays.'

'Ahhh.' I can see he's working it all out.

I drive along the M8. It was Scotland's first motorway, connecting Glasgow and Edinburgh; now there are motorways springing up all over the country. I think back to the last time I visited Maryhill from Seafield – I'd to take a bus to Bathgate, another one to Glasgow then another one to Maryhill. About two and a half hours' travelling.

Now it's just a case of into the car and off I go. A mere fifty-minute journey.

As I near the city centre, I know I'm in Glasgow – but not MY Glasgow. There are no trams. This is maybe the third time I've been in the city since they did away with them in '62. The corporation buses still have the same cream, green and orange livery – and the grand city coat of arms. Ah, but it's not the same. The cobbled setts have been lifted; I'm driving over tarmac; there are no overhead wires to carry power to the trams. For me, the trams are the biggest miss of all.

I drive over the St George's Cross junction. It was criss-crossed with tramlines when it was MY Glasgow. On a winter's night, with the tram's windows misted with condensation or spattered with snow, you always knew when you passed through St George's Cross – the car would jerk and shoogle, the wheels grinding and squealing in protest. Now it's smooth. Well, at least there's one compensation – I'm driving up the Maryhill Road in a Volvo. What about that, Ma? Who'd ever have thought it?

Trouble is, if she knows about the Volvo, she'll also know I'm screwing up my marriage. I try not to think of what she'd say. I can't stop myself . . .

'You're jist like your bloody faither, you!'

'Ah'm no', Ma. Ah don't knock her aboot the wye ma faither used tae knock you aboot.'

'There's worse things than knockin' yer wife aboot.'

I drive past Sammy's close and turn right into Hinshaw Street then right into Doncaster Street. I stop and look down 'my' bit. As ever, my first reaction is how small it looks. When I was a boy it seemed so big. It looks really scruffy now. Then I realise why – most of the houses have their windows boarded up. The street's not swept anymore. Jeez. They're obviously getting it ready for demolishing. As each family moves out, they block the windows up. It's almost empty. Nothing but sightless windows face out onto the street now. Next time I visit, it'll all be gone. I lean forward in my seat, fold my hands on top of the steering-wheel

Doncaster St. 'MY' Street: 1967. Although I left in 1955 it looks just the same. My close, No. 14, is the first one past the wee shop on the right. All demolished in the late seventies.

and rest my chin on them. Better take a good look, boy – this is your last chance. So many memories. The church hall is on my right; I used to go in there for the Lifeboys and Boys' Brigade. There's the spot opposite my close where the two bonfires were, on VE Day then VJ day; Peggy Jarvie's shop. At the bottom of the street is Lizzie's. There's not a soul walked up or down the pavements these last ten minutes. It used to be full of weans. Girls with their skipping-ropes, boys playing football or soldiers.

I drive further down and stop at my close. I look at the square, enamelled 'No.14' plate. I'm having that! I get a screwdriver out of the boot: The two screws loosen easily; it's mine. I look towards the bottom of the street. Jeez, I wish there were some workmen with a ladder about – I'd bung one a couple of quid to climb up and unscrew the blue and white enamel Doncaster Street plate.

I drive round the corner and park in Trossachs Street. Well, at least the Blythswood Cinema and Cocozza's Café are still going strong. But for how much longer?

I'm at Sammy's door. Aw, man! There's nobody in. The familiar plastic plate bearing the name 'F. Johnston' is still there. The thought enters my head – maybe I should unscrew that, too! There's been no familiar uproar behind the door. The terrier, Sally, always races along the passage to give a load of cheek to whoever has rung her bell. I'll just have to stand at the mouth of the close and wait until one of them turns up. Ah! Just a minute. I remember Sammy saying Lottie isn't averse to dropping into the Shakespeare pub for a wee refreshment. It's worth a look.

I come out of the close, turn right, then take the next right into Raeberry Street. I cross over to the Shakey. I enter through the street door and open one of the two inner doors. It's nearly empty. Two young guys sit over on the far right. I bend my head to the left and look into the corner made by the side of the entrance lobby. Lottie looks up at me!

'Hello, Lottie me darling!' I lean forward and give her a kiss.

The incomparable Lottie Johnston, my friend Sammy's Ma. Late 1970s.

'Fuck me! Whit ur you daein' here?'

I could have taken a bet that those would be her first two words. 'Ah'm looking for you. Ah've been up tae the hoose, there's naebody in.'

'Frank's at the shoaps. It takes him ages, he's getting awfy slow nooadays.'

'Will ye manage a wee half?'

'Och, aye. Put a wee drap watter in it.'

I return with a double and a glass of lager for myself. I sit beside her. 'So, whit's happening? Is auld Sam (Sammy's Grand-ad) still going strong?'

'Aye, jist!'

'Is Sammy still at hame?'

'Och, God, naw. Sammy's merrit wi' weans and livin' ower in Partick.'

'Is he, be damned? That'll keep him oot o' mischief!'

We sit and blether for half an hour, then Lottie says, 'C'mon, we'll away up the hoose. Frank should huv toddled hame by noo.'

We rise and step out towards the middle of the floor. Lottie links her arm through mine. One of the two young guys who are sitting on the far side speaks up. 'Eh, who's that, Mrs Johnston? Are ye aw'right?'

Lottie pulls me in even closer. 'Ah! Youse are aw'right, boys. This is Robert Douglas. Sammy's pal from when they wur at the school. He used tae belang tae Doncaster Street.'

The lads smile.

'Aye, youse are all right, boys,' I say, 'she's in good hands.'

We come into the house. Frank is at the table, drying dishes. He looks to see who it is.

'It's Robert Douglas,' says Lottie.

It takes a second for it to sink in. 'Oh, aye. Aye. Hello Robert.'

He's looking quite frail. Sort of bewildered. Jeez, I wish we were like Italian or Spanish folk and I could give him a hug. He's such a lovely man. 'So, are ye retired now, Frank?'

'Oh, aye. This good wee while.'

'Ach, he's loast withoot his job at the hospital,' says Lottie. Frank turns to the sink and empties the basin. She leans forward. 'He's no' the man he wiz. Workin' as a nurse at Ruchill kept him going. Kept him alert.'

'What aboot auld Sam?'

'Well, he's very frail noo. As usual he's huvin' a wee lie doon.'

'Ah noticed when ah rang the bell, there wiz nae Sally running up the passage?'

'Oh, aye. That wee sowel went a few years ago.'

'And what aboot Toby?'

'She's no' that long away, that yin. She wiz nearly twenty when she went. Cats nearly alwiz ootlive dugs.'

The time flies by. Old Sam comes through for a wee blether. He's so frail, yet his mind is still sharp, recalling things way back to when he was a young soldier in the Boer War. I look at my watch. 'Well, I don't want to, but I'm going to have to go. It's been really great seeing ye all again. Tell Sammy I'm asking for him.'

I rise, give Lottie a kiss and a hug; put my arm round Frank's shoulder for a moment; gently squeeze old Sam's hand as he sits in his chair. His skin is like parchment. 'Cheerio, Sam.'

'Cheerio, Robert. Cheerio, son,' he says, his voice tremulous.

'Don't wait so bloody long till the next time,' says Lottie.

'Ah've got a car, now. So it shouldn't be so long till ah see ye again.'

Frank and Lottie stand at the door as I start down the curved stairway. 'Cheerio, son.'

'Aye, bye. Ah'll see ye soon.'

I cross the Maryhill Road. The shops are all there but it doesn't look right without the cobbled setts, overhead wires and trams. I try to cheer myself up – I've got my close number. I climb into the car and drive off down the Maryhill Road.

I'm filled with a great sadness. I feel I've just seen Lottie, Frank and old Sam for the last time.

The Fine Art of Reverse Psychology

Townsend is a big black guy. He reminds me of an out of condition George Foreman – with a bad Afro. He looks quite fearsome, but over the last four years I've deduced he's another one who uses his menacing appearance to try and get his way. If that doesn't work, he'll become verbally aggressive. Only as a last resort will he threaten violence. Even then, I've noticed he makes sure he picks on one of the smaller, less assertive screws.

He's doing seven days down the block. I'm in charge of 'bathing punishments' and I've got Sandy Smollet with me. We take Townsend on his own to the bath-house. As he gets undressed I get a good look at the bad scar he has on his neck. It's rope burns. About twenty years ago, when he was in his teens, he was doing a spell of Borstal. Sharing a wooden hut with another couple of dozen youthful offenders, Townsend had become such a bully that, late one evening, his fellow detainees decided to hang him. After a struggle they managed to get him strung up. Only the intervention of some officers saved him. He was left with a badly scarred neck to remind him that, now and again, bullies get their come-uppance.

He's in the bath. Sandy and I have nothing to do but wait until he's finished. Suddenly, from inside the cubicle, Townsend starts to chant. 'Fuck the Prime Minister, fuck the Home Secretary, fuck Harold Wilson, fuck Rab Butler . . .' I look at Sandy. He's gone a bit pale. He's probably glad I'm the S.O. I give him a wink. I walk over and stand at the half-door, looking at Townsend as he sits in the bath. He continues his litany while staring at me . . . 'Fuck Prince Charles, fuck the royal family . . .' I continue looking straight at him, a half-smile on my face. He begins to falter. 'Fuck Field Marshal Montgomery, er, fuck Enoch Powell . . .' He stops, still looking at me. He no doubt expects me to start remonstrating with him, threaten to put him on Governor's report; the usual knee-jerk reaction. The ball is in my court. I haven't taken my eyes off him. Now I start . . . 'Fuck Jomo Kenyatta, fuck Idi Amin, fuck Malcolm X, fuck Sonny Liston—' Suddenly I'm interrupted.

'HAH!' Townsend slams his clasped hands into the water, making a big splash, then laughs out loud. 'You got me, boss!'

I turn round. Sandy's looking paler than ever. I amble over. 'You have to play them at their own game, Sandy. He expected me to act the heavy screw. Instead, I put the ball back in his court – what's he gonny do about it now?'

It's a couple of months later, April '74. I'm on evening duty on the Centre, assisting P.O. Owens, who is orderly officer. It's almost nine p.m. I'm in the process of allocating this evening's receptions to the empty cells on the various wings. We're supposed to finish in fifteen minutes' time. Not tonight. The receptions are late. The sooner I get them all sent off to the wings, the quicker they'll be locked up, THEN we can get finished. There are still eight or nine prisoners standing along the wall, bedrolls at their feet, waiting to see where I'm about to locate them. I've already sent a dozen or more up onto the various landings. One of the receptions I've already allocated to a cell is Armstrong. I've put him on D Wing. I got rid of him right away as he can some times cause a bit of trouble. He's a big lad, early thirties, and is, as they say, not quite the full shilling. If something upsets him he usually starts shouting and bawling while waving his arms about. It normally takes four or five screws to bundle him back to his cell. This is why I got shot of him quickly. There's only George Patten and me on the Centre.

Things are going well until George, whose nickname is 'Cousin', sidles up to me. 'Shit! Don't look now, but Armstrong is making his way doon from the fours, he's carrying his plastic jug. It'll be some complaint or other. Ye kna what he's like. This is ahll we fucking need at this time o' night!'

I don't bother turning to look. I don't want Armstrong knowing that we're talking about him, that we're in the least worried about him. I look at my watch; it's twenty past nine. 'Right. We haven't time to waste on this. When he arrives, Cousin, just leave him tae me.' As I speak, I can hear Armstrong's purposeful footsteps getting nearer. 'Now, listen Cuz, don't think I'm having a nervous breakdown. I'm gonny go ballistic wi' this fucker – start shouting before he does. It's all put on, so don't worry about it.' I pretend I'm busy with my lists of empty cells. George moves back out of the way. Armstrong appears at my side.

'Boss, this jug has a hole in the bottom. The screw on the wing says there ain't a spare one to be had. I'm entitled to have a jug.'

I can tell he's hyping himself up ready for a good rant if he doesn't get a serviceable jug. I haven't got the spare officers or the time to start running after this normally objectionable fucker.

'Give us a look.' He hands me the jug. I look inside it. There's a hole the size of the Tyne Tunnel in the bottom. He has a point. But I haven't got time for points – or for Armstrong. I hold the jug for a moment, looking inside it as though I can't believe my eyes. I start mumbling, low at first, but swiftly increasing in volume as I begin to 'crack' from the stress . . . 'Who would leave a jug wi' a hole like this in a fucking cell, eh? The screws are supposed tae check the cell equipment whenever a cell is emptied.' I look into the jug again. I suddenly snap my head up and look at Armstrong. 'EH?' I scream. He takes a step backwards. 'IMAGINE LEAVING A JUG LIKE THIS IN AN EMPTY CELL!' I turn to my right. 'I HAVEN'T GOT THE FUCKIN' TIME FOR THIS!' I raise the jug above my head and smash it onto the tiled floor. It makes a loud 'BANG' at first then, as it's made from thin plastic, to my delight it bounces about 20 feet up into the air. Cousin Patten, Armstrong, me and the eight or nine cons watch in silence, heads moving as though at Wimbledon, as it comes back down, bounces up maybe 12 feet this time, then comes down neatly onto the top of the steps leading to B1. With a grace that would turn Fred Astaire green with envy, it daintily tumbles down them – two at a time – tap dancing onto the ones while emitting a lovely 'blump, blump, blumpety-blump' which descends the tonic scale as well as the stairs. Alas, I have to spoil the moment. I turn, take a step towards Armstrong – who almost falls backwards to get away from me – and yell, 'HOW AM I EXPECTED TO GET A MAN A JUG AT THIS TIME O' NIGHT?' I'm wild-eyed by now. Armstrong has turned pale. He's the one who should be doing the shouting – not the screw. 'Boss! Boss! It's okay, don't worry about it.' He holds both hands out, palms facing forwards as though to placate me. 'Ah'll just fill me mug and that'll dae me the neet. It'll be ahll reet.' He's obviously glad to see I'm calming down. 'Ah'll manage fine till the mornin', boss.'

'As long as you're sure,' I say. He hurries off, glad to get away from the nutcase on the Centre.

Decline and Fall

Hard men have the same length career as professional boxers. Both lose it by the time they hit their mid- to late thirties. The only difference is, a pro boxer is allowed to go gracefully when the bell rings for the last time. A criminal with a reputation for being hard isn't allowed the same courtesy. Once they lose the fire in their belly it shows. They begin to get flabby. Don't look as smart as they used to. During the last twelve years I've seen it so many times. Guys who were full of hell, always aggressive – suddenly burn out. The young Turks soon spot that the 'main man' is going soft, ready to be taken. The parallels with boxing are obvious. In the late fifties I remember watching Sugar Ray Robinson – arguably the greatest 'pound for pound' fighter of them all – begin to lose fights to guys he wouldn't have hired as sparring partners ten years earlier. His opponents weren't beating him – it was Old Father Time. The Sugar Man had turned forty.

Frankie Metcalfe is a case in point. He was the number one in Newcastle when I came north in 1970. Though when he's inside he always makes sure he doesn't cross swords with John Bryden. He knows he'd come second.

Only once did I have any bother with him. He'd been put on report for some offence and I had the job of taking him down to A1. Armed with three other screws, I open his cell on D Wing. 'You'll have to pack your kit, Frankie. You're going down on A1.' As I speak, I shoot the lock. 'They've not fucking put me on report for that? It was just a difference of opinion with the shop instructor. Ah want to see somebody. I ain't fucking having that.'

I move into the cell. Two of my officers come in behind me. The third stands at the open door.

'Frank, you've been long enough at the game to know the routine. I've come up here with orders to take you down the block. I'm not gonny run back down and say to the Chief or the Governor, "Oh, Frankie says he's not going down the block till somebody comes and sees him." Here!' I hand him the chit. 'It's all on there. The instructor says you wouldn't do what he told you, and you also gave him a good slagging. You know you'll see the Governor in the morning, and that's when you'll get your chance to put your case.'

'I'm gettin' put down the chokey block for fuck-all!' I can see he's on the edge of losing it, weighing up if he should add 'assault screws' to the original offence. I've already told my officers that if he does start, they've immediately to draw their sticks and use them.

'Frank?' I say. He looks at me. 'Now you're far too big for me to tackle. Probably knock fuck out o' me in two minutes flat. But if you do start, it'll be really messy. I've ordered my laddos here to use their sticks. If needs be there'll be more screws come up. Whether it's the easy way or the hard way – you'll still be going down the block. We all know you're a hard man. You don't have to keep proving it. You're on report for next to nowt. Add assault screws and you'll finish up down the strongbox for a couple of weeks AND lose remission. Just cool it, eh?'

He stares down at the floor, thinking. I hook my thumbs in my pockets so my right hand is almost touching Charlie Wood. Just in case.

'Ah, fuck it!' He starts packing his kit.

As we come away from A1, Davey Sanders falls into step beside me. 'You handled that well, Bob. I thought he was about to go at one point.'

'You know what did the trick?' I don't wait for him to answer. 'When I said to him "You're far too big for me. Probably knock fuck out o' me in two minutes flat." Too many screws feel they've got to stand toe to toe with that type. You don't. The thing is NOT to challenge them. Don't set yourself in front of them as if you're ready to take them on. When I said that, it defused the situation – and also did his ego a bit of good. I'm acknowledging he's a hard case, I'm not threatening him, BUT I'm also saying that he's going down the block. Easy way or hard way.'

All that was nearly five years ago. Frankie's been in quite a few times since then. He just got sent down a few months back. Jeez, what a change. It's been almost a year since he was last in. I nearly didn't recognised him. Now he's fat and has his hair trimmed as short as can be. As soon as I saw him, I knew his time had passed. The great days have gone. The King is dead. Long live the King!

For years he and his usual entourage – four or five lesser-spotted shitbags – have gone round many of Newcastle's pubs and clubs. They're usually just in for ten minutes. The landlord puts up a drink for them, slips Frankie a couple of tenners, and on they go to the next premises. It's normally a Saturday night. If the landlord doesn't oblige, a 'fight' will be started. One or two chairs will be hoyed at the collection of glasses, bottles and mirrors behind the bar. It's cheaper just to pay up with a smile.

Now and again he comes up against someone who has 'insurance'. I've been a few times to one of the better clubs in the 'toon' and the boss has got to know that I'm a screw. We're sitting talking. 'You'll know Frankie Metcalfe?' he says.

'Frankie? He's such a regular in the jail he gets invited tae the staff dances.'

'He thought he'd try a bit of muscle up here a while back. I told him nothing doing, so he threatened that next time he appeared there'd be a bit of bother if I didn't cough up.' The manager laughs. 'What he doesn't know is, we have "friends", shall we say, in London. So by the next Saturday I've got it all organised. One of my staff, who knows Frankie, is standing outside at the entrance. When he sees him appear with his usual hangers-on, he gives a whistle up the stairs to warn the "reception committee". In comes the bold Frankie with his team and they start to climb the stairs. Just before they reach halfway, two rather large gentlemen from London step out onto the landing. "Just stop there," they say. They both open wide one side of their topcoats to let Mr Metcalfe and his cohorts see that they have guns in shoulder-holsters. "Don't EVER come back into this club. Be warned!" So Frankie and his chums turn tail, and that's the last I've seen of them.'

I laugh. 'Well, you won't be seeing much of him at the moment. He's inside again.'

A few days after my visit to the nightclub, I'm doing suppers on D Wing. I open Frankie's door. After our face to face of a few years previously he and I have got on fine and I never get any bother with him. 'So how is Francis this evening?'

'Nowt's a bother, boss.' He lifts his jug, about to go for some fresh water. I can't resist it.

'I was somewhere up the toon on Saturday night, where you can't go!' I flash him a smile.

He gives an assertive shrug of his shoulders. 'I don't think so, boss. Ah can gan anywhere ah like in the toon. Anywhere!'

'That's not what I heard in ________'s club.'

He's lost for words for a moment, then he recovers. 'Ah well, don't play fair them bastards. Bring in guys wi' shooters, don't they?' He stomps off down the landing, trying to keep his dignity.

That was more than a year ago. Now he's back. Fat, out of condition, and not yet forty. The great days are over. Well, what he would consider as great days. He got himself into bother about a week ago, finished up doing seven days on A1. While he was down there he got into more trouble – so now he's down the strongbox. He's doing seven days in there. The strongbox is situated at the end of D Wing. It has no windows; the bed is just a raised dais with the thinnest of mattresses on it. No sheets, just a few blankets. No table, no chair, just a piss-pot. There's no reading material either. It wouldn't be any use if there was, since they spend all their time in there in the dark. Frankie's on bread and water. He's only unlocked to slop out and have his one hour of exercise a day. Otherwise he sits in there in the pitch dark, for hours on end. It's a waste of time trying to make a noise, as no bugger can hear you. The cell is isolated. You go through two doors to get to it, then there's the cell door. You can shout and bawl, bang your plastic piss-pot on the wall, but what's the point? You're not bothering the screws. You're not bothering anybody. Nobody even knows you're doing it.

We've done the suppers, got the wing locked up. 'Right, we'll do Frankie.' My officer follows me as I unlock the doors, then his cell. The light spills in from behind me. There's not much of it, but after the pitch dark it's enough to make him blink as he rises.

'Good evening, Francis. You want to use the recess?'

'Aye, might as well. Ah'll fill me mug wi' fresh watter while ah'm at it. Ah knocked the bugger ower in the dark.' He goes stiffly off in the direction of the recess. As I watch him, I think back to the shape he was in just a year or so ago. It's amazing how rapidly some of them lose it. It must suddenly hit them one day – 'I can't hack it anymore' – and they just let go. I look in through the cell door. A chunk of bread lies on the boards of his bed. He might get a bit of that weight off on his enforced diet. He comes back, goes into the cell, sits on the raised dais. His eyes have got used to the light during the last few minutes. I stand at the heavy door.

'Many days you got left to do?'

'Just two.'

I reach into my pocket and take out a wrapped chocolate caramel. 'Here!' I throw it to him. He catches it.

'Thanks, boss.'

'Make sure you get rid of the paper.'

'Ah'll put it in me piss-pot.'

I bang him up, then lock the other two doors. I walk along a quiet, suppered D Wing. What was that old movie that was on TV the other day? Anthony Quinn was in it. I read the book years ago. Yeah. *Requiem For a Heavyweight*. That was it.

A Parting of the Ways

In June '74 we have a fortnight at Morecambe. For the last twelve years, since I joined the Prison Service, we've always taken our two weeks with Nancy's folks at Seafield. No doubt Nancy hopes this family holiday will make me realise what I'll be giving up if we part. It doesn't. Mainly because I won't let myself think about it. Instead, I count the days until we get back and I can see Barbara. She has proved to be the longest lasting of all my affairs. So far. It has now been going on for more than a year. Although physical attraction is a major part of our relationship, we've also grown extremely fond of one another. There are times when we talk about how wonderful it would be to live together, but at the moment she feels she's not quite ready to make that commitment. Her kids are still quite young, she'd rather they were a bit older.

When we come back home, I feel more down than ever. During our stay at Morecambe we were out and about every day; there was always something to do. I took great pleasure in Scott and Nancy's enjoyment of being let loose on all the seaside attractions. Now there's nothing to look forward to and I'm also becoming more and more disenchanted with working at Durham. Worst of all, though I try not to think about it, I know I'm treating Nancy very badly. I attempt to justify it by telling myself I don't love her anymore, that if we stay together 'just for the kids', that isn't the basis for a marriage. I tell myself that if we do part, she'll come to realise it was all for the best. At last, as I knew would happen, it wears Nancy down. It's a month or so after our return from the summer holiday . . .

I walk into the kitchen. Nancy turns to face me; she's just lit a cigarette. 'Do ye no' think we should talk? We just go aboot aw the time and we know things are gettin' worse between us.'

I stop in front of her, spread my arms, then let them fall to my sides. 'I don't see what there is to talk about.'

'Aboot us. Oor marriage, aboot the kids. We used to be happy . . .'

'Huh! We were happy when we were at Birmingham, aw'right. I never used to go anywhere. You were gettin' oot tae the bingo four nights a week, you were trying tae dictate how often we had sex – and even when we did, you made it plain it was just something you had tae put up with. YOU were quite happy 'cause you felt you were running things.'

'Well that's why ah feel we should talk. Ah'm willing tae change tae save oor marriage. Surely it's no' too late tae . . .'

'You can't see it, can you? I don't love you anymore. I don't want tae live with ye anymore. I know if we part I'll be losing the kids – but I'm prepared tae pay that price. Can't you understand, I really don't want to live with you, be in the same house as you . . .' As I speak, the tears start rolling down her face. She looks so forlorn. I realise, see it in her face, the hurt I'm causing her. I burst into tears. I step forward, take her in my arms, kiss her cheek then just hug her tight. 'Nancy, I know it's terrible for you. But I don't love you anymore. I just don't want to live with you. The longer we're together the more I realise I don't want to be with you, sleep with you, be around you. I'm sorry, but that's the way it is. If you were to say, "Look, ah'll change completely, be exactly how you want me to be", it wouldn't make any difference now. Even before we left Birmingham I was beginning to feel a bit like this, so it hasn't all happened since we came up here. Being at Durham and going out and about has just sort of speeded things up. It's too late now to save it. As far as I'm concerned, it's over.'

The next few weeks bring no rows, no arguments. We live together in a strangely peaceful, sociable way. I go out when I want. When I return there are no accusations, no baleful looks or long silences. Towards the end of July, Nancy reaches a decision. I come home from work just after five thirty p.m. She's cooking the dinner and turns her head as I come in.

'Ah've decided tae go back up tae Scotland wi' the kids.'

'Oh!' I get a pang in my stomach. I can't figure out if it's pleasure or pain. Pain, really. But I have to see it through. 'Are ye gonny stay at your mother's?'

'There's a house vacant on the Miners' Rows, you know, the ones that run along the main road?'

'Oh, aye. I know the ones ye mean.' Instantly a picture comes into my mind; Nancy in her camel-hair coat as we stand behind those rows, in the shadows, doing a bit of kissing and cuddling before she goes home. Jeez, I was crazy about her then. 'So will you get it?'

'Aye, ma brother, wi' him working for the council, he made enquiries. They'll let me huv it.'

'Oh, well, that's good.' This obviously isn't a snap decision.

'What aboot furniture? Ah'm gonny need some stuff.'

'Yeah, of course. Take what ye need. Obviously all the kids' bedroom furniture. Ye can take anything ye want as long as you leave me a bed and some cooking utensils. Remember, ye can't take the telly. It's rented.'

'Aye, ah know.'

I waken up just as the alarm gives a click. It'll start ringing in a few seconds. Nancy lies next to me. I wonder if she's sleeping? Probably not. It's Tuesday 6 August 1974. Her brother Alec is coming down with a van today to collect the furniture and Nancy. And the kids. I get up. All the time I'm getting ready it's continually on my mind. Nancy's leaving with the kids today. I sat with Scott and Nancy yesterday and tried to tell them that their mother and me breaking up doesn't mean I don't love them anymore. Nancy junior's okay about it; she thinks I'm too strict. Scott doesn't want to take it in. He's my best pal, we're always playing together. He's losing his dad and his pal. Once he's up in Scotland and realises he'll only see me a couple of times a year, it's going to take him a long time to get over it. Both their birthdays are this month – he'll turn thirteen, Nancy eleven.

I have no appetite; I just have a cup of tea. I put my uniform jacket on. Nancy comes into the kitchen and I stand up. 'I'll just go up and say cheerio to the two of them.'

I climb the stairs, enter the bedroom. I give little Nancy a gentle shake.

'Mmmm?'

'Daddy's away tae his work. You're going up tae Granny's the day. Don't forget, your daddy loves ye.'

'Mmm, Mmmm . . .' I kiss her on her cheek. I wish I could kiss her longer. I turn to Scott. He's lying with his eyes open. 'Hiyah, pal.' He doesn't say anything. I stroke his hair, kiss him on the cheek. I whisper, 'Scott, it's VERY important you realise your daddy loves you as much as ever. It's just Mammy and me aren't gettin' on so it's best we don't live together anymore. You're still ma best pal. You and Nancy will be coming down for holidays, we're still gonny see each other. Anyway, I've got to go to work. I'll be seeing the two of you soon.' I give each of them another kiss. 'Bye.'

Scott barely whispers, 'Bye.' Nancy just 'Mmmm's.

I go downstairs, put my mac on, go through to the living-room. Nancy's standing by the fireplace, smoking.

'Well, I'm gonny have to go.'

She draws on her cigarette. 'While ah'm away that might help ye make your mind up whether ye want me or not. It's up to you tae decide what ye want tae do.'

'I know. Right, I hope everything goes okay. Do ye want a kiss before I go?'

'Might as well.'

I go over and kiss her on the cheek; I squeeze her forearm as I do.

'Right, ah'll see yah.'

'Cheerio.'

I climb into the Volvo and drive away. There are tears in my eyes. God, I feel so fuckin' rotten.

As the time nears one o'clock I keep having terrible doubts. It's like a pain in my stomach. Should I say to the Centre P.O., I'll have to have an hour off. Domestic problems,' and fly home in the car. The van will be at the door, probably half loaded. Should I say to Nancy, 'Look, will we have one last go at making it work? I don't want you to go. I don't think I can stand losing the kids, so we'll HAVE to make it work.' Should I say to Alec, 'Sorry for wasting your time . . .'

I look at the large clock above the Centre. Should I? C'mon, think logically about it. You know that within a fortnight – within ten days – you'll be saying to yourself, 'Why didn't I let her go? It's never going to work.' In a few short years, and they *will* be short years, the kids will be up and away. You'll be left with just Nancy – and you'll rue the day you didn't let her go.

I look at the clock. It's gone two. They'll be well up the road by now. It's for the best. In the long run it's for the best.

At last five thirty comes. I drive home to Langley Road. The house looks the same from the outside. I go inside. The kitchen looks pretty much like always. I go into the living-room. The fireside rug has gone. I'm surprised she's left the suite. The mantelpiece is bare, most of the pictures are gone. The ones that I appear in have been left. I go upstairs. Our double bed is still there. I slowly push open the kids' bedroom door. The room is empty. Stripped. I think back to being in here this morning; those two innocent sleepy heads. I go downstairs. Sit on the sofa. And cry.

Getting Used to It

I miss my kids. To come home to a house without Scott and Nancy running around takes a long time to get used to. Yet the decision to split with Nancy must have been the right one. I find I don't miss her.

I decide that keeping busy and, whenever possible, having a laugh, are the best ways to help me get through this difficult period. For a long time I've toyed with the idea of learning a second language. I've been appointed to the job of gatekeeper. I find when I'm on the gate there are spells of time when I've little to do, especially on evening duty and when I'm weekend 'on'. Instead of spending my time reading books or magazines, I buy a beginners' course in German. The main reason for my choice is because, being Scottish, I have no problem with the pronunciation. Soon, whenever I have spare time on the gate, I can be found studying my primer. The hours begin to add up. At home I play the cassettes which came with the course. Like all beginners in German, at first I get the impression it's going to be dead easy, until I come up against grammar – and gender! Masculine, feminine and neuter. In English we say, 'the table', 'the lamp' and 'the car'. In German we have *der Tisch* (m), *die Lampe* (f) and *das Auto* (n). This stage is what sorts out the dedicated student from the rest. Many fall by the wayside when they come up against the complexities of grammar and gender. Being someone who hates to be bested, I knuckle down and eventually reach that wonderful plateau where all of a sudden it becomes clear – I finally get it.

* * *

My study of another language fulfils my need to keep busy. There's also that eternal quest of most Glaswegians and, I'm sure, others, to have a laugh when you're at work . . .

The great days of sessions and assizes have finished. A Crown Court has been established at Newcastle, and I'm on my fortnight there. The same judges and recorders try the same types of cases in the same courtrooms, but no longer do they sit for certain periods of time – as in quarter sessions. Crime is a growth industry. Not only do courts now run all the time without a break, but there are more courtrooms and more judges needed to deal with the rising number of cases. Crown Courts, which combine the duties of the old sessions and assizes, are now the norm in all cities.

I'm at the Moot Hall in Newcastle. A beautiful Georgian building, dating back some two centuries, it boasts a couple of impressive courtrooms downstairs, all polished wood and brass, which were probably last updated when Queen Victoria ruled supreme. Underneath these courts are an extensive network of passageways and rooms. At the far end of this honeycomb, furthest away from the room where the officers normally sit, is a small cell complex. By the Friday of my second week there are only two cases to be dealt with. One prisoner has been brought from Durham, the other has been on bail. With such a small list it's been decided I can take charge without the need for a P.O. to be there – an S.O. will be enough. I have three officers with me: Jack Walton, Alan Briggs and Brian Slater. Jack and Alan are good mates of mine and regular drinking companions. With my lifelong aim of 'having a laugh', I've brought along a rubber skull mask which was originally bought to play ghosts with the kids now and again.

By mid-afternoon things are quiet down below. The remand we brought from the jail this morning has been dealt with by means of a non-custodial sentence, so he's been discharged. The guy who came off bail is up in the dock of number one court. Jack and I are stationed downstairs. Brian has come down for a coffee. When he returns to the dock, Alan will come down for a break. I suddenly remember I've got the skull mask with me. As Brian leaves to go back upstairs, I take the mask from my mac pocket.

'I'm going to the cells. When Alan comes down, tell him to go along and ask "the prisoner" if he wants a cuppa. I'll frighten the crap out of him.'

We don't actually have anyone in custody, but I assume Alan will have forgotten that. The cells are far removed from where we sit. At the far end of a long corridor, on the right, is an ancient, heavily-studded door. Upon opening this door, an officer is faced by one of the half-dozen or so cells. The top half of this cell's door consists of thin iron bars, through which you can see into the cell. Whenever we have prisoners in custody, the lights in the block are always on. Today, of course, the lights are off. There's nobody in there except . . .

I pull the heavy main door closed behind me, then, in almost complete darkness, open the cell door which faces it. Once in the cell I put the skull mask on, close the door behind me and stand towards the rear. I'm wearing dark trousers and a navy blue pullover. I pull my jersey up so it covers my white shirt collar and place my hands behind my back. The only thing that is pale now in all this blackness is – the skull! I await Alan.

Soon I hear his footsteps coming along the corridor. As briefed, Jack has asked him to 'see if the prisoner wants a cuppa.' He stops outside the studded door and swings it open. As he will tell us later, 'I wondered why the lights were out. If we've someone in cells they should be on.' I watch through the eyes of the skull as a quizzical look comes over his face. The cells are unlit. Obligingly not switching on the lights, he takes a step inside. I move my foot slightly to make a scuffling noise to attract his attention. He looks up, then through the bars into the cell. As the place is in darkness, all he has to see by is the spill of light from the corridor behind him. There, in the gloom of the cell, floating in mid-air, is a skull! I watch his face. He freezes, his eyes growing wide; he emits an 'ooooOOOOH!' and turns quickly, pushes the heavy outside door shut and makes off smartly along the corridor to the comfort of company.

'Does he want one?' asks Jack.

'Eh, no. There's nobody in the cells,' he says.

'Oh, of course,' says Jack, 'I'm forgetting, the other lad got away, didn't he?'

'Yeah,' says Alan. He seems a bit distracted.

A few minutes later I enter the room. 'Everything all right, lads?'

'Yeah.'

I turn to Alan. 'You just been down the cells?'

'Yeah.' The penny drops. 'Was that you, yah bastard? Ah nearly shit meself!'

'How come you never said anything to Jack when you came back here?'

'Ah wasn't that sure what I'd seen, then I thought, these gits won't believe me. So ah said nowt!'

A month or so later, I'm on a week of nights. The skull mask goes on duty with me . . .

It's coming up for six a.m. All is quiet. Big Brian McLachlan, a Scot, is A Wing patrol. A Wing is remote from the Centre. It runs off, in a curve, from the far end of D Wing. The oldest wing in the prison, it has long had the reputation of being haunted. When you're down the far end of it, pegging the night clock, you are as remote from your few colleagues as it's possible to be. The P.O. and me are the only two with keys. I have the ordinary cell and pass. The P.O. has the night keys. To save electricity, during the night every second or third landing light is switched off. This makes the wings gloomier than ever and creates areas of shadow.

We sit companionably in the rest room. The other pair of night patrols know what my intention is. For the last twenty minutes I've been steering the conversation round to tales of patrolling certain parts of the grounds at night – especially the area where those convicts executed over the last two centuries lie in unmarked graves. Brian obligingly brings up the subject of A Wing himself. 'Mind, ah'm never ower happy when ah'm doon the far end o' A Wing. Ah've heard some tales aboot that wing.'

I shake my head. 'Aye, so have I. When ye think o' the folk that have been locked up doon there, and occasionally died, ower the last two hundred years. The first prisoners in there were Frenchmen, taken during the Napoleonic Wars.'

'Aye, but ah've heard it's maistly a wumman,' says Brian. 'They say it's that Mary Ann Cotton.'

'Oh, aye. The poisoner. She got hung some time in the 1870s or '80s. She'd done away with nearly two dozen. That was an evil woman, that yin. I've heard she's been seen a few times over the years.'

'Ah'm quite sure it's her that's the "presence" doon there,' says Brian. He looks at his watch. 'Anywye, time ah was away tae dae ma mornin' check and get the lights oan.' He rises and without much enthusiasm, sets off for the isolated wing.

'Right!' I say. 'My moment has come.' Not only have I brought the skull mask, but when I came on last night I opened up the cleaner on D1 and got a spare bed sheet from him. I now head for A Wing. I sneak a look round a corner and spot Brian as he slowly makes his way along one side of A4, switching on cell lights, flicking spyholes open to check his numbers, then taking off the outside night bolt. As he progresses above me I'm one landing below, on A3, directly underneath him. The entire wing, including empty cells, was locked up last night and the night bolts slipped into their slots.

Choosing an empty cell, I quietly take off the bolt, unlock it and leave the door wide open. Although the cell light is off, I reach up and take the bulb out just in case Brian tries to switch it on. I then stand at the far end of the cell, under the window. On goes the skull mask and I wrap myself from head to foot in the bed sheet. Then I wait for Brian.

I listen as he comes down the stairs and starts on the threes. As he comes along the dimly-lit landing, he expects to find things exactly as they were last evening when he checked his numbers: all cells, including empties, locked. He approaches the cell in which Mary Ann Cotton waits for him. When he's just a couple of steps away, he notices the door is wide open! How can that be? I watch as he stops at the entrance to the cell. He looks in to the darkness.

'FUCK ME!' He takes off.

Though I'm convulsed with laughter, it only takes me a few seconds to reach the door of the cell. I look along the landing. Nobody there! It's almost 100 yards to the end of the wing. In spite of being 6 feet 2 inches and around 15 stone, Brian has easily shaved about 3 seconds off the world record. Alas, it hasn't been ratified.

I spot him down on A2. 'Don't forget you've got the threes to finish.'

'Yah bastard! Ah nearly filled ma troosers just noo!'

The Best Laid Plans . . .

The ambience of the Dun Cow surrounds me. I'm amongst friends. Light reflects off the bottles lining the shelves behind the bar; the different coloured spirits sparkle like fairy lights. Tommy's busy filling my pint glass with draught Carlsberg lager and I've replied to the seven or eight greetings which met me as I slid open the door. It doesn't seem too busy tonight – it's only crammed. The perfect pint is placed in front of me.

'What's thy fettle?'

'Oh, not so bad, Thomas.'

'Getting used to being on your own?'

'Wellll . . . I miss the bairns. But, like they say, time's a great healer. It's almost two months now.'

'Mind,' says Tommy, 'I liked the look of that lass you brought in last Sunday afternoon. Barbara, wasn't it? She's the one you've been seeing for a while if ah mind right.'

'Aye, that's her.' I take a long draught of lager. 'Over a year, now.'

'So, is she gonna fill the vacancy?'

'No. There was a time when it looked like it. But she won't leave her kids. Not at the moment anyway. I think it's gonny peter out. It's not going anywhere, Tom.'

'What you gonna do?'

'I intend, as they say, to play the field. I'm as good as free, so I'm going to have one whale of a time. There's a lot of women out there who need a good fettling.' I finish the last of my pint and slide the glass over to Tommy for a refill. 'And I'm just the lad for the job!'

* * *

I don't know it yet, but I won't even get off the starting blocks.

On Monday 7 October 1974 I start another fortnight at Newcastle Crown Court. It's around ten a.m. I've detailed the officers to their various jobs: dock officers; cells; records. I climb the stairs up to the dock of number one court and make my way out into the grand entrance hall. I knock on the door of the police office which is situated under the broad staircase. I open the door and find, as expected, the usual suspects – Tommy and Leo, two long-serving constables and Inspector Collingwood, better known as 'The Bugler' – though not to his face.

'Hello, Jock. Is thoo back here again?'

It had been on my first or second spell of duty at Newcastle, in 1970, when I'd first heard the inspector's nickname. Of course, I had to make enquiries . . .

'How come your inspector gets called "The Bugler", Tommy?'

'Eh, lad. Noo mind, divn't cahll him that tiv his face. He hates it. It's a full twenty-five years since he first got it. He'd come oot the army after war service and right away joined the polis. So yee can imagine, he's this fresh-faced young constable, "fruit salad" on his tunic, dead keen, anxious to do well. He's on duty one Saturday up the Bigg Market and there's a bit of a demonstration gannin' on. Ah can't remember now, but ah think it were the market lads, ye kna', stallholders or summat. Anyways, it were gettin' oot o' hand, bit o' fisticuffs here and there, and the polis were ootnumbered and they'd had tae retreat. So their sergeant is trying tae rally them tae make a baton charge, restore order. And young PC Collingwood is trying to help. Not being lang oot the army, and kna'ing most of the lads are ex-service like himself, he has a brilliant idea. There's a rag man nearby with his horse and cart – and they ahlwis have a bugle tae blaw so's folk kna' they're aboot, divn't they? So the bold lad sprints ower tae the cart, grabs the bugle off the lad – and sounds the Charge!'

'He didn't!'

'He did. And from that day tiv this they've never let him live it doon at Pilgrim Street Station.

It was during my second week at the Crown Court that it happened . . .

It's just gone ten a.m. I'm standing in the hall talking to Leo, the duty policeman. There's an upstairs landing that runs round the inside of the building above our heads, giving access to a couple of large rooms and the court offices. I happen to look up. 'Gee whizz, Leo! Who's the blonde?' A girl is walking along, carrying some papers.

Leo glances up. 'Oh, that's our Pat. She's a smasher, ain't she?'

'Not half.' I watch until she vanishes through one of the doors. I have GOT to get to know her.

The courts have risen. Down below, the screws are busy getting the records done to save reception some work back at the jail. One of the last jobs we do at the end of the day is go up to the office and collect the various committals, remand orders and any other documents needed to show those prisoners in our cells are being held legally, and for how long. Normally I just phone upstairs, speak to someone called Vi, and tell her which prisoners I still require orders for. She'll ring me back when they're ready and I send one of my lads up to collect them. But not today. I intend to call for them personally. If I'm lucky, the blonde will be there. She is.

'Hello, I'm Bob Douglas. You must be Vi.'

'Hiyah! I am.'

'We're always speaking on the phone. So I thought it was time to put faces to voices.' I nod in the direction of Pat. 'And what do they call your friend the movie star over there?' The two of them laugh.

Vi turns towards Pat. 'I think you'll have to watch yourself with this 'un, Pat.'

I decide to go in head first. 'She's right! I saw you walk along the landing this morning, so I've decided that from now on I'll be coming up to collect the warrants myself!'

Pat blushes. I look up on the wall. There's a large poster of Sinatra with his trademark snap-brimmed fedora. I nod at it. 'There's obviously someone works in here who has good taste.'

Vi smiles. 'That's mine. I love him.'

'Me too – though probably not quite in the same way as you.'

I stay chatting for a while. Pat mentions that on Saturday night she's going to a barn dance at Haydon Bridge. 'It's a long time since I've been to one of them,' I say.

'You're welcome to come if you want,' she blushes again, 'but I live at Corbridge. That's a bit of a long way for you to come.'

'Not if I'm going to be in your company.'

'My mum and dad are also going.'

'Good! It'll be a chance to meet my future in-laws!'

'Eeeeh, Pat!' says Vi, 'Isn't he the bold one?'

I smile. 'I've always believed you can't get into trouble for telling the truth. See you on Saturday night.'

As I go downstairs I'm walking on air. If this was a musical, I'd tap-dance all the way back to the cells. Oh, well – that's my plans for playing the field just gone out of the window. She's single, I'm separated. I'll have to let Barbara know it's time to call it quits. If this works out the way I hope it will, I intend to play it straight down the middle. IF Pat and I become a steady thing, I intend to see only her. No cheating. Jeez! And all this from just a glance up at a girl walking along a landing. I haven't even taken her out on a date. Yet I know. *This* is the one!

Goodbye to All . . . What?

It all just falls into place. I meet Pat's mum and dad, Ethel and Sid Alfrey, and we hit it off right away. Ethel will tell me later, 'As soon as I met you I thought, he's the one for our Pat.'

'That makes two of us!' will be my honest reply.

Within a month, Pat has moved in with me and we settle down to living in sin. At twenty-six, she's nine years younger than me. We are instantly compatible, liking the same movies and music. On one of our early dates we're sitting in a café. A record comes on the jukebox. As soon as I hear the first few bars I say, 'Oh, I just LOVE this rec—' She interrupts me:

'Maria Muldaur, "Midnight at the Oasis", me too!' It becomes 'our' record. The following week we go up the toon to see *That's Entertainment* and love every toe-tapping, all-singing, all-dancing minute. We regularly go to the Tyneside Cinema, which is also up the toon. It specialises in the best of foreign movies and classics from the great days of Hollywood. I feel I'm in a time machine as we sit in the dark and watch, on a small square screen, Humphrey Bogart and Ingrid Bergman in *Casablanca*, Joan Crawford in *Mildred Pierce* or the wonderful *Seven Samurai*. Now and again there are new movies; ones which haven't been given a general release into the big chains, yet, thanks to the nous of the enthusiasts who run cinemas like the Tyneside, they will gradually build up a cult following until word of mouth leads to them being shown nationwide. A prime example is Mel Brooks' *The Producers*, starring Zero Mostel and Gene Wilder. Considered too way out at first, it is now acknowledged as a classic.

* * *

The first time I take Pat to a dance at the officers' club on a Saturday night, I know exactly how it will go. As I come striding in with her on my arm, conversation dies. All heads turn to watch as I deliberately amble diagonally across the dance floor with this gorgeous blonde on my arm. There's more than a whiff of sexual jealousy. From both sexes.

My life now slips into a happy, settled phase – outside the jail. When I'm weekend off we're regularly over at Corbridge. As '74 turns into '75 I have Scott and Nancy down a couple of times for visits. We enjoy ourselves, but I probably get more out of it than they do. They're growing up – and growing away from me. Seeing each other occasionally does not build, or maintain, the closeness that living together does. Scott and I still play-fight and fence with one another, but it is now with a slight feeling of embarrassment. He knows I'm doing it to try and please him, to rebuild the bonds that have been broken. Nancy was becoming quite independent even before the split. Still only twelve, she's continuing on that route. They both know I love them, they get told regularly, and there are always plenty of hugs and kisses. But from now on, the closeness I wish for will only be given to their mother. I can't have my cake and eat it. Nancy senior will prove to be generous in matters to do with Scott and Nancy. She doesn't try to use them as a weapon, or turn them against me. I can ring up at any time and speak to them. They are free to come down to Durham whenever they want. That's as good as I could hope for. Perhaps more than I deserve.

On 13 July '75 I do my last shift as gatekeeper. I'm asked if I'd like to go into the prisoners' canteen. It's a two-year post. I've no doubt that, as with the gate, these posts are to keep me away from the mainstream jobs in the wings – I upset too many officers and P.O.s with my pointed remarks and criticisms. I refer to them as my 'malicious truths'. I'm quite happy to say yes to the job, especially as my best mate, Jack Walton, is on the staff. Soon

I'm immersed in the world of double entry bookkeeping and stocktaking. Prisoners at this period in time are not paid in cash, though this will shortly change. The earnings they make in their workshop are credited to them. When they file through the canteen they come to the counter, give us their name and number, and we tell them how much they have to spend. This varies from the basic £1.50 up to £3.50 or so. The major purchase is tobacco, followed by such items as a tub of margarine, a pot of jam or various sweets. Other items are on sale; birthday cards, ball-point pens etc. For canteen, read corner shop.

I'm taking over from S.O. Jack Sunter. Jack is very much my type of screw. Around fifty years of age, he is a Second World War veteran who was wounded in the landings at Anzio in 1943. Maybe 6 feet tall, well built and with a good strong jaw, he stands no nonsense. We work together for my first month in the canteen, so he can show me the ropes. The barometer of Jack's mood is always expressed in his jaw. When a con begins to annoy him the jaw seems to jut out and slightly to one side. The word 'belligerent' comes to mind . . .

There has been a riot at Hull Prison and several wings were wrecked. We receive a large intake of homeless – or should that be 'cell-less' – convicts. Unlike Durham, Hull is a prison which doesn't do court duties. The prisoners there have all been sentenced and are serving their time. The majority of those we've received have taken no part in the riot. Unfortunately we don't know who has, or hasn't, been involved. All of these cons have been earning somewhere from £3 to £4 a week on piecework. As we have no record of what they've been earning, or how much credit they might have saved up, all we can pay them is the basic £1.50 – less than half their usual wage. The eighty or so ex-Hull inmates we've received are not happy bunnies.

* * *

Jack and I are behind the counter. The first of the refugees enters. This is now their third week at Durham.

'What's your number and name?' I say.

'406334 Duncan.'

I look down the sheet and half turn towards Jack. '£1.50, Mr Sunter.'

'£1.50?! I've got nearly £5 in credit from Hull, boss.'

'We've never had any paperwork yet from Hull. Till we get it, all you'll be getting is thirty bob a week,' says Jack.

'This is three weeks now. 'Ow long are we gonna 'ave to wait to get our rightful money?'

I watch Jack's jaw begin to stir into life. 'I haven't a clue,' he says.

'This ain't right. How come they 'aven't sent up the paperwork yet?'

Jack leans forward, his jaw fully engaged. 'Because the screws down at Hull are clearing up a wrecked jail. It'll be months before the place is back in action. The canteen was one of the places that was ransacked – robbed, then wrecked. So finding the wages sheets, if they still exist, is not a priority for the Hull screws. In fact, it's probably bottom o' the list. Until we get them, if we ever do, we don't know how much you had. Right, now you've got thirty bob to spend in here. Do you want it, or don't yah?' His jaw is now on full jut.

The con, wisely, reads the signs. Muttering under his breath, he makes his purchases. I decide to go outside and warn the others.

'Ah'll just go and put the rest of this Hull lot in the picture, Jack. Two minutes.' I go out onto D2. There are thirty to forty lined up. 'LISTEN UP, you Hull lads. To save time, and to save repeating the same thing over and over, we have NOT received any paperwork from Hull. I don't think the Hull screws see searching for the wages sheets as a priority. They've got other things to do.' I pause for the expected mutters, 'rhubarb rhubarbs' and other sounds of dissatisfaction. I give them a nice smile. 'If you've any complaints, make them to the fuckers who wrecked the jail. It wasn't the screws – it was your fellow cons. If you start moaning on or arguing in here, you'll finish up GETTING NOWT! So you've been told in advance.'

Although their faces betray their real feelings, the rest go through without complaint.

Pat and I settle into a steady routine. Every second weekend, when I'm off, we either go over to Corbridge or Ethel comes to us – alone, since Sid sadly passed away not long after Pat and I met. We've also become great friends with Pat's cousin, Kathleen, and her husband, Bobby. They live in Kirkintilloch. Kathleen's mum, Noeleen, is Ethel's sister. She is also a widow, and lives in Glasgow. Noeleen had met her husband, George Clarke, a Glasgow man, when he was stationed locally during the war. So I'm not the only Glaswegian to have thrust himself upon the family! Sadly, George, who became a taxi driver in Glasgow, died before I came on the scene.

As we go into 1976 I find I'm becoming more and more disenchanted with working at Durham. I'm coming up for fifteen years in the job, then there comes a chance to – perhaps – get out of it. There is a vacancy for a P.O. in Spandau Prison in West Berlin. Most members of the public believe that it's the military who guard the dwindling number of major war criminals in Spandau. It's not. They only guard the perimeter. Inside the jail, since 1945, it is prison officers from Britain, America, France and Russia – the 'Four Powers' – who guard the inmates. Vacancies rarely come up. Once a P.O. gets this job they are there until they retire, or die. Considered a plum job, it carries extra wages and allowances to cover accommodation and living expenses for staff and their families. Over the years the small number of inmates has dwindled until, with the release of Albert Speer and Baldur von Shirach in 1966, Rudolf Hess becomes the sole inmate. Three of the four allies would be willing to release him, but the

Russians refuse. While Hess is in Spandau, the Russians have the right to regularly take their turn parading through West Berlin when they mount the military guard at the prison. They don't wish to give it up.

As I'm about due for promotion to P.O. I apply to be considered for the post. I'm added to the list of applicants. I hope the fact I'm still studying German may swing it for me.

Alas, late in '76 I'm extremely disappointed when a P.O. from Stafford Prison gets the vacancy. Just as in the army, the chance of a posting to Germany ends in disappointment. My growing dissatisfaction with working at Durham, missing out on the Spandau job, and becoming more and more fed up with the long hours I work, all help me to make up my mind. It's time for a change. I know it'll mean a big drop in wages, but I want a five-day week, more time off. Quality of life is my new maxim.

As 1977 begins I decide to work on until I complete fifteen years' service, then resign. When I leave, my pension will be frozen. When I joined the Prison Service in 1962 I brought two years' National Service and almost eighteen months with the gas-board with me. As one was a government job and the other with a nationalised industry, they are added on to my Prison Service years. I've now got over eighteen years for pension. It's better than nothing.

On Saturday 9 April 1977, I step out through the wicket-gate of Durham Prison for the last time. I've just been up to the Chief's office to hand in my key chain, whistle and truncheon. My resignation is now effective. I head down to the Dun Cow.

'Well, that's it, Tommy. I'm no longer Senior Officer Douglas.'

'Aye, you've done it now, Bob lad. Any regrets?'

'Oh, jeez, no. You've no idea how sick I was of the job. I just hated going through that gate every day.' I finish my pint. 'Right, time to get off home. I'll see you when I see you, Thomas.'

'All the best, Bob.' There's a few officers and some of the regulars in. I leave with good wishes ringing in my ears. I stride along Old Elvet to where the Volvo is parked.

I follow the familiar road out of Durham. Up the hill, under the railway viaduct and on out towards Framwellgate Moor. Time to take stock. I'm thirty-seven years old and I don't have a job. But I'm glad I'm no longer a prison officer. I think back to my teens. Whenever I'd pack a job in I'd always feel confident that, as Mr Micawber would say, 'Something will turn up'. It's fifteen years since I was last unemployed. I don't have any skills, except maybe man-management – and how to INcorrectly use a truncheon to best advantage. Yet, just as I did at seventeen or eighteen, I somehow feel confident that something WILL turn up. Betcha!

Back in the Old Routine

There it is, in the 'Situations Vacant' – a position for a meter reader/collector with the North Eastern Electricity Board (NEEB). With my previous experience of doing the same job for the Scottish Gas Board after I left the army, I write off with my hopes high. I'm called to the HQ of the company on the Team Valley, Gateshead for an interview. A week after that a letter arrives. The job is mine!

Not only have I quickly landed a job, but it's a five-day week one. No more working late in the evenings either. A straightforward eight till four thirty. Though I'll have plenty of time off, it comes at a price. My earnings are cut by half. Adjustments will have to be made. Out goes the Volvo, in comes a Mini Clubman Estate. I'll also have to vacate the married quarters. Now I'm no longer a screw, I have to pay rent. I decide to sit tight until I'm served with an eviction order – it'll give us time to work out what we're going to do. Anyway, the rent's cheap. I sit tight for as long as possible. When the eviction order arrives, we start looking for somewhere to buy. Soon we're moving in to a new two-bedroom flat at Chester Le Street, a few miles from Durham. £7,700. Jeez! There isn't that much money in the world!

I quickly pick up the meter-reading and emptying of slots again. When I left the gas board in 1962 they'd just started to bring in two-shilling meters. Now, fifteen years later, the 'heavy users' have 50p-meters and it won't be long until £1 slots will be installed. Time marches on. I work with a good bunch of lads and I soon become part of the group.

Now and again I meet old customers from my previous life . . .

It's a nice sunny morning. I'm working round Saltwell Road in Gateshead. The area consists entirely of red brick terraces; it's all door-to-door stuff, which makes it easy to get my day's work done. I ring a bell. The householder appears; he's a thin guy in his fifties.

'G' morning. Electric man.' I know his face.

He looks at me. 'Yah bugger! Hello, boss! What are yee daein' here?'

'Hello, Smithy. Well ah'm here tae read yer meter.'

He stands aside, opens the door wide. 'In ye come. Have ye time for a cuppa?'

'Why aye. Ah'll manage a cuppa nae bother.' As I walk in, I think to myself, it was bound to happen. A lot of our 'customer base' at the jail came from Gateshead. He was never any bother, Smithy. In and out every year or two. Bit of thievery now and again; nothing big, never any violence.

'Ah'll get oor lass tiv make a brew. Mary! This is Jock Douglas, used tiv be a screw at the big hoose doon in Durham. Put the kettle on, pet.'

Pat and I have been together now for the best part of two years. We're sitting on the sofa watching Morecambe and Wise. Why not? I turn to face her. 'Do you fancy gettin' married?'

'Are you serious?'

'I've just been sitting here thinking, we seem to work well as a couple – so why not?'

'Eeeeh! That would be lovely. When were you thinking of?'

'As soon as you like. You choose the date.'

She does.

It's the big day. 23 July 1977: a Saturday. With Bobby McKenzie, husband of Pat's cousin Kathleen, as my best man, we are married at Hexham Register Office in the morning. Then it's back to Corbridge where we receive a blessing from the Rev Chadwick at St Andrew's Church in the market-place. So that's me nuptials done!

The reception is held at Piper Close, a grand house on the outskirts of the village. Ethel, Pat's mum, worked for many years for the owner, Mrs Craig, who has kindly offered to let us hold the reception there. Amongst my guests are Tommy Wilson from the Dun Cow, and Jack Walton, Jack Sunter and Ralph Kirby from the prison. As they arrive at Piper Close and walk through the grounds to the impressive house, the consensus seems to be, 'Bob's married into money!' Just for devilment I go along with it!

'By! This is a bit of all right, Bob.' Jack Sunter slowly looks round the drawing-room, takes in the paintings, silver and china.

Pat and me. Durham, 1978.

'Fell on your feet here, Bob lad,' says Tommy.

Mark Kirby, ex-Chief Petty Officer, RN, also casts an eye round the premises. 'Grand big house, this. I'd 'ave trouble finding me bedroom if I supped too much in here one night.'

'Yeah,' I say. 'They're thinking of getting a bigger place, actually.' I keep my face straight.

'Bugger me!' says Kirby.

Right to the present day there are retired prison officers who continue to believe that I can still be found, living in the grand style, somewhere in Northumberland.

With money being somewhat tight, we have a couple of nights in the two-star King's Head Hotel in Kelso, then it's off to Blackpool for a few days. There, we see a couple of really good shows, one with Les Dawson, the other with Eric Sykes, Hattie Jacques and Derek Guyler, which is based on their long-running TV series. Then, all too quickly, it's back to work.

As I get older, I'm finding years don't last as long as they used to. I think back to when I was at school. As the seemingly never-ending summer holidays finally did draw to a close, I'd lay out my books ready for the return to school on Monday. 'Aw, Ma! It's a year until the next summer holidays. A whole YEAR. They'll NEVER come!'

She'd laugh. 'Aye, don't worry, they'll come. Jist wait till you're a bit aulder, you'll find a year is'nae as long as ye think it is.'

Huh, you were right, Ma. They're just flashing by. For me, I think seeing old movies on TV is what really highlights just how short years have become. One day, I open the *Radio Times* . . .

'Oh, man o' man!'

'What's the matter?' Pat's busy in the kitchen.

'They're showing *The Robe* on Tuesday afternoon. I remember every detail of going to see that doon in the Seamore wi' Sammy. We bought a bar of Highland Cream Toffee, five

Woodbine tae split between us . . . I've just looked at the date – 1953! That's twenty-six years ago! It cannae be. It just seems like ten years, yet really it's more than a quarter of a century! Whit's happening tae years? We're getting short-changed. They're only lastin' aboot three months nowadays! It's time there wiz an enquiry. Questions should be asked!'

She shakes her head. 'Are you finished?'

'Aye, for the minute.'

'Good. Come and get your dinner.'

'Right, pet.'

It's February 1979. I'm about to turn forty. Jeez! If my poor ma had lived she'd still only be sixty. Instead, she's been dead for twenty-five years. As it's a milestone birthday, Pat throws a party for me. She asks me what I'd like for my main prezzie. 'Mmm, I've always fancied painting. What about a box of oil paints? Now I'm on a five-day week I've got time to take up a hobby. Yeah. That's what to get me.' So she buys me a nice wooden box full of tubes of paint, and a few weeks later I tentatively put brush to canvas. I love it, even though a few of my early efforts have to be binned. Not only are they bad, but I haven't read enough about technique; the mixing of paints with a medium of turps and linseed oil to make them thinner, workable. I soon join Hexham Art Club and begin to improve somewhat – but only to a certain level. I realise I lack flair. During the next few years I sell three paintings – that's three times more than Van Gogh in his early years – so at least my ears are safe! Even though I know I'll never be more than a moderate painter, I still enjoy it and always have a picture underway. It's not just a hobby, it fulfils a need for self-expression.

A couple of months after my birthday, in April '79, I'm reading meters along Coronation Way in Sunniside, near Gateshead. I'm having a cuppa with a lady who always offers one to the readers . . .

'You're quiet this morning, Jock.'

'Oh, aye. I'm miles away. What it is, I got a message yesterday that my father's very ill. On his way out, so it seems. He's asking for me. Wants to see me.' I half laugh. 'That's a first! He never wanted to know me most of his life. Treated my ma and me very badly. Unloaded me into the RAF Boys' Service after Ma died, so as he could go off with his fancy woman.'

She tops up my cup. 'The same thing happened to me. I didn't gan to see him.'

'That's exactly what I'm thinking. I know what it'll be . . . "I was a terrible father to ye. Ah know ah treated your mother badly. Can ye forgive me, son?" That's why he's asking for me. But I really think there's no point in me going. This man told my mother, weeks before she died of cancer, "Look, I'm just waiting for you tae die so's ah can get married again – so fuckin' hurry up, will ye!" I know that I'll say to him, "No, I can't forgive you." And if there's other folk at his bedside, they'll be making ME out to be the villain. That's why I think it's best I don't go.'

She sits back in her chair. 'I agree with you. I did exactly the same around fifteen years ago, and I still think it was the right decision.'

Our conversation helps me to make up my mind. I decide not to go. During the next few weeks there are no more letters. We aren't on the phone, so Beenie can't ring us. The weeks became months; then years. With no word. No doubt Beenie would think I'm heartless because I never came to see him. But she never knew the whole story. A few years later I discover that the week after he'd been 'asking to see me' he died. Unforgiven.

Flitting

'How does the idea of living in Corbridge strike you?' Pat tries to look non-committal.

'Ah like it.'

'Mum is moving to Ralph's at Dilston. If we fancy renting her cottage, she'll have a word with the landlady.'

'Yeah, I'm fine with that. Even though it means selling this flat and just renting at Corbridge, I still think it's worth it to get into the village. You obviously want to do it?'

'Oh, yes. It'll be nice to move back.'

'Right, ask your ma to have a word with her.'

Number 14 Watling Street lies across the road from St Andrew's Church, barely 50 yards from the market-place. To save money I hire a large van and do the removal myself. It doesn't take long to settle in. I love it. One of the oldest streets in England, Watling Street – also known as Dere Street – is the Roman road that ran from Londinium (London) all the way north to Hadrian's Wall. Many centuries later, long after the Romans had withdrawn, mail coaches would thunder along the same road, carrying passengers and the royal mail. It was now called the Great North Road and mostly followed the original route first chosen by Roman engineers.

In the 1950s, whether in RAF or Army uniform, I'd sometimes stand at the side of the Great North Road (or A1 as it had become) hoping for a lift. Little did I realise that just a foot or so down lay the original cobblestones of Watling Street so painstakingly laid by the legionaries. Nor could I have dreamt that one day I'd be living in this ancient road I used to hitch up.

In 1988 I have a bit of luck. The electric board decides to reorganise itself and the area we cover from South Tyneside is expanded westward to as far as Haltwhistle. To cut down on the driving time needed to get to the farthest reaches of our new district, it's decided to set up a small section of meter readers at Hexham Depot. This is good news for me. Corbridge is less than 4 miles away. I apply for, and get, the job of charge hand. I have two lads with me at first, Johnny Brooks and Adrian Jarman, who have transferred in from Newcastle. We're later joined by a third, Ray Cummings. Like myself, they all live nearby and wish to move to Hexham to cut down on the travelling time needed to commute to work every day. But there's an extra bonus for all of us. We leave behind us the housing estates and built-up areas of Newcastle and Gateshead. Our new environment is now made up of small towns and villages and vast areas of heath, moor and farmland. From Kielder and Bellingham in the north, Prudhoe, Riding Mill and Corbridge in the east, Haltwhistle in the west and Allendale, Allenheads and Carrshield in the south – and everything in-between – I now spend my working days roaming a large part of England's Best-kept Secret – Northumberland! It's a shame to take the money.

Like most things in life, at first it isn't easy. It's not so bad when I'm reading meters in one of the many villages: if I can't find a property, I simply walk back a few yards to the house I've just left and ask those folks for directions. But when I'm doing one of the country rounds which consists mainly of scattered farms and cottages, I might be having difficulty finding the lane which will lead me to, for example, Dunterley Farm. My last call could have been 3 miles back over the moor. So I decide to go on to the next place, read their meter, then ask them how to get to Dunterley Farm. Alas, when I get there, I find they're not in. I drive on to the next call. I've now covered around 8 miles. They give me directions to the farm I've missed. BUT, if I decide to go back to it, this will now entail a round trip of 16 miles – for just one reading. I'm faced with frustrations like this on a daily basis because it's all new to me. Johnny Brooks knows the district like the back of his hand. Each morning I get him to give me directions to my first call. Once I find that, the rest of the day is spent either asking directions or using the invaluable Ordnance Survey maps. I begin to keep a notebook in which I write down directions to the hard-to-find farms and cottages. It will be more than two years before I can do a farm round without picking Johnny's brains before I leave the depot, or asking locals for directions. In spite of those early frustrations I quickly learn to love my new area. I get to see it in all its beauty in the four seasons. Perhaps being a 'city boy' makes me appreciate it even more.

Having read all the immensely popular vet books by James Herriot, I now feel I'm experiencing many of the things he wrote about – such as driving onto farms when the tups are being kept well away from the ewes . . . I approach one of the three or four gates leading up to the isolated farm. As I climb out of the van and approach the first gate, a couple of dozen tups gather on the other side of it. Testosterone coursing through their veins, they'll be through it if I give them a tenth of a chance, never mind a half. As one of the hill shepherds once said to me, 'Sheep ALWAYS want tae be where you don't want them tae be.'

I undo the catch then start waving my arms around and shouting 'HUP! HUP! HUP!' The sheep back off, but not as far as they normally would. Their hormones and the proximity of a few hundred ewes are making them bold. I chase them off a bit further, run back to the van and race through the gate. Even as I'm braking they begin to surge forward. I sound my horn and throw open the van door. They halt. I leap out of the van and do my 'HUP! HUP!' and arm-waving thing. Over a period of weeks this will be a daily routine. It's essential that tups and ewes are kept apart, especially on the hill farms. If a ewe is 'caught' and she lambs too early, she and her lambs – they usually have twins – will have to be brought into the barn to shelter, otherwise the lambs won't survive on a wintry hill. The higher a farm is, the later the shepherd wants his ewes to lamb, so their chances of survival are increased.

Many farms have their meters located inside the outbuildings. At this time of year it's a regular thing to find a little 'pend' made of wooden pallets in which half a dozen orphan lambs are snuggled together under a heat lamp.

I'm driving up towards a farm. The shepherd's attending to a ewe which is lying on its side. I know him, having read his meter many a time. I pull up beside them. 'Is she about to lamb?'

'Aye, she is that.'

'Would ye mind if ah watch? I regularly pass ewes who've just lambed, but I've never actually seen one being born.'

'Aye, ower ye come.'

I switch off, climb out of the van and stand beside them. Though the ewe's on her side, she occasionally lifts her head to have a look and see what's going on at her nether regions. The man inserts his hand inside her vagina, moves it around a little, then draws out a lamb by its two back legs. It is all slimy and wet. He rubs it briskly with a handful of straw, gives it a couple of slaps, then inserts his fingers into its mouth to ensure the airway is clear. He then lays it on the grass near to the ewe's head. She sniffs it to confirm it's hers, then starts licking its face. Minutes later, the twin is born and receives the same treatment.

'So that's how it's done?'

'Aye. Fifty times a day, hinny.'

Later in the day I'm on another large farm. There's a long track leading down to the house. I stop the van for a moment. 'Jeez. I wish I had my camera with me.' One of the sons of the family is riding a dark, fat-as-butter pony; two black and white collies follow him. He has a capacious home-made canvas hammock slung round his back. As he rides amongst his flock, they don't move; they're obviously used to him and the pony. He stops now and again to look. Without getting out of the saddle, he defies gravity as he leans way down to the side and plucks yet another lamb up by the scruff of its neck, then reaches back to drop it safely into the bag with the others. They'll obviously all be spending a cosy night in the buildings.

There are also plenty of cattle to contend with. As a child, whenever I made one of my rare visits to Mulguy (Milngavie) with my pals, I'd always give cows a wide berth. As far as I was concerned they were bigger than me, and big meant dangerous. Now, I often drive up to a gate and find there are cows, accompanied by a bull, standing a few feet away on the other side. From somewhere on my travels I've assimilated the knowledge that most of the time, bulls won't bother you. They are even less likely to be aggressive when surrounded by cows. It's known to keep them calm. I climb out of the van, open the gate, and give them a blast of 'HUP! HUP!' The cows shy off; the bull looks at me like I'm nuts. But he doesn't move. I give him a longer, louder dose. He ambles off a few feet. It's enough to get the van in.

Even though I'm just a few yards from him, I now get out and shut the gate. I look around; I'm quite alone. As I walk back to the van I stop. 'HEY, TORO! TORO!' He begins to graze. Probably doesn't understand Spanish. I think he's Aberdeen Angus. Och well, disnae detract from my bravery. If only my pals could see me now.

Write? Get Out of Here!

'Ah've just been thinking.' Pat's sitting beside me on the sofa. We have our dinner on our laps so as she can watch *Coronation Street*. She makes no response. Too involved in Deirdre's latest troubles.

'Ah say, ah've been thinking.' She still doesn't answer. She knows that, just for devilment, if given the chance I'll make a big dramatic thing out of being made to take second place to her favourite soap.

Without taking her eyes off the screen, she speaks. 'This'll be finished in about three minutes. Deirdre's about to make an important decision.'

'Great! Deirdre makes an important decision – usually the WRONG one – aboot every three weeks. I'VE just made an important decision. But it looks like its gonny have tae take second place tae *Coronation Street*!'

'I'm not biting.' Her eyes are fixed firmly on the screen.

I do a lot of sighing and shoot pointed looks at her.

'Stop it!'

At last Deirdre chooses wrongly and the soap's signature tune fades in.

'Well! What's this important thing you urgently had to tell me?'

'Ah'm no' tellin' ye now.'

'Good!'

'Aye, but it'll no' be good when ye come hame fae your work – and find ah've moved!'

'Why do you always have to revert to a strong Glasgow accent when you do this carry-on?'

'Cos it makes it funnier.'

'I've never noticed!'

'Ohhhhh!' I curl up, as though in pain. 'You really know how tae hurt a guy, dain't ye?'

Against her will, she laughs.

'Ahhah! Got ye. Okay, now that my honour's been restored, I'll tell ye what ah was gonny tell ye.'

She shakes her head, at the same time looking heavenward.

'Dae ye realise that next year I'll turn fifty?'

'Yeah. So?'

'Well, it's all very nice living here at number 14, paying a low rent, but don't you think we'd maybe better think of getting a place of our own? You know, taking out a mortgage? It just suddenly hit me that at fifty, I might not be able to GET a mortgage!'

Indeed it does prove to be slightly tricky. We finally do get a mortgage, but it has to be a twenty-year one because of our ages; I'm forty-nine and Pat's forty. It also turns out that Pat is the major partner in our joint loan, because she's younger AND the biggest earner. Oh, the shame of it all!

There's no problem over the house we buy. Since 1946, 'Glendue' had been the home of George Twist, the village cobbler. A great character, George had carried out his business from a medium-sized hut standing on some spare ground in Watling Street. Pat had known him all her life. Since his death in 1986, the house has lain empty for more than eighteen months. At first glance it appears rather sad and neglected. Quite a few people have looked at it during this period, but because it needs quite a bit of work, nobody has made an offer. We immediately fall in love with it. We like the look of it and, once inside, like the feel of it too. Constructed in 1880, it's a brick built, stone-fronted, semi-detached property. The roof and chimney stack will need attention as soon as possible. It has a small kitchen and tiny bathroom which will eventually have to be knocked down and rebuilt. Even so, this doesn't deter us at all. It's a nice house in a quiet street in the centre of the village. We want to live in it. The asking price is £40,000. We offer £38,000. After a wait of almost six weeks, George's son, Peter, accepts our bid. Glendue is ours! But £38,000! There DEFINITELY ain't that much money in the world. Early in September 1988, we move into our house. Jeez! If Ma could see me now. Two living-rooms and THREE bedrooms!

'Ah've just been thinking.'

'Again?'

'Yeah, even though it makes my head hurt.'

She sits back in her chair. 'Well? Are you going to tell me?'

'Come 17 December, it'll be twenty-five years since that lad was hung at Bristol.'

'So?'

'Well, you know how newspapers, magazines, they all love anniversaries – ten years, twenty-five years, that sort of thing? I think I'll ring the *Bristol Evening Post*.' I pause. 'Or was it the *News*? To see if they're interested in me doing a piece. They'll pay me for it.'

'Mmm. Suppose it won't do any harm to ask.'

'*Bristol Evening Post*. Can I help you?'

With surprising ease, we establish that they would indeed be interested to read my article. Just as I'm about to hang up, a thought strikes me:

'Eh, probably a stupid question, but if you do like it, and publish it, I take it I'd get paid for it?'

'Oh, yes. If we use it, we'll pay you for it.'

'Right, grand. I'll have it done in a few days. Bye.'

'Goodbye.'

* * *

For the next few days I come home from work and sit with an A4 pad until I have a first draft done. I decide to write it just as though I was talking to somebody. Narrative style, I think they call it. I don't have a typewriter, so the first couple of drafts are done in pencil. After I've finished the second one I read it over a few times, do a bit of rubbing out and rewriting here and there, then decide it's time for the final version. This is neatly hand-printed in Biro. As I do it, I still find there is the occasional word, or even sentence, that can be improved. When I'm finished I painstakingly count the number of words. Just over 2,300. I post it off to Bristol.

Six weeks later, an A4 size envelope comes through the door. Inside it is a copy of the *Bristol Evening Post* for Friday 16 December 1988. The day after that was twenty-five years to the day after Pascoe was hanged. I leaf through it. There it is! Spread over two pages is my article. I'm pleased to see they've published it more or less just as I wrote it. The editing is minimal. A few days later a cheque for £100 arrives. Jeez! I didn't expect as much as that.

Audrey Graham lives two doors along from me. She's a fellow Scot. Although we've only been in Glendue for just over two months, I know Audrey from when we lived in Watling Street. She writes, and has had pieces published in such as *The Scots Magazine* and *The Lady*.

I bump into her a few days after my piece has been in the Bristol paper . . .

'You write, Audrey, don't you?'

'Mmm, now and again.' She smiles.

'I've just had an article published in a Bristol evening paper. I'll push a copy through your letter-box and you can have a read of it.'

'Oh, good. What's it about?'

'Well, I won't tell you. Just let you read it. Be a bit of a surprise.'

She laughs. 'Right, I'll look forward to seeing it.'

The day after I've put it through her letter-box, she knocks on my door.

'Hiyah, Audrey. What did you think of it?'

'Did you write that yourself?'

'Well of course, who else?'

'No, what I mean is, did Pat help you?'

'No – as they say, it was "all me own werk!" I'm afraid.'

'Well, I'll tell you something, you should write!'

I laugh out loud. 'Audrey, I left school at fifteen withoot an O level to my name.'

'I don't care.' She points to the paper. 'This is good. If you wrote that, I'm telling you – you should write!'

'Well, that's very complimentary of you. But this is just a one-off. You know – I've done the job, so I can write about it. But really, that's it. The first and the last.'

'Aye, well I think you should find another subject you could write about. See if you can do it.'

'It's nice of you to say so, Audrey. But this is IT!'

At regular intervals over the next three months, whenever I bump into Audrey she'll say, 'Have you tried writing something yet?'

'Audrey, painting's my hobby. Folk who left school at fifteen don't write. I've been an avid *reader* since childhood, but I don't think that makes me a writer.'

'Well, I think you could write.'

It's March 1989. Pat and I usually go out on a Saturday, but the weather's so bad this weekend we've decided to stay in. I look out of the window into the backyard. 'Blustery' just about sums it up. Frequent squalls of rain; trees swaying in the wind. Man, this is boring. I'm not used to being in on a Saturday. 'I know what I'm going to do to pass the time.'

'What?'

'I'm going to try and write something. Audrey's always on at me every time she sees me. I'll see if I can think of a subject, write it out like the Bristol piece, and send it to a magazine. THEN, when it comes back with a "thanks but no thanks", she'll maybe give me some peace.'

I sit for three hours or more and finish up with a small article, maybe a thousand words, all about Glasgow and its love affair with the trams; how Glasgow folk loved their 'caurs' and how sad we were, in 1962, when we became the last major city to give them up. I decide to send it to *The People's Friend*. That'll show Audrey!

It's perhaps a fortnight later. Audrey opens her door. 'Remember I told you I'd written this wee piece about Glasgow trams and sent it to *The People's Friend*?'

'I do.'

I hand her the letter. 'They like it. They've sent me a cheque for £25!'

'Am I allowed to say "I told you so"?'

Something's Got to Give

As the eighties turn into the nineties, I finally get to know our vast district as well as Johnny Brooks and Adrian Jarman. John and I do the majority of the country rounds between us. I get to know every nook and cranny, every lane and track. As the years go on our customers know they can rely on us, trust us. We're told where spare keys are hidden; if no one's in we take the key, let ourselves in, then leave a note to say the meter's been read. When doing the small towns and villages, such as Haltwhistle, Bellingham and Bardon Mill, we know that Mrs Jones works at the hairdresser's so we call in to get her house key from her; that Mrs Hall doesn't get home until three fifteen, so on the way back to the depot we divert slightly and read her meter. All this local knowledge and willingness to oblige our customers builds up a rapport and goodwill which I often feel management doesn't fully appreciate. Our customers do. John and I regularly come back to the depot laden with free-range eggs and enough home-grown lettuces, cabbages, potatoes and tomatoes to open a greengrocer's.

Meanwhile, I continue to paint and write. I take out a subscription to *Writers' News* and find it invaluable. Because I work on my own and have no contact with other writers, the articles in the magazine provide the only input I have as I try to improve. I slowly begin to grasp the techniques of story construction, plot and pacing. By the early nineties I still don't have a typewriter. Most of my output is short stories for competitions and the occasional piece or article for newspapers or magazines. My *modus operandi* is the same as when I first started – do a few drafts in pencil, then, when I think it's good enough, print out a neat, final draft in Biro. This doesn't seem to do me any harm. Maybe I'm looked on as a bit of an oddball? Over a period of five years, I sell half a dozen or more pieces to publications such as *The People's Friend*, the *Sunday Post*, *Weekend Magazine*, the *Newcastle Journal* and the *Hexham Courant*. In that same period I also win first, second and third prizes in competitions. Therefore, I just carry on with the mixture as before. As they say in sport – 'Never change a winning team!'

Meanwhile, at work, things are changing. In the late eighties, the national electric boards are privatised. They are broken up into twelve regional electric companies. Ostensibly it gives Joe Public a chance to buy shares in them. In reality it leads to the worst kind of corporate greed. We at NEEB become Northern Electric. The old chairman and board are swept away. In come the 'suits'. Their first task is to award themselves a massive pay rise compared to the salaries the old board members had, plus almost unlimited cheap share options, plus a 'profits bonus'. As they are new to the job, how they earn that first year's bonus remains a mystery to this day. The profits bonus is ONLY for the chairman and board of directors. Not the 5,000-plus workforce. The National press and consumer groups complain bitterly about the way these new bosses, of the former Nationalised Industry, appear to be 'filling their pockets'. The furore lasts for a few days, then fades. Nothing changes.

Just before I'd left Gateshead to come to Hexham I had, by default, become the shop steward for the meter readers and collectors. Nobody wanted the post so rather than go unrepresented, I'd said, 'Okay, I'll do it. But remember, I'll probably be the only right-wing shop steward in the history of the GMB Union!'

Like most of my fellow workers, I'd also bought some of the shares we were allocated. I don't have the money to take up the limit of £12,500, which I could buy at £2.40 a share. I can only afford £2,000 worth. Even then I have to pay this amount monthly, on instalments. Nevertheless, whenever I have any meetings with management and I want to ask any questions which I know will embarrass them, I always preface my enquiry with . . . 'Now, may I point out that I'm not JUST asking this as a shop steward, but also as a shareholder, an employee AND a customer of Northern Electric!' When they hear that, they always know I'm about to ask an awkward question. I can almost hear their teeth grind.

The chairman, David Morris, visits us at Hexham. He had been an unemployed executive when he'd applied for, and got, this position. Now well on his way to his first million, he must have thought all his birthdays had come at once when he was appointed. I stand up and give my usual preamble, then comes my question. As ever, it's meant to make him squirm. 'It's over a year now, Mr Morris, since you and your new board of directors took up your posts. One of your first acts was to institute a profits bonus for yourselves. Seeing as the efforts of the workforce contribute to the profits of the company, why is there no profits bonus for us?' The sixty or so staff at Hexham turn from looking at me to look at him. He looks distinctly uncomfortable. He eventually manages to stammer, 'Eh, well it has been discussed, you may be hearing something next year.'

I can't prove it, but I feel certain he's just made that up. About a year later we hear that a profits bonus has been brought in. We are to receive less than 1 per cent of our wages. The average bonus that management give themselves EVERY year for the next few years varies between 11 per cent and 13 per cent. That percentage of their salaries is more than a normal employee's annual wage.

Another embarrassing question I ask, at a monthly works' committee meeting, is why the splendid apprenticeship scheme is being dismantled. All the districts of the national electric boards nationwide, ran apprentice training schemes. At any given time, each area had from thirty to fifty young lads doing four- or five-year apprenticeships. One of the first acts of the new companies upon privatisation was to announce that no more apprentices would be taken on. Once the existing trainees finished their time, the schemes would be dismantled. It was done solely as a cost-cutting exercise, to help increase profits. I ask the directors sitting round the table, 'Don't you think this is short-sighted? Where are tomorrow's electricians going to come from?' I get the usual waffle and management-speak type of answer.

At a later meeting, I tell the chairman straight: 'Mr Morris, I used to like working for the North Eastern Electricity Board. I DON'T like working for Northern Electric.'

Since the days of Northern Electric, which was bad enough, at the time of writing – November 2006 – the company has passed through the hands of one American company and is now owned by another. The workforce has shrunk from over 5,000 to less than 3,000. Most of the small local depots have been closed, the buildings demolished and the land sold off. The milch cow has been milked dry. Even the beautiful headquarters of the once proud NEEB, Carliol House in Newcastle, has been sold off and is now a bar cum nightclub. Having a prestigious art deco head office in the heart of the area's major city doesn't matter any-more – not if it will fetch big bucks on the open market.

What was it Gordon Gecko said in the movie *Wall Street*? Ah, yes – 'Greed is good!'

Off Into the Sunset

In February 1994 I have my fifty-fifth birthday. If I'd stayed in the Prison Service I could have retired by now. I'd always fancied retiring at this age. Over the years, I've come to the conclusion that the younger a man is when he retires, the longer he lives. I've also noticed that folk who have a hobby, an interest, are the ones who seem to keep going. As a meter reader I call at every house in the district. I soon come to realise that it's the old folks who are always busy every time I call; those who complain that 'the days aren't long enough' are the ones who, over the years, I watch go into a ripe old age. Some seem as though they're determined to live for ever. Then there are the houses where, every time I call, the only one I ever see is the wife. The man is always at work. Then one day I call and there he is, sitting in the living-room, watching TV . . .

'Good morning. I don't usually see you when I come to read the meter. Usually just madame.'

He's sitting on the sofa, arms folded, trying to get interested in breakfast TV.

'Aye, I've just retired, hinny. Trying tiv fill me time in. Got bugger all else to do.'

His wife speaks. 'Gets under my feet, that's what his job seems to be now. Doesn't know what to do with himself.'

So many times, almost word for word, that scenario is repeated in umpteen houses. For the next two or three years, every time I call, I know that when I open the back door I'll find the wife busy in the kitchen and the sound of the TV coming from the front room. A glance through the door will give a view of the back of her husband's head.

Then I'll call one day . . .

'Morning. Electric man.'

'Oh, hello Jock. Time for a cuppa?'

'Why aye. Ah can always force a cuppa.' I read the meter and enter it on the sheets. I sit myself at the kitchen table, glance through the living-room doorway. The room is in darkness, the TV off.

'Where's himself this morning?'

'Oh, did ye not hear, hinny? He died. Aye, about five months ago. Heart attack.' Her eyes fill up.

'Eeeh, no, I didn't. I'm sorry to hear that.'

For the last few years I've been having increasing problems with osteoarthritis in my knees and hands. The fact that I have so many scattered calls in my area means I'm in and out of the van all day long, opening and shutting gates – not good for someone with troublesome knees. By the middle of '94 the company announces there will be a programme of redundancies and early retirements, although it's not expected there will be any job losses on the meter reading sections. I decide to make an application for voluntary redundancy, but without much hope – the company still needs its readers. I'm the only one who applies from all our districts. To my surprise and delight, they tell me I can have it. There are a few readers, especially amongst the dozen or so I used to work with at Team Valley, who would also like to take it. They are told it's not an option. Could it be that the board have seen a chance to get rid of this troublesome shop steward who regularly embarrasses them?

In October '94 I walk out of Bridge End Depot for the last time. I got my wish. I've retired at fifty-five years of age. The following day, management starts sending meter readers out from South Tyneside to Hexham to fill the gap left by my departure. There wasn't really a case for redundancy. I'm the only reader who gets it. It's nice to know I must have been quite a thorn in their sides. Not only do I leave with a large lump sum of severance pay, but I also leave with a good pension. All the years of contributions that I brought with me to the electric board have been added to the seventeen years I've just spent with the company. The maximum pension it's possible to get under their scheme is one for forty years' service. I qualify for a thirty-seven-year one. As I'm fifty-five I'm entitled to start drawing it right away. I use part of my lump sum to pay off a chunk of our mortgage, thus reducing our monthly outgoings.

Although I miss roaming the Northumberland countryside in all its seasons, and the relationships with our customers, I take to retirement like the proverbial duck to water. For quite some time I've known that there is a WEA (Workers' Educational Association) writing group that meets in Hexham on Tuesday afternoons. I was never able to go because I was working; but now I join it immediately. There are some fourteen members, the majority of them women, ranging in age from their fifties to their seventies. The tutor is an Irish lad in his thirties, Brendan Cleary. He is very popular – and rightly so. Whether he's dealing with poetry or prose, Brendan is always able to give input to the writer. The group is exactly what I'm looking for, and what I need. It's very much a working group. As soon as you finish reading your piece, your fellow members and Brendan will let you know if it works, and how it can be improved. As well as Brendan, I find that another member, Philippa Collingwood, is also unerring in her ability to home in on the weak spots in my work. I like the contrast between Philippa and me. A southerner, tall, slim and in her late thirties I find her delightfully posh – as I regularly remind her.

It's the practice to turn up at the group every week with something to read out. One of the dictums for aspiring writers is write what you know. Therefore, I've begun to write small pieces of around 1500 to 2000 words about growing up in Glasgow in the forties and fifties. They're nearly always 'fun' pieces. If I do write something serious or sad, it'll be about folk who lived in Doncaster Street. My street. I don't write about the death of my ma or my father's bad behaviour. I don't yet know it, but I've started to write *Night Song of the Last Tram*, which will become my first book.

Very quickly, Tuesday afternoons become the highlight of my week. It's always with a tingle of anticipation that I walk through the doors of Hexham's Queen's Hall and climb the stairs to 'our' room. I open the door. Gellie, who is Dutch and speaks better English than me, looks up and says, 'Hiyah, Bob.' So does Marjorie. I take a seat. 'Hello girls.'

'Oh, isn't he nice?' says Marjorie. 'Girls!'

Over the next ten minutes, the members arrive in ones and twos. Brendan, our tutor, is usually last. He has to catch a local train from Newcastle to Hexham and sometimes it's a few minutes late. He always reminds me of a latter-day Bob Geldof. Although he's the youngest of us all, he has no problem in running this class of older pupils. I don't think he realises how well liked he is, and how highly regarded as a tutor.

The poets normally print off copies of their work and hand them out, one sheet between two. Because I write prose, and it usually runs to four or five pages, I only do a copy for Brendan and one for myself to read from. I always rehearse my readings at home so that, hopefully, I'll read them well in class. Some other members just read their pieces straight off, unrehearsed, which means they often make mistakes. This spoils it for me. I'm becoming absorbed in their work; they're putting pictures in my mind – then they'll mispronounce a word, or stop and say, 'Eeeh, I can't read my writing.' Then they've lost me; broken my concentration. This is why I always rehearse. It's a courtesy to your listeners. What would they say if they were listening to the afternoon short story on Radio 4 and the reader kept stuttering and stopping?

I finish reading my piece. It's all about how, as kids, we used to go over to what we called 'the toffs' houses' and rake their middens to see if they'd thrown away anything worth salvaging.

Brendan looks around. 'Any comments?'

'Yes!' It's Philippa. 'I wouldn't start it where you've started it. It REALLY begins further down, where you have your first section of dialogue.'

Brendan nods. 'That's what I was going to say. The dialogue takes us straight into the piece. It's always your strong point, Bob. It comes alive with the dialogue. The info you have in those first two paras, you can feed that in later.'

'Right.'

One or two other classmates make comments, then Philippa comes back in.

'I don't think you need all of that explanatory prose in the middle section. We know what a midden is, simply because you're showing us as you and your friends are raking it. That dictionary definition isn't needed. It slows things up.'

'But I put that in for the benefit of southern softies like yourself, Philippa.'

'Well I don't need it, thank you. I know what a midden is.'

'Ah'll bet that when you were a kid in Bournemouth, just like Hillhead folk, you were so posh that you used tae take yer ashes doon tae the midden in a briefcase!'

In spite of herself, she laughs. 'Just take that middle bit out.'

'Yes, miss!'

Now that I'm writing Glasgow pieces on a weekly basis for the class, I find my painting's taking a back seat. I've barely been retired a fortnight when I realise it's going to be a bit unfair if I sit and indulge myself in my hobbies all day, then expect Pat to come in at six-fifteen and start making the dinner. That evening, she comes through the door . . .

'I've been thinking. To help out, what if I get a few recipes together – nothing too difficult – and start doing the dinner Monday to Friday? It's gonny be a bit much expecting you to do the dinner when you come in from work.'

'Oh, that would be a help.'

It's a few weeks later. Pat comes into the kitchen while I'm chopping veg. I turn round. 'You know what? I'm really enjoying this cooking lark.'

About a month later, I have another rush of blood to the head. 'I've had an idea. Just to share out the work a bit, when you've got some clean washing ready to be ironed, I'll start doing most of it for you. Might be the odd item I leave for you to do, if it's something difficult. When I was in the army I often did my own washing and ironing to save money. I'm not, as you might say, a stranger to an ironing-board.'

Eventually, as time goes on, now and again I indulge in a bit of light dusting. Behind closed doors, of course.

Ron

I'd known Ron Tierney almost twenty years before we became friends. Good friends. Pat introduced me to him in 1974. A slim man with a Ronald Colman moustache, he was then in his fifties. He and his late wife, Moira, had been next-door neighbours of Pat's mum and dad. After we moved to Corbridge in 1981 I'd occasionally run into him in the village and we'd always stop and speak. My first impression of him, which never changed, was that he was very much a gentleman. Retired from teaching at Hexham's Queen Elizabeth High School, most of his days are now spent on the golf course with his small group of cronies. I soon realise that the company of his pals is just as important to him as the golf. He's been a widower since 1968 and by now his three children; Ian, Lorna and Kevin, have flown the nest and live in different parts of the country.

When Pat and I moved from Watling Street to St Helen's Street in 1988, I was pleased to find we now lived just three doors away from Ron. If I'm doing calls in the area I often come home for lunch. Frequently I pull up just as Ron and his golfing friends are about to leave for Hexham . . .

'Is that you away for a round of the "gowf", Mr Tierney?'

He laughs. 'Well, if you can call it golf. This lot would make a good golfer weep!'

'Here! I resemble that,' says one of his mates.

I often go along to the Wheatsheaf for a pint on a Friday night. As I walk home, some time after eleven p.m., I know exactly what I'll see as I pass Ron's. He never draws his curtains. He sits to the left of the window under a standard lamp, still trying to finish the *Telegraph* crossword. On the other side of the room the TV flickers, unwatched. Twenty years on, he still misses Moira. Hopper could get a painting out of this.

It's late October 1994. I've only been retired two weeks and I haven't yet got used to it; it feels as if I'm on holiday, or off sick.

'I'll tell you what,' I say to Pat, 'it's all right in the morning when I'm writing. But after I've had lunch and a kip, the time really drags until I start the dinner.'

'Why don't you pop along to Ron's for half an hour? He's usually back from the golf by late afternoon.'

'Mmm, suppose I could.'

That was the start of it. A few days later I drop in and Ron and I hit it off straight away. Now into his late seventies, though looking younger, Ron has a sharp intelligence and, even in his old age, an enquiring mind. Always within reach of his chair is a heavy, one-volume Chambers Dictionary; its red board covers darkened and worn from daily use. Whenever we're discussing something and can't arrive at a consensus, he'll say, 'Let's have a look in Chambers.' It's surprising how often we find the answer.

My visits start off at just two half hours a week. Within a couple of months it has become six. The only day I miss is Saturday. Pat and I always have a run out somewhere.

Ahead of me lies five years of one of the great friendships of my life. It will pass all too quickly. Now and again, maybe once a month, he'll come along and have dinner with us when Pat comes home from work. He'll arrive at six p.m., twenty minutes or so before she's due. As soon as Pat joins us I immediately make the two of them a gin and tonic, with ice and lemon. As I beaver away in the kitchen, cooking dinner, the pair of them enjoy a blether in the living-room. It nearly always takes them back thirty years to when he and Moira lived next door to Pat's family. She's known him since she was a girl and is very fond of him.

As 1994 becomes '95, then '96, the relationship between Ron and me becomes an easy-going friendship. Sadly, by 1996 he is beginning to be troubled by osteoporosis. This puts a stop to his great love, golf. He still goes to the club, walks round nine holes with his friends, but he finds it too painful to play. Also, slowly but surely, his small group of pals begin to die. Soon there are only two left, Dennis and John. He now visits the club just once a week.

During these years I get to know his grown-up children – and assorted grandchildren, who are mostly in their teens and visit 'Gramps' regularly. His daughter Lorna often thanks me for 'keeping an eye on him'. I always assure her that I don't consider I'm doing any such thing. I call in every day because I enjoy his company.

As his discomfort from the osteoporosis increases, and he turns eighty, he slowly begins to grow frail. His mind is as sharp as ever, but old age is claiming him. Often, as I come along for my visit, I'll glance through the window. There he sits, newspaper open wide, dozing off, coming to, then dozing off again. Right. Time for action! I knock on the door and open it at the same time. The sweeping brush leans against the wall just inside. I upend it, put it under my arm like a crutch, but don't yet appear in the doorway. Out of sight, I go into my best Robert Newton/Long John Silver impression . . .

'Har har, excuse me bothering 'ee, Jim lad. H'ive been told an old matelot has dropped anchor in theses premises, an' any former seafaring man is allus welcome to a dish of tay. Has Long John been informed correctly, sur?' I wave the tip of the broom back and forward in the open door.

'Come in you daft bat,' he says.

'Har, now mind 'ee, sur. If it be a problem, Long John would just as soon ship out. Twenty years afore the mast – man and boy – I be one old tar who never likes—'

'Just go and put the kettle on, you silly bugger.'

'Now, as long as 'ee's sure, sur.' I step into view, framed in the doorway. I've bent my left leg up behind me, there's nothing to see below the knee. I have the crutch under the wrong arm, supporting my good leg. I look down. 'Har, I think me crutch should be . . . AHHHR!' I topple over to the left – and out of sight.

'You're mad as a bloody hatter!' he says.

We sit drinking tea and eating slices of fruit cake. I know that any minute now he'll say, 'I remember one time, during the war it was . . .' Then he'll tell me one of the many stories from his wartime service as a petty officer in the Royal Navy. During the five years of our friendship there will not be one single day, when he will not tell at least one of his tales. As he grows older and frailer, I'm happy to indulge him. I once remark to Pat, 'When I called in this afternoon he was almost in a torpor. Never heard

My great pal, Ron Tierney. Gentleman and scholar. 1995.

me knock. I was in the living-room before he began to surface. By the time we'd had a cuppa and a good blether he was firing on all cylinders. When he tells me his tales the years just fall away. He's "there", he sees it all. He's Jack-the-Lad again.'

By the late nineties our friendship is so comfortable it's beginning to take on aspects of *The Odd Couple*. On a daily basis Ron continues to tell me anecdotes from his nine years in the Navy, which include the tale of two of his ships being sunk by enemy action, but he has increasing difficulty recalling names. We're sitting with our mugs of tea . . .

'Hah! I've never forgot the night, before the war it was, and I'm in this pub. Just across the road from Plymouth dockyard's gates it was . . . Oh, man! What was its bloody name?'

'The Anchor,' I say.

He points at me. 'That was it. So I'm in the Anchor. I'm the only one in there off the old *Bridgewater*. There's a dozen or more bootnecks (Royal Marines) who are all off . . .' He pauses, 'What was its name? Battleship, she were . . .'

'HMS *Rodney*,' I say.

'The *Rodney*! That was her. I could tell these buggers were spoiling for a fight. I didn't have my petty officer's hat on, but I was wearing my mac, so they knew who I was. Anyway. I'm thinking, I'd better try and slip out of here. Then, by good luck, in comes . . . oh, man! I can see him – boxed heavyweight for the Navy. Off our ship he was . . .'

'"Digger" Thompson,' I prompt.

'"Digger" Thompson! That was him. Comes and leans on the bar beside me. "All right?" he says. "All right now," I says. "Will you have a pint, Digger?"'

Then there are the jokes. I have a large repertoire of them and they're mostly 'blue'. I divide them into 'upper mess deck' and 'lower mess deck' stories. We both agree that the only criteria for a joke is not that it's blue, but that it's funny. Ron doesn't just have trouble with names, he quickly forgets jokes too. This means I can recycle them on a monthly basis. All except one. And it's clean! He never forgets it. It's one of those which I've adapted and tell as if it were true.

Ron loves nature documentaries, especially those featuring David Attenborough. He's telling me about a programme I missed yesterday and I suddenly remember 'the joke'.

'Did you see that one about the pygmies the other night?' I enquire.

He pauses. 'No, I must have missed that.'

'It was about a group of pygmies called the Foohkawie Tribe.'

'Mmmm,' he sips his tea, 'never heard of them.'

'They're just 3 feet tall – and they live amongst the 4-feet tall elephant grass. That's how they get their name. Every couple of minutes they jump up into the air shouting, 'Where the foohk are we? Where the foohk are we?'

Ron lets out a great bark of a laugh then goes helpless. I've never seen him laugh so much since I've known him. He never forgets it and takes great delight in telling it to all his grandchildren.

He often talks of Moira. 'The lassie', as he likes to call her. A Highland girl from Ballahullish in Argyll, they'd met in Dunoon. She was a Wren. In 1943 they got married; she died from cancer in 1968. He would mourn her for the rest of his life.

It's 22 December 1999. Ron's grandson, Duncan, has come up to stay the night, then drive Gramps down to Lorna's in Derbyshire for Christmas. It's only a few weeks since Ron was down there, to welcome his first great-grandchild, Izzie. As I'm interested in family history I say to Lorna, 'Make sure you take a photo of him holding the bairn. It's not so much for now, but just think, in fifty years' time, around 2050, she'll be able to show it to folk and say. "This is me with my great-grandfather. Over a hundred years ago, in the middle of the last century, he was in the Royal

Navy during the Second World War!" That's when she'll be glad you took a photo.'

It's after 9 p.m. I've seen Ron this afternoon, but I've gone in again to say hello to Duncan before they leave tomorrow. As he always does when I'm leaving, Ron comes out to the gate with me. He stands on one side of it, smoking a cigarette. I stand on the pavement. 'Well, you'll be doing your paterfamilias for the next few days, eh?'

He laughs. 'Aye, and the familias is getting bigger all the time.'

It rained earlier, it's cold and damp. 'Well, I think I'll get away in, Ron. If I'm up and dressed early enough I'll pop in for five minutes before you go.'

'Right, okay mate.'

I like it when he calls me 'mate'. Being an ex-sailor, he doesn't use the term lightly. 'Fine. I might see you the morra' morning.' I turn and raise my hand in the air as I walk away.

'Aye, I'll see you the morn's morn,' he says. That's a phrase he picked up from Moira.

I smile; half turn. 'Aye, the morn's morn.' It's a while since I heard that.

The phone rings at about 9 a.m. 'Bob? It's Duncan. I'm afraid I've got some bad news. My grandfather took ill during the night. He, ah, died early this morning.'

'Oh, jeez! Right, I'll get ready. I'll be along as soon as I'm dressed.' That's a blow. I know he's been failing this last wee while. He's told me he's weary. Ready to go. I'm not half going to miss him. What am I gonna do with my afternoons, now?

Ian, Lorna and Kevin soon arrive. And some of the grandchildren. We're all sad. They've lost a much loved father and grandfather. I've lost my old mate.

'Is there anything you'd like to have, Bob? To remember him by?' asks Lorna.

I laugh. I point to the old, red-covered Chambers Dictionary. 'Believe it or not, I'd like to have that. It's been such a feature in my life these last five years.'

It's still in regular use. He'd like that.

First Steps on a Long Road

I sure miss having Ron as my sounding-board. All the late afternoons I'd call in, four or five pages of manuscript in my hand, and say, 'Right, Tierney, pin your lug'oles back. I've got some deathless prose here for your delectation.' He'd sit there, eyes shut, concentrating on every word, as I'd read yet another chapter of what would eventually become *Night Song of the Last Tram*. When I'd finish he'd then give me his opinion as to what had, or hadn't, worked. More often than not, what I'd just read would remind him of something from his own childhood, and off we'd go at a tangent. It was always great fun.

Some time in the late nineties Brendan, our tutor, decides to move away from the area. For the last couple of years of his tenure he has continued to urge me on, asking, 'When are you going to get these Glasgow pieces of yours together and off to a publisher?'

I always give him my stock answer. 'Well, the trouble is, Brendan, there's quite a bit of "bad" stuff to write about. I will eventually get round to it. Honest.'

As we go into the new millennium I finally run out of 'good' stuff. It's decision time. What ya gonna do, Yogi? Should I carry on writing short stories for competitions – or concentrate on putting a book together? My fellow members of the WEA writers' group continue to give me great support and input when I finally decide to attempt an autobiography. I start on the 'bad' stuff. Chapters which will tell of my rotten father – and the death of my ma at just thirty-six.

After Brendan's departure, I'm further disappointed when my great supporter – and pal – Philippa Collingwood also decides to leave the group, shortly after the distinction of getting an MA from Newcastle. All is not lost, however. For the next couple of years, as I apply myself to the task of producing a manuscript which will one day interest a publisher, I send new chapters, edited chapters, then revised and rewritten chapters, to Philippa on a weekly basis. They always arrive back a few days later suffering from a severe outbreak of redpenitis. My spirits are lifted now and again when she awards me an (occasional) tick!'

I find writing the sections about my father are not too much of a problem. It just makes me sad when I remember how much I'd looked forward to him coming home in 1945, only to discover what a nasty piece of work he was. The last few chapters,

At the Portpatrick Hotel for my 60th birthday, with Pat. I always said I'd go back – 1957, kitchen porter. 1999 guest!

describing the illness and lonely death of my ma, are heavy going. It's hard to type when you can't see the keyboard for tears. By 2000, it's done. The title is *Of Trams and Tenements*. It covers my young life from birth until I've just turned sixteen. I look at it as it lies on the kitchen table, all neatly typed and in a blue folder. I'm about to start sending a synopsis and three sample chapters round to publishers. Will someone say, 'We love it! We want to publish it'? I know from articles in *Writers' News* that it's 99.9 per cent certain that WON'T happen. At sixty-two years of age, I'm also aware that all my life I've had to struggle to get what I want. Good things never just *happen* to me. Other folk have good luck. I have hard graft. All I'm certain of is that I've written the sort of book I like to read. Will a publisher somewhere give it more than just a superficial glance? Maybe even read some of it?

It's three years later. I have a growing collection of rejection slips. Most are of the 'thanks, but no thanks' variety. But not all. Now and again there will be an almost full-page letter from an assistant editor: 'This is good, but it's difficult to sell an autobiography if you're not famous. Or infamous.' See – I knew I should have become a criminal instead of a screw. Even though I'm continually being disappointed, my belief in my book never wavers. Every nine months or so I read through it and always find myself unable to resist rewriting and editing. Then I finish up having to sit down at my word processor to type out, yet again, another brand-new manuscript. All 90,000 words of it. Every time I do this I have the satisfaction of knowing that the new version is just that little bit better than the previous one.

In late 2003, I spot a small piece in *Writers' News*: 'Hodder & Stoughton have decided to set up a Scottish list. Any manuscripts should be sent to their newly appointed agent, Bob McDevitt, at . . .' It gives a Paisley address. My first reaction is to immediately send out my increasingly frayed sample chapters. Then I think about it. No, the guy will almost certainly be inundated. Play it cool. Who are ye kidding? You don't dae 'cool'! Well, you'll jist have tae. Common sense prevails. I actually wait until March 2004. Surely the tidal wave of submissions he'll have received will have subsided by now? While I've been waiting I've put the whole manuscript through yet another edit. I hold it up in the air. I'm sitting at my workplace – the kitchen table. 'This is IT, Pat. Do you realise every chapter in this book has been through a minimum of ten drafts? Some of them have had another five or six on top of that. This is as good as it's going to get. I either sell it to a publisher, or it doesn't get published. I'm certainly not going to have it vanity published. That wouldn't mean a thing. If it's good enough, someone will want to do it.'

With the usual feeling of *déjà vu*, I start getting the three sample chapters ready to send up to Paisley. I decide to type out a new letter. Och, why not be a bit bold . . .

Dear Bob McDevitt. Would you like the chance to publish Glasgow's *Angela's Ashes*? Except mine is funnier – and sadder. (Jeez! I hope nobody tells Frank McCourt.)

I send the brown A4 envelope off to Paisley with my hopes high. Huh! I always send them off with the certainty that this is it – it will definitely be This Time! This is my twentieth publisher.

It doesn't take long to read three chapters and a synopsis. Three days later, the phone rings . . .

'Hello?'

'Is that Bob Douglas?' It's a good, strong voice. Glasgow, but with a soupçon of the West End. At least he's no' trying tae talk 'pan loaf' jist because he's landed a joab wi' a big publisher. Ah think ah can work wi' this lad. (I didn't REALLY think all that, this is a wee bit of added colour.)

'Yeah, it is.'

'Hi. I've read the sample chapters you sent me. I take it there's a manuscript?'

I laugh. 'There certainly is.'

'I'd like you to send it up to me.'

Jeez-oh! Now don't get too excited. The hair tingles on the back of my neck. 'Oh, yes, of course. I'll put it in the post tonight.' I'd love to say, 'You must have liked the sample chapters if you're asking for the manuscript?' With an effort of will that is entirely foreign to me, I resist.

'Yes, I enjoyed what I read in the sample chapters. I'll look forward to reading the manuscript.'

'Right, eh, eh, that's good. I'll look forward to hearing from you, then.' I wish he would stay on the phone for an hour or so. Tell me things like, 'If the rest of it is as good as the three chapters I've just read, we're talking best-seller, here!' He doesn't.

'Fine. I'll be in touch, hopefully in a few days.'

'Okay, I'll look forward to hearing from you. Bye.'

Five days later, Bob McDevitt calls again: 'I've just finished it. It's a cracking read!'

'Pat? It's me. I've just had that Bob McDevitt on the phone again. You know what he said? I quote, "It's a cracking read!" He's sending it down to London to a guy called Nick Sayers for him to read. If he likes it, we're as good as published!'

'EEEEE!'

You Couldn't Make It Up!

We're driving up the A1 from North Yorkshire, heading for Newcastle. I glance at Pat. I let out a long 'Ohhhhhhh! Ah'm aw excited!' That's about the seventh one since we set off.

'DON'T START!' she says, in mock severity.

'But can you believe it? We're going tae meet two guys from Hodder and Stoughton. They're wanting to see me – ah mean, *moi*.'

She gives a loud 'Tut!' (Maybe that should be 'Tsk!')

'Dae ye think ah should start wi' all that air kissing stuff?'

That earns a louder 'tut/tsk'. 'Why do you keep reverting to a broad Glasgow accent?'

' 'Cause ah don't want them thinking ah'm putting oan airs and graces.'

'Don't be stupid! If you speak like that, the chap from London won't understand a word you're saying.'

'You kin translate.'

'Tut/tsk!'

Bob McDevitt had rung just days before we were about to leave for a week's break in North Yorkshire. 'Nick and I would like to meet with you next week, if that's okay? To talk about your manuscript, contract etc. Can you suggest somewhere that will be handy for the three of us?'

'What about Newcastle Central station? You can get trains direct from London and Glasgow.'

'Sounds good. I take it that's all right for you?'

'Well, as it happens we're gonny be down in Yorkshire – but

it's still no problem. It's only about an hour and a half straight up the A1. Nae bother.'

We're approaching Scotch Corner. This is the old, original A1; the Great North Road. I never thought I'd be DRIVING up it in my own car. Or going to meet a couple of publishers . . . 'Ohhhhhh!'

'Stop it!'

We meet in the Centurion bar at the station. The walls are covered with original, late Victorian majolica tiles. Nick Sayers has read my manuscript and both he and Bob are very complimentary about it. Nick will be my editor and asks, 'How much more is there to come after this?'

In chronological order I give them a brief synopsis: 'Nine months in the Boys' Service, back to Scotland, working down the pit, working in a hotel in Portpatrick, back to Glasgow to work down the docks for eighteen months, two years in the army, getting married, fifteen years as prison officer – I begin to get to the end – working with the electric board, starting to write, retiring from work . . .' I laugh, '. . . and I finish up sitting here with you two guys!'

'Mmmm. How many books do you think it'll take?'

'Oh, I would hope just two.'

Nick shakes his head. 'I would think you'll need three.'

'Yeah, I wouldn't think you'll cover it all in two volumes,' says Bob.

'Anyway. For the moment we'll offer you a contract for *Of Trams and Tenements* with an option for a second,' says Nick. 'You don't have an agent, do you?'

'No. I'm a one-man band.'

'Well, I can assure you we won't be ripping you off or anything like that. You'll be offered the standard Hodder contract. You can always get yourself an agent if you want?'

'No, thank you. I've done all the hard work myself. Sold my

book. Why present an agent with an author who's already done the business for him – then pay him 15 per cent of my earnings for just looking at my contract? I'm quite capable of reading a contract. Anyway, I've known the name Hodder and Stoughton since I was about eight years old and joined the Woodside Library. And after meeting you two today, I get the feeling you'll look after me. As my old mate Ron Tierney would've said, I like the cut of your jib!' I point to Pat. 'Anyway, if you try and do me – I'll set her onto you!'

'Good!' says Nick, 'I think we've covered everything at the moment. I feel we can work well together too. Hodder would really like to publish your book. We think it's a wonderful read, so I'd like to offer you a contract.' He offers me his hand. So does Bob. Then they both shake hands with Pat. 'Welcome to Hodder,' says Nick.

Just before we leave, I say, 'Do you know something? When the book comes out, I'd love it if I got a review in the *Sunday Times*. I've been a reader since the 1960s. I take it mainly for the book reviews – I just love them! It's the section I always turn to first. I find they're so well written. Just think what a thrill it would be one Sunday to open it and find MY book in there!'

'Well,' says Nick, 'I can promise you that we'll SEND them a copy for review. But I'm afraid I can't guarantee that they will do it.'

The next few months seem to fly by. At regular intervals, sometimes weekly, different sized envelopes drop through the letterbox. Every time I see the Hodder and Stoughton logo on them it gives me a tingle. Jeez, this is from my publisher. I've got a publisher! If Pat's in, when I bring the mail through I always go 'Ohhhhhhhhh!'

She just shakes her head.

In the second half of 2004, I open a heavy, padded package. It contains a couple of 'proof' copies. My book is now called *Night*

Song of the Last Tram. We had earlier agreed that the original title might mislead some folk into thinking it's all about Glasgow tramcars. Anyway, I like the new title. I hold a proof in my hands. It's just like a large paperback. How wonderful to see it as a book. Exciting! I dip into it here and there, read a few sentences. Every line and sentence is so familiar; I've pored over each word for years and to see them in the pages of a book is really special. Nick tells me there will be 600 proof copies, some of which will soon be winging their way out to newspapers and magazines where, hopefully, the reviewers and critics will consider it good enough to merit a review.

Bob McDevitt rings. 'Your first review is in!'

'Ohyah!' Around 3,426 butterflies take wing in my stomach. 'Where?'

'*Publishing News*. It's a trade paper. They're always one of the first.'

'And?' I take a breath.

'They've made you Book of the Month for November!'

'Get out of here!'

'Seriously. Gave you a big column all to yourself. The reviewer, Sue Baker, she's the editor. She finishes by saying, "A quite exceptional autobiography".'

'Jeesusjohnny! This is even more than we could've hoped for, ain't it?'

'Not half.'

As we go into 2005 it just gets better and better. Glasgow has decided to hold its first ever book festival, the 'Aye Write' festival. I'm to be launched there on the evening of Friday 25 February. I'll be speaking and reading. Imagine, my first book and it's to be launched in my home town at its inaugural book festival! As January becomes February I find I'm regularly up and down to Glasgow. I'm interviewed by Maureen Ellis of Glasgow's *Evening Times*. On 5 February they do a lovely big spread.

It includes a photo of me superimposed against my painting of Cocozza's Café. Within a week, Peter Cocozza – whom I remember as a wee boy – gets in touch. To my delight, he tells me that his mother, Maria, is still alive and well at eighty-four. I give Maureen a ring at the *Times*, simply to tell her how pleased I am. 'Oh, good,' she says, 'we'll do a reunion piece in front of where the café used to be!' A couple of months later, in April, we do.

Meanwhile, another special event happens. To mark the opening of the book festival, I'm invited to a civic dinner at Glasgow's City Chambers in George Square. One of the Hodder party can't make it – so that means Pat can have the ticket. We are put up for a couple of nights in the Millennium Hotel which overlooks George Square and the City Chambers. I look out of our room window. This view never seems to change. I have postcards dating from before the First World War; it looked exactly the same back then. Statues and formal flower-beds. I look at the centre of the square. I think it would be round about there where

2005. Reunited with Maria Cocozza.
The family café stood where the flats are.

the Spitfire stood. It was just before my father went abroad – that makes it 1942 – and I was coming up for three and a half. We queued for a fair while until, at last, it was our turn. He lifted me up and sat me inside the cockpit. It was getting to be dusk. I remember there was a cloth-covered twirly piece of flex – the same kind as you got on the telephones then – with a small bulb burning on the end of it. I was so excited. I tried to take it all in; all the instruments, the control column. I touched things, waggled things, then all too soon I was lifted out. Now here I am, back in Glasgow, sixty-three years later. 'Ma? I'm going for dinner the night wi' the Lady Lord Provost in the City Chambers. Can you imagine that? You know ah've got a book coming oot, dain't ye? And you're the star. It's dedicated tae you.' My eyes brim with tears.

The reviews start coming thick and fast. All good. In fact, all very good – but I'm too modest to say! I especially like the comment by Tom Kyle in the Scottish *Daily Mail*, '. . . made me laugh until the tears ran down my legs!' I'm also very gratified to see a review in the *Independent on Sunday* by the novelist Louise Welsh. A few weeks previously I'd been invited to a Burns Supper in Edinburgh hosted by the Scottish book trade. At the end of the night, as folk were beginning to leave, I'd congratulated Louise on her punchy 'Reply for the Lassies' speech. I'd picked up a couple of spare proof copies of *Night Song*. 'What's that under your arm?' she asks. I tell her. 'I wouldn't mind a read at it.' I give her a copy. As I've just met her, I'm not aware she reviews books. She kindly takes it on herself to review it. Alas, there's nothing from the *Sunday Times*. Och well, you can't have everything.

I'm being launched at the Mitchell Library, one of the venues for the 'Aye Write' festival. I spend quite a bit of time up in Glasgow beforehand. I do a Scottish TV interview and three radio interviews: Saga, Clyde and BBC Radio Scotland. With Bob McDevitt as my guide, I go round all the major bookshops, Waterstone's,

WH Smith and Ottakars, meeting the managers and signing stock for them. We also have a nice wee break as we run out to Loch Lomond Books, have lunch with the owner, Beth, then I do a reading and sign some books. It'll tune me up for my big night! There's further excitement when I'm told that both Waterstone's AND WH Smith are making *Night Song* Scottish Book of the Month for March. Jeez-oh!

Suddenly, it's the BIG NIGHT! I'm being launched. Well, the book is. The Mitchell Library is the biggest reference library in Europe! I'm pleased the launch is being held there. The Mitchell is very much part of the Glasgow scene. Although it's in a beautiful old building and has such a grand reputation, the Mitchell feels far from remote and austere. It's very much 'the people's library'. Strangely enough, I'm not too nervous as the time nears. All the years of reading my 'work' to my writing group back in Hexham has made me confident. I'm also well rehearsed. Quite a few of my childhood pals have turned up: Billy Ferrie, Tommy Finnegan, James Gibson and Jim McDonald. There's a hundred or more folk in the audience. I get up, thank them for coming, then give a wee résumé of what started me off writing. I then read them a piece where we're playing 'guesses' in Lizzie's shop window and nobody can get it. Wee Hughie has a lisp – and he thinks 'caramels' begins with a 'T'.

Afterwards, I sit at a table like a real writer, and sign around fifty books.

We all hang around for a while. I especially enjoy talking to the lads I grew up with; they're all mentioned in the book. It's one of those evenings you don't want to end. Bob McDevitt has booked a meal, so we'll have to make a move. I thank the Mitchell staff for all their good work and we make our way down the grand staircase and out onto the pavement. We should turn left. 'Come this way,' I say. 'Don't ask! Just come with me for a minute.' We walk along the side of the Mitchell to where the library ends, and a tenement building starts. After a few yards I stop at one of its closes. 'This street, as some of you may know, is Granville Street. And this is number 32. Late on the evening of 7 January 1959, I stepped out of this close for the last time. I was nineteen years of age and about to go down to the Central to catch a train for Portsmouth tae start my National Service. I point up the building. I rented a room in a house on the top floor for thirty bob a week. That was the last time I lived in Glasgow. Now, who would have thought that forty-six years later I'd be back in Granville Street – at the Mitchell – tae launch a book!'

We begin to walk off. I turn for a last look at the close, then further down the street at the library. I link arms with Pat and Bob McDevitt. I smile. 'You couldn't make it up, could you?'

On Sunday 13 March, Pat and I are at home having our breakfast. Silently, she hands me the Culture section of the *Sunday Times*. There it is. It's a great review!

Loose Ends

For those of you who have followed me through three books, perhaps you'd like to know what has happened to some of the main characters who have featured in my life . . .

My childhood pal, John Purden, married an American girl and emigrated to the USA in 1968. Sadly, he died in New Jersey in the late 1990s. For around thirty years I lost touch with my other great pal, Sammy Johnston. In 2005, weeks after *Night Song* was published, he was driving up the Maryhill Road. A friend of his attracted his attention from the other side of the street. 'SAMMY! You're in a book! You and your ma and da, you're all in a book!' I'm now back in touch. His wonderful parents, Lottie and Frank, died twenty or more years ago.

Of my other childhood pals, the first book has led to many reunions . . . Robert Purden, John's older brother; his wife, Helen, formerly Burns. Margaret Mulholland, daughter of 'Big' Dan, Margaret Maloney, Tommy Hope, Jackie Brittain, Jim Loan, Aly McLean, Tommy Finnegan, Ernie Thomson, James Gibson, Andy Kennedy, Ian Ferrie, Eric Robertson, Bobby Calder, 'Chic' Wright. Then there are those I've never lost touch with . . . My cousin, Ada Ure; Ina and Nancy Cameron, daughters of Ma's great pal, Aunty Nicky. Billy Ferry; Jim McDonald.

From my time in the RAF I was in contact with Lyn Thomas from Camarthen. Sadly, he also died a few years ago. From my National Service in the army I'm still in regular touch with Brian 'Titch' Gurney, 'Butch' Palmer and I recently spoke to Pete Smith (Crispian St Peters).

Of my fellow prison officers, I've lost touch with the officers I served with in Birmingham – most, I would think, are now dead. From my time at Durham my friendship with Jack Walton has endured; we're still pals to this day and he visits often. Pat and I regularly spend a Saturday in Durham and I frequently bump into officers I served with. Norman Hutcheson, my favourite P.O., died a few years ago. Alan Briggs is still going strong.

My Uncle Jim and Aunty Jenny died, both aged eighty-six, within weeks of one another in 2006. My ex-wife, Nancy, died in 2005. We spoke on the phone a few weeks before her death. I see Scott and Nancy regularly. They visit and also come to many of my book events. I'm settled at last.